Outsourcing Welfare

Outsourcing Welfare

*How the Money Immigrants
Send Home Contributes to
Stability in Developing Countries*

ROY GERMANO

OXFORD
UNIVERSITY PRESS

OXFORD
UNIVERSITY PRESS

Oxford University Press is a department of the University of Oxford. It furthers the University's objective of excellence in research, scholarship, and education by publishing worldwide. Oxford is a registered trade mark of Oxford University Press in the UK and certain other countries.

Published in the United States of America by Oxford University Press
198 Madison Avenue, New York, NY 10016, United States of America.

Library of Congress Cataloging-in-Publication Data
Names: Germano, Roy, author.
Title: Outsourcing welfare : how the money immigrants send home contributes to stability in developing countries / Roy Germano.
Description: New York, NY : Oxford University Press, [2018] |
Includes bibliographical references and index.
Identifiers: LCCN 2017046507 (print) | LCCN 2018002073 (ebook) | ISBN 9780190862855 (Updf) |
ISBN 9780190862862 (Epub) | ISBN 9780190862848 (hardcover : alk. paper)
Subjects: LCSH: Emigrant remittances—Developing countries. |
Developing countries—Economic policy.
Classification: LCC HD5701 (ebook) | LCC HD5701 .G47 2018 (print) |
DDC 332/.04246091724—dc23
LC record available at https://lccn.loc.gov/2017046507

9 8 7 6 5 4 3 2 1

Printed by Sheridan Books, Inc., United States of America

For Candice and Violet

CONTENTS

ACKNOWLEDGMENTS

The earliest seeds of *Outsourcing Welfare* were planted many years ago when I worked with immigrants from Mexico, South America, and Eastern Europe in Chicago. I would like to thank Leobardo Torres, Henrietta Cipkova, and Jorge López for answering questions I had in those days about why people migrate and why they send money home.

In the years that followed, I benefited from the generosity, time, and expertise of countless people while conducting fieldwork in high-emigration areas of Mexico and Central America. I am especially grateful to Iván Montoya Zepeda, José Martín Álvarez Pantaleón, Juan Carlos Duarte Escalante, Ignacio Daniel Galván Martínez, Ángel García Pineda, Leticia García Pineda, Selene Maldonado López, Ana Martha Mora Ruano, and Ana Paula Steck de la Vega for their assistance collecting survey data in Michoacán, Mexico. I would also like to thank Douglas Massey and Jorge Durand for inviting me to work with the Mexican Migration Project team in Morelos, Mexico; Solomon Rodd for his guidance in the Mexican Huasteca; and Renato Lacayo, Ray Jesus, Dan Cain, and Spencer Chumbley for their support and assistance in Honduras and Guatemala.

My fieldwork was only possible because hundreds of families volunteered to tell me their stories. I would like to express my gratitude to the 768 families in Michoacán, Mexico who participated in our face-to-face household survey; families in Guerrero who participated in survey pretests; and dozens of families throughout Mexico, Honduras, Guatemala, and the United States who welcomed me into their homes for long discussions about migration and its impact on their households and in their communities. I am particularly grateful to Agustín Cisnero Rincón, Carolina Coria Rueda, Juan González, Olga Guerra, Alejo Froylán Guzmán, Kacie Jesus, Ray Jesus, Carlos Portillo, and Francisco Vanegas for their insights and hospitality.

While writing *Outsourcing Welfare*, I benefited from the feedback of many friends, colleagues, mentors, and students. Thanks to Katherine Bersch, David Crow, Michael Dennis, Gary Freeman, James Galbraith, Terri Givens, Ken Greene, Jim Granato, Christopher Haid, Austin Hart, Alan Kessler, Devesh Kapur, Tse-min Lin, Douglas Massey, Ernest McGowen, Paulomi Mehta, Clarisa Pérez-Armendáriz, Jessica Price, Saskia Sassen, Ryan Schmitz, Clint Wallace, and Kurt Weyland for feedback on drafts and ideas. I'd like to extend a special thanks to Faisal Ahmed, Katrina Burgess, Suheyla Cavdar, David Doyle, Nicolle Galteland, Sarah Louden, Tatiana Marroquin, Kathleen O'Sullivan, and Shai Tamary for extremely helpful feedback on the manuscript in its late stages. Thanks also to James Cook and Angela Chnapko, my editors at Oxford University Press, for their enthusiasm for this project and for all they did to bring *Outsourcing Welfare* to market.

A number of organizations and institutions helped make this book possible. Thanks to Afrobarometer, Arab Barometer, Caucuses Barometer, the Latin American Public Opinion Project, and the Mexico Panel Studies for making their data available. Major financial support for my fieldwork and writing came from the National Science Foundation Graduate Research Fellowship Program, the National Science Foundation Political Science Program, the Tinker Foundation, and the Department of Government, Center for Latin American Social Policy, College of Liberal Arts, and Office of Graduate Studies at the University of Texas at Austin. I completed various stages of research and writing while in residence at the University of Texas at Austin, the New School for Social Research, and New York University.

Last but certainly not least, I would like to thank my wife Candice for supporting me and pushing me to make this project better. I could not have completed this book without her love and encouragement.

Outsourcing Welfare

Remittances and the Politics of Austerity

oping with poverty and risk is a way of life for the world's poor. Droughts, natural disasters, political instability, violent conflict, economic crises, public health emergencies, and other shocks create great suffering for people living at the margins. To insulate themselves from market, environmental, and life course risks, many poor families do their best to diversify income, pool resources, and self-insure through saving.[1] But often the very economic conditions that families aim to guard themselves against cause their coping and self-insurance strategies to fail. It is difficult, for instance, to diversify income if one's local economy is limited to rain-fed agriculture or poorly paid informal work. It is impossible to save much when wages are low and economic crises or natural disasters are frequent.[2] To more effectively manage poverty and risk, some families spread themselves out geographically, sending members to work in places where wages are not only higher but also uncorrelated with economic cycles at home.[3] If all goes as planned, those who emigrate will be in a position to save and send money home to support or insure those who were unable or unwilling to leave. By diversifying their income portfolios across different industries and locales, poor households can use remittances—money that migrants send home—to mitigate poverty and reduce the pain of economic shocks.[4]

Some people emigrate as part of an explicit household coping strategy. They leave home for a few months or a few years with the goal of saving and sending as much money as possible to spouses, children, parents, and siblings who have remained in the home country. They keep their expenses in the destination country to a minimum—sometimes living in tight quarters with other migrants to save money on rent—and work long hours, often in difficult, low-wage jobs. At some point, they hope to return home and reunite with their family members more prosperous than when they left.

Javier, for instance, a small-plot strawberry farmer from Mexico, migrated to the United States when he could not pay back debts after a bad harvest. His wife Carolina and their young children remained at home in Mexico while he worked as a line cook at a Tex-Mex restaurant in Atlanta, Georgia. In Atlanta, Javier worked long hours and barely spent anything on himself—"fasting," as Carolina described it. He sent much of the money he earned back to Carolina so she could purchase things like food, shoes, clothing, and school supplies for the kids. The rest went to savings. After a few years of hard work in the United States, Javier returned to Mexico with enough money to build a brick home to replace his family's wooden shack.[5]

In contrast to Javier, millions of people emigrate with their families, or with the intention of starting one, and plan to settle indefinitely in their new country. They are motivated by the prospect of finding work or starting a business, escaping violence or persecution, or giving their children opportunities they would not have back home.[6] And while they may not migrate as part of an explicit household coping arrangement like Javier did, many send remittances to friends and relatives back home out of a sense of duty, love, and genuine concern for their welfare.[7]

Alana, for example, migrated to the United States in 2006 from Trinidad and Tobago. She supports herself and her three kids, all of whom live with her in the United States, with money she earns working as a nanny and doing other odd jobs, such as braiding hair. Then she takes whatever amount she can spare—usually about two hundred dollars a month—and sends it to relatives back in Trinidad. The family members she helps support include her father, her grandmother, her sister, and her aunts. Typically, they spend her remittances on basics like food, medicine, and school supplies. In addition to the regular amounts she sends every month, Alana often sends extra money when relatives call or text asking for more help. She says this usually happens when food prices in Trinidad are high or a relative has a medical emergency. In these instances, Alana says she assesses the situation and thinks about how much she can afford to send and how much she thinks her family members need.

I asked Alana if she ever expects to be repaid when relatives contact her asking for extra support. "Never," she replied. "If somebody back home calls me and says, 'I don't have food at my house,' I think, *What if I didn't have food?* So I send them money. When I give, I know a blessing will come back to me, so I don't look back for anything from the person I am doing it for."[8]

Rasel also immigrated to the United States in 2006. Although he is married with a baby and making a life for himself in New York, Rasel still manages to set aside two hundred dollars every month from his salary as a community organizer to send to his sixty-seven-year-old mother in Bangladesh. Rasel's mother uses the money primarily to buy medicines to treat her diabetes and high blood pressure. When he has a little extra money to spare, Rasel tries to help extended family members or people in his home village, such as a young girl who had an accident and needed a surgery that her family could not afford.[9] Similarly, Adolfo religiously sends one hundred dollars a week back to his native Guatemala—an impressive feat considering that he doesn't earn much more than minimum wage stocking shelves at a corner deli in Brooklyn and has a wife and child of his own in the United States to support. Adolfo usually sends money directly to his mother and younger sister, which they use to buy food and other basics. When I asked Adolfo why his mother needs the money, he said because she is too old to work. Her husband, Adolfo's father, passed away. She would be destitute without her son's assistance.[10]

It is tempting to think of the money people like Javier, Alana, Rasel, and Adolfo send home simply as a gift from one family member to another.

Taking a broader view, however, these transfers of cash start to look like much more. International migrants, in fact, are filling a significant welfare gap in many developing countries and, as I will argue in this book, helping to reduce the severity of economic grievances that fuel political instability and civil unrest.

REMITTANCE FLOWS TO THE DEVELOPING WORLD

The United Nations estimates that about a quarter of a billion people live outside their country of birth.[11] Millions of these migrants—no one knows exactly how many—send relatively small sums of money to friends and family back home on a regular basis. Some send remittances from Western Union or through their banks. Others wire money from internet cafes, twenty-four-hour check-cashing shops, currency exchanges owned by conationals, or automated kiosks inside of small convenience stores. Some immigrants send money using the latest text messaging and smartphone technologies—through mobile apps like WorldRemit and TransferWise—while others still send money the old-fashioned way as cash or money orders mailed in envelopes or in the pockets of friends who are returning home.

How much do they send? No one knows the exact quantity of remittances that flow between countries because so much of it is difficult to track. However, based on records of money sent through formal remittance channels like banks and wire transfer services, the World Bank estimates that international migrants transferred about $5 trillion to developing countries between 2000 and 2017.[12] In 2017 alone, migrants sent an estimated $450 billion to the developing world through formal remitting channels—nearly twice the amount they sent through formal channels a decade earlier.[13]

To put this amount into perspective, Figure 1.1 shows the flow of remittances and government aid to developing countries from 2004 to 2014. We can see that remittances grew significantly over this period (some of this growth, however, was due to better record-keeping) while the flow of aid remained relatively constant. The gulf between remittances and aid

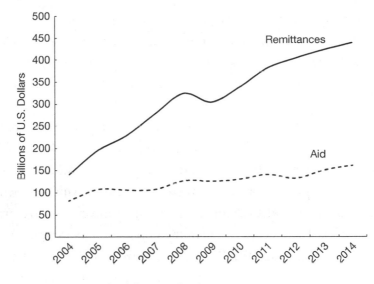

Figure 1.1 Remittances and aid flows to developing countries, 2004–2014.
SOURCES: World Development Indicators (rev. August 2016); World Bank Migration and Remittances Data (rev. April 2016).

reached its highest point yet in 2014 when international migrants sent an estimated $443.8 billion to developing countries and the world's richest governments donated $135 billion in the form of aid and official development assistance.[14] This difference is worth emphasizing. International migrants, many of whom work low-paying jobs that few others want, contribute more than three times as much toward fighting poverty in the developing world than the governments and taxpayers of the world's richest countries.

Remittances are a large and important source of income to dozens of developing countries. The top remittance-receiving countries are India and China, which received an estimated $62.7 billion and $61 billion from international migrants in 2016. Other countries with large remittance incomes include the Philippines (estimated at $29.9 billion in 2016), Mexico ($28.5 billion), Pakistan ($19.8 billion), Nigeria ($19 billion), Egypt ($16.6 billion), Bangladesh ($13.7 billion), and Vietnam ($13.4 billion).[15] For the most part, the top remittance-receiving countries have relatively large populations and large economies. When we measure remittances only in total dollar amounts, we therefore run the risk of overlooking the importance of remittances to many smaller developing countries. Figure 1.2 demonstrates just how large remittance income is relative to the size of the domestic economy in twenty-five small developing countries. Starting at the top of Figure 1.2, we can see that remittances are equivalent to more than 20 percent of gross domestic product (GDP) in Nepal, Liberia, Tajikistan, Kyrgyz Republic, Haiti, Moldova, and the Gambia and 10–19 percent of GDP in Honduras, Lesotho, Jamaica, El Salvador, Lebanon, Kosovo, Jordan, Armenia, Senegal, Palestine, Georgia, and Guatemala. Remittance income is furthermore equivalent to 5–10 percent of GDP in the Philippines, Nicaragua, Yemen, Guyana, Togo, Sri Lanka, Bangladesh, the Dominican Republic, Pakistan, Vietnam, Ukraine, Ghana, and Egypt. Overall, remittances are equivalent to 5 percent of GDP or greater in more than fifty developing countries.

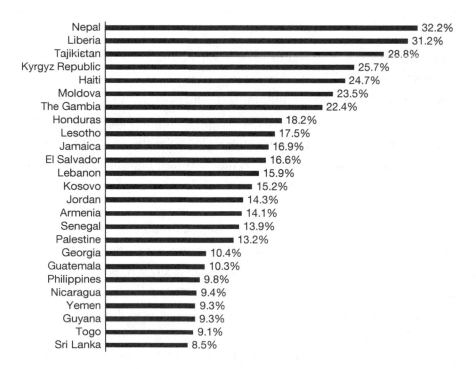

Figure 1.2 Remittances as a percentage of GDP in 25 developing countries in 2015. SOURCE: World Bank Migration and Remittances Data (rev. April 2017).

Yet another way to measure the flow and importance of remittances is in terms of how many people in a country receive them. Figure 1.3 shows aggregates from nationally representative surveys conducted in recent years in the Middle East, Africa, Latin America, the Caucuses, and the Caribbean. Listed is the percentage of respondents who reported receiving remittances from a family member abroad at least once or twice a year. As we can see from these surveys, remittance recipients make up a significant share of the population throughout the developing world. A staggering 49 percent of the population in the small island countries of Haiti and Cabo Verde, for instance, reported that they receive remittances at least occasionally, as did 46 percent of the Jamaican population. Remittance recipients make up a large

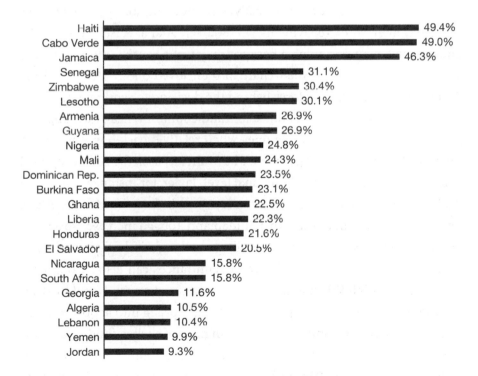

Figure 1.3 Percentage of national populations that reported receiving remittances at least once a year.
SOURCES: Afrobarometer (2009); Arab Barometer (2011); Caucuses Barometer (2013); Latin American Public Opinion Project (2014).

share of the population in a number of other countries. About 30 percent of people living in Senegal, Zimbabwe, and Lesotho receive remittances at least occasionally, as do 20–27 percent of people living in Armenia, Guyana, Nigeria, Mali, the Dominican Republic, Burkina Faso, Ghana, Liberia, Honduras, and El Salvador. Moreover, 9–16 percent of the population receives remittances at least occasionally in Nicaragua, South Africa, Georgia, Algeria, Lebanon, Yemen, and Jordan.

REMITTANCES AS SOCIAL WELFARE

Remittances are impressive not only because they are such a huge source of income to so many developing countries but also because migrants send most of this money altruistically without conditions or expectations of profit, interest, or repayment.[16] Like Javier, Alana, Rasel, and Adolfo, most people who remit do so because they feel a sense of duty to family and genuine concern for the welfare of their loved ones.[17] Because altruism is so often the driving force behind the decision to send money home, remittance flows tend to be both stable and countercyclical, meaning that migrants typically send more money when relatives back home are facing some sort of crisis or emergency.[18] We have already seen the countercyclical nature of remittances at the individual level. Javier, for instance, emigrated and sent money following a bad harvest on his farm in Mexico. Alana sends more when food prices in Trinidad and Tobago increase. Rasel sent more money when a member of his village in Bangladesh needed a critical surgery. The countercyclical nature of remittances can also be observed at the macro level. When a devastating earthquake struck Nepal in 2015, for example, the Nepali diaspora immediately sprang into action and sent millions of dollars to family and friends in need of shelter, food, and medical assistance.[19] Similarly, remittances to the Philippines increased after a deadly typhoon in 2013; to Haiti after a massive earthquake in 2010; and to Sri Lanka after a catastrophic tsunami in 2004.[20] Remittances also rise when human-made crises cause suffering. Remittances to Yemen, for instance, surged between 2011 and 2012 amid the political, social, and economic upheaval that surrounded the resignation of President Ali Abdullah Saleh and much of his government.[21] Remittances also rise when economic crises strike developing countries.[22] For example, citizens abroad pumped more money into the Mexican economy during its 1995 currency crisis and into the Thai and Indonesian economies during the 1997 Asian financial crisis—periods when many foreign investors were pulling money out.[23]

Remittances are a critical lifeline for millions of families. Although some remittances are invested in income-generating ventures, like small businesses and agriculture, and in long-term investments like health and education, the vast majority are spent on immediate consumption needs and basic goods and services. In a survey I conducted in ten Mexican communities with high rates of out-migration, a majority of respondents who received remittances (57 percent) said that food is the most common item they purchase with remittances. When asked to name the top three things they buy with remittances, respondents mentioned food 30 percent of the time; medicine and healthcare 21 percent of the time; utilities like electricity, gas, and water 18 percent of the time; clothing 10 percent of the time; and education 4 percent of the time.[24]

Similar spending patterns have been observed throughout the developing world. A study by the Bank of Jamaica found that Jamaicans spend 85 percent of their remittances on basic goods and services, such as utilities, food, housing, and education.[25] A survey in Kosovo found that 90 percent of remittances are spent on food, healthcare, education, clothing, and housing.[26] A survey in Ghana found that 90 percent of remittance recipients use remittances for food, 70 percent for clothing, and 20 percent for education.[27] A survey by the Bangladeshi government estimates that about 39 percent of remittances to Bangladesh are spent on food, while 24 percent are used to repay loans taken out to pay for expenses associated with moving abroad, including labor recruitment fees.[28] In Indonesia, 96 percent of respondents whose only income comes in the form of international remittances said they use remittances to buy food; 74 percent said they use remittances to pay for utilities; 73 percent said they use remittances to fund transportation costs; and 70 percent said they use remittances to pay for education. Among respondents who have income in addition to remittances, 68 percent said they use remittances to buy food, 55 percent for utilities, 57 percent for education, and 27 percent for home maintenance and repairs.[29] According to the Central Bank of the Philippines, 93 percent of remittance-receiving households use remittances for food, 72 percent for education, 63 percent for healthcare costs, and 50 percent for paying off debts.[30] Remittances are largely spent on food, healthcare, and education in Burkina Faso and Uganda, and overwhelmingly spent on food in Senegal.[31]

By allowing households to continue consuming even when local economic conditions are unfavorable, remittances reduce poverty, raise standards of living, and give families more freedom to make long-term investments in housing, education, and health.[32] The largest beneficiaries of remittances, of course, are the people who receive them directly, but the positive effects extend to others in the community when remittances stimulate local spending and commerce. When remittance recipients spend money on food at local markets, purchase new appliances at local shops, and hire neighbors to help them build new homes or till newly purchased land, this puts money in the pockets of other people in the community, creating or sustaining jobs and stimulating another round of spending.[33]

OUTSOURCING WELFARE

The citizens of wealthy Western democracies are able to count on any number of social insurance and subsidization programs in times of need. Unemployment compensation and trade adjustment assistance help households manage job loss. Agricultural subsidies and crop insurance provide a safety net to farmers and help them compete in global markets. Food assistance programs, social security, and public health insurance help poor families, older people, the disabled, and entire societies manage unforeseen economic shocks.

Most people living in the developing world, on the other hand, lack adequate social welfare protections. In the absence of a strong commitment from the governments of developing countries to provide a safety net, migrants abroad fill a significant welfare gap. Their remittances insulate poor households from macroeconomic crises, economic mismanagement, and political and social upheaval.[34] They keep smallholder farmers from going into debt during droughts or when they are priced out of local markets by foreign competition.[35] They help families rebuild after natural disasters. They keep food on the table when harvests are bad, when food prices surge, when jobs are lost, when family members fall ill, and when small businesses go under. For hundreds of millions of people around the world, it is their family members abroad—not their governments—that have assumed the primary social responsibility of ensuring a minimum level of economic security.

Remittances can therefore be thought of as *transnational safety nets*. They are *transnational* because they flow over national borders. Their transnational nature is advantageous because it means that flows are less likely to be disrupted by the same economic problems that remittances are sent to address. Remittances are a *safety net* because they help poor families more reliably meet basic consumption needs during times of economic crisis. As a transnational safety net, remittances serve a function similar to the kinds of social protections that many wealthy governments provide to their citizens.[36] Like unemployment insurance and trade adjustment assistance, remittances allow people to keep paying the rent even when they are put out of work by foreign competition. Like food stamps, they allow families to buy food even when global food prices are on the rise. Like fuel subsidies, they help families afford cooking gas and heating fuel even when global fuel prices surge. Like agricultural subsidies and crop insurance, they allow small farmers to keep their heads above water when they have a bad harvest. Like health insurance, they help poor people make doctor's visits and afford medicines they need to survive. Like social security programs, they compensate people who cannot work due to disability or old age.

Remittances have become a particularly critical safety net in the current era of neoliberal globalization. Developing countries have become more open to the vicissitudes of global markets in recent decades, but instead of establishing robust welfare states like their counterparts in postwar Europe and North America, most governments in the developing world retrenched or have engaged in procyclical social spending that falls far short of the kinds of universal welfare programs established in Western democracies.[37] In many developing countries, spending cuts were a precondition for establishing more market-oriented systems. The governments of many developing countries, for example, once used public funds to subsidize (i.e., artificially lower) the prices of agricultural inputs like seeds and fertilizer so that smallholder farmers could spend less to grow their crops. Moreover, many governments used, and to some extent still use, food, fuel, and transportation subsidies to keep prices artificially low in urban areas where the potential for civil unrest is high.[38] Many governments eliminated or greatly reduced these subsidies as part of structural adjustment reforms adopted since the 1980s. Prices on everyday goods and services rose, and poor people were left spending more of their hard-earned income just to survive.

Austerity has come at a time when people in developing countries need more, not fewer, social protections. Neoliberal globalization has made the poor increasingly vulnerable to economic shocks. Trade liberalization, for instance, has opened small producers in developing countries to competition from behemoths abroad, pricing poor farmers and mom-and-pop businesses out of local markets and creating legions of angry, unemployed citizens in need of a social safety net. National economies have furthermore become increasingly interdependent, leaving the poor more vulnerable to the booms and busts of global capitalism and the whims of international investors living thousands of miles away. The economic pressures resulting from austerity and global market integration have torn at the social and political fabric of many societies. Between 1976 and 1992, 146 grievance-fueled food and austerity riots took place in thirty-nine developing countries, including El Salvador, Jamaica, Sierra Leone, Bolivia, Zambia, Poland, Jordan, Nepal, and Egypt.[39] In some countries, like Peru and the Dominican Republic, riots led to the ascendance of opposition candidates; in others, such as the Philippines and Haiti, leaders were overthrown.[40] Unrest related to austerity and globalization continued through the 1990s. In Mexico, the violent Zapatista uprising in 1994 was an explicit rejection of suffering caused by austerity and Mexico's integration into the global economy. In Indonesia, the suffering and job loss caused by the 1997 Asian financial crisis were made more excruciating by cuts to food and fuel subsidies. Violent demonstrations broke out across the country, fracturing Indonesian society and bringing an end to the thirty-one-year reign of Suharto.[41]

The risk of grievance-fueled instability has remained high in the twenty-first century. In 2007 and 2008, skyrocketing food and fuel prices—a phenomenon driven largely by speculation half a world away—exacerbated poverty throughout the developing world.[42] From Mexico to Haiti, Indonesia to Egypt, Honduras to Burkina Faso, Peru to Mozambique, poor people took to streets banging pots and pans, demanding that their governments do something to ease their suffering. Their grievances were further inflamed by the global financial crisis that began in 2008. In the initial phases of the crisis, most countries increased public spending in efforts to stimulate their economies and avoid falling into recession. As the economic crisis deepened, however, public revenues dropped off and attention turned from recovery to austerity.[43] Between 2010 and 2013, dozens of developing countries cut fuel, electricity, water, transportation, and food subsidies, reduced health and pension obligations, and laid off public workers.[44] Half a decade later, many developing states are spending far less than they were before the crisis and continue to reduce spending. Meanwhile, economic shocks, like a spike in food prices in 2011, triggered demonstrations and political instability in North Africa and the Middle East.[45] High food prices, volatile markets, and inadequate social protections continue to threaten social and political stability in the developing world.[46]

By prioritizing austerity, many governments have implicitly assigned greater responsibility to families and other social institutions to guarantee social welfare.[47] Austerity, however, has caused not only the privatization or "familialization" of social welfare provision but also its transnationalization. Migration and remittance flows have risen precipitously over the past three decades in response to the vulnerabilities exacerbated by neoliberal policies. When citizens cannot count on their governments to compensate them for market risk and volatility, unemployment and underemployment, or man-made and natural crises—and when adverse local economic conditions prevent local solutions to economic problems—more citizens cope through emigration. When the vicissitudes of global capitalism are not mitigated by government social programs, those families that have access to foreign labor markets rely increasingly on remittances as a safety net. It is therefore not surprising that remittance flows have surged with the spread of neoliberal policies in the post-Cold War era. Emigrating to remit has become an increasingly critical coping strategy in the absence of adequate social protections in developing countries whose populations are increasingly exposed to the ravages of global capitalism.[48] By sending back growing sums of money, global migrants—like other non-state actors—have assumed a greater share of the state's welfare burden in the neoliberal era. No longer is social welfare necessarily something administered via universal, countercyclical government programs, as it came to be in interwar and postwar Western democracies. Rather, *welfare has been outsourced to citizens abroad*, obtained increasingly through a self-help system that requires families to divide themselves across national borders. Developing country governments that are unable or unwilling to spend on universal welfare states count on migrants to fill the welfare gap with their remittances. Counting on people to emigrate and send money home has become a de facto social welfare policy in many developing countries.

REMITTANCES, ECONOMIC SECURITY, AND POLITICAL STABILITY

This book is about how the social welfare impact of remittances promotes economic security and political stability in developing countries. A key argument of this book is that by filling such a large welfare gap, remittances make people in developing countries feel more economically secure and less economically aggrieved. I argue that this economic security effect makes remittance recipients more optimistic, enhances their assessments of government performance, and makes them less likely to blame or punish incumbents during bad economic times. As a result, remittances contribute to political and social stability in developing countries during otherwise destabilizing periods of economic crisis.

Economic conditions, of course, are critical determinants of social and political stability. Public approval of governments plummets when the economy is bad. High unemployment, rising prices, stagnant wages, economic volatility, natural disasters, and pessimism about what the future might hold contribute to suffering, grievance, and the aggravation of social, political, and ethnic tensions. The resulting anger fuels the rise of populists and demagogues who promise a better economy and an undoing of the political establishment. Their directives can ignite demonstrations, violence, and instability, and their policies can lead to the erosion of democratic institutions.[49]

Wealthy countries spend large sums of money on social welfare programs and subsidies to help ordinary people manage economic downturns, natural disasters, and life course risks. Social welfare programs keep food on the table and the rent paid despite job loss and other economic hardships. They allow families to continue making long-term investments in health and education when prices rise. They create a buffer for those at the margins of poverty. By absorbing economic shocks and compensating people for losses tied to integration into the global economy, government spending plays an important social and political function: it helps reduce the kind of suffering and anger that lead to civil unrest and political punishment.[50]

As a substitute for—or complement to—government spending on social welfare, remittances perform a similar stabilizing function.[51] As I will show through case studies and statistical analyses in later chapters, the social welfare impact of remittances has a distinct calming effect on people. Remittance recipients are less aggrieved and more optimistic about the future because remittances allow them to continue consuming despite the poverty, risk, and crises that are endemic to life in developing economies. As one man I interviewed in rural Mexico put it, remittances "lift the mood" in his community despite what feels like a constant stream of economic crises. My argument is that by reducing economic suffering and "lifting the mood," remittances, like social welfare benefits, leave people less motivated to blame, oppose, or mobilize against the party in power during bad economic times.[52] While remittance recipients may not completely approve of how their government is managing the economy, they are more forgiving of government performance and more willing to wait for better times. They have more to lose and less to gain from rioting or seeing the political order completely upended. They are less inspired by the calls of populists and demagogues to punish those in power, take up arms, or scapegoat minorities.[53]

To sketch out the logic behind this idea further, let's first assume that people derive utility from their capacity to consume and that everyone has a preferred minimum consumption threshold. For some people, the minimum consumption threshold may simply be the ability to keep food on the table and a roof over their heads. For others, the preferred threshold may include more than what is needed to survive—a comfortable home, appliances, a car, and the ability to purchase luxury goods. For our purposes, the important thing is *the difference* between the level at which citizens are actually consuming and their preferred minimum consumption threshold. When this difference is positive—meaning that people are consuming beyond their preferred threshold—voters will, all else equal, be more likely to approve of government performance. When this difference is negative—meaning that people are consuming below their preferred threshold—voters will be more likely to disapprove of government performance.[54] What matters most here is whether people are suffering or doing well—not necessarily the role leaders' policies, actions, or inactions play in determining consumption levels. People, in other words, often misattribute the difference between actual consumption and preferred minimum consumption to government performance. Christopher Achen and Larry Bartels show, for instance, that incumbent approval tends to plummet after droughts and floods even though every rational person understands that governments do not cause, nor can they prevent, bad weather and natural disasters.[55] Similarly, Daniela Campello and Cesar Zucco show that voters systematically reward and punish incumbents for

booms and busts in global markets that are clearly beyond domestic policymakers' control.[56] The same logic of misattribution applies when people
receive remittances. By boosting consumption and reducing economic
grievances, the welfare effect of remittances makes people more forgiving
of a poorly-performing government despite the fact that remittances are
non-governmental transfers.[57]

In addition to this welfare effect, remittances relieve governments of
pressure by providing some citizens a quick and effective option for securing economic relief. When faced with an economic crisis, someone with
a family member in another country has the luxury of being able to pick
up the phone, write an email, or send a text message to a family member
abroad and ask for money. For most poor people, calling upon a family member abroad for relief makes far more sense than dealing with a
corrupt, unfair, slow, or unaccountable political system.[58] Consistent with
the neoliberal ideal, they find ways to cope with economic adversity independent of the limited state. Remittance recipients therefore have less
demand for government-provided welfare because they find it more effective to resolve economic problems by other means. Reduced demand for
government-provided welfare—combined with a welfare effect that softens economic and political grievances—means that remittances relieve
government officials of some pressure to solve economic problems or
guarantee a minimum standard of living. In this way, remittances act as a
safety valve that reduces some of the social and political tension that arises
when markets fail and states are slow or inadequate in their response.

Figure 1.4 summarizes these arguments. In the first place, remittances fill a welfare gap. This does two things. First, remittances reduce
economic grievances and leave people feeling more optimistic about the
economy. Second, people who receive remittances have less demand for
government-provided welfare, both because they have fewer economic
grievances and because they know that it is more effective to turn to family
members abroad when they have economic problems. Reduced economic
grievances also reduce the risk of grievance-fueled civil unrest and lead to
improved assessments of government performance, which boosts support
for incumbents in elections. In these respects, remittances contribute to

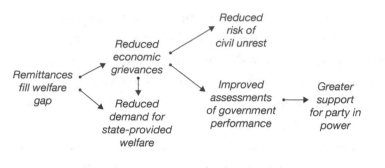

Figure 1.4 Remittances, Economic Security, and Political Stability.

economic, social, and political stability in countries that are vulnerable to frequent bouts of economic crisis.

CASES AND ANALYTICAL APPROACHES

This book is based on ethnographic fieldwork and survey research I conducted in Mexico, Central America, and the United States and on analyses of publicly available survey data collected from 120,000 individuals living in Africa, the Middle East, Latin America, and the Caribbean.[59] My focus here is on individuals, not aggregates, hence my use of ethnographic and survey methods. Although aggregate country-level data on remittances do exist, they are notoriously incomplete because so many remittances flow as cash or through informal networks, making them difficult to track. Moreover, the quality of the aggregate data varies from country-to-country due to the fact that some governments make it a priority to closely monitor and record remittance flows, while many others do not. Generally speaking, record-keeping has improved since universal definitions of remittances were established by the International Monetary Fund and World Bank in the mid-2000s and as more people use formal remitting channels in many parts of the world. Still, these improvements have been uneven and it is not usually clear how comparable or complete the data are from country-to-country and year-to-year. Although a number of researchers analyze aggregate time-series data on remittances, I think it is anybody's guess what such analyses really tell us since the quality of the data varies so much between countries and over time.

In keeping with my focus on individuals, when I speak of remittances in this book, I am referring to funds sent from individuals abroad directly to family members and friends in the homeland, usually in relatively small and frequent sums. These "family remittances" make up the vast majority of money that migrants transfer home and are usually what people are referring to when they talk about remittances. Family remittances can be distinguished from what are known as "collective remittances," a type of transfer that is largely beyond the scope of this book. Collective remittances are funds that groups of migrants raise and use to underwrite community projects in their homelands. The people raising and pooling money often come from the same hometown and have settled abroad in the same area. In some cases, they form clubs or formal associations in their new countries and use their combined economic power to fund large projects. Groups of Moroccans living in France, for example, have funded the construction of electricity networks and roads in their villages of origin.[60] Mexican migrant associations in the United States have raised funds to refurbish rundown plazas and old churches and construct wells, roads, and stadiums throughout rural Mexico.[61] Ghanaians living in the United States, United Kingdom, and Germany have organized and pooled their money to underwrite schools, fund the construction of libraries, and purchase equipment for hospitals back in Ghana.[62] Some migrant associations have become economic powerhouses that have accumulated political clout in their home countries.[63]

With my primary focus on remittances sent from individuals to families, I see remittances as a substitute for or complement to spending on subsidies and social welfare programs by national governments, such as food subsidies, agricultural subsidies, unemployment compensation, social security, and public healthcare. My focus thus excludes the ways in which migrants replace governments, sometimes formally, in funding public works projects. Instead, I am interested in drawing a comparison between family remittances and the kind of money many states spend (or once spent) to subsidize prices and otherwise insure ordinary people against economic, environmental, and life course risks. I do not argue that, by sending remittances, migrants have become institutionalized providers of social welfare in the sense that there has been a formal transfer of power or responsibility from governments to migrants. Rather, as I explain in more detail in the next chapter, migrants have assumed this responsibility in particular times and places by default, often as a means for coping with austerity and surviving economic shocks. Migrants are compelled to fill this gap because they feel a sense of duty to their family members.

CONTRIBUTIONS

The principal contribution of this book is to a burgeoning literature in political science on the effects of emigration and remittances on political outcomes in developing countries.[64] Remittances have traditionally been studied by anthropologists, economists, and sociologists for their social and economic causes and effects. Scholars have explored the reasons why people remit, the macroeconomic forces that drive the global flow of remittances, how transnational engagement (including remitting) alters social and economic relations in migrants' communities of origin, and how remittances impact poverty and growth in developing countries. Over the past decade, more scholars have started to ask how these large flows of money affect politics in migrants' home countries. Earlier studies focused primarily on the impact of collective remittances on migrant-state relations and the formation of pro-migrant policies. Increasingly, attention in recent years is turning to the micro- and macro-level political impacts of remittances sent by individuals. This book adds to the growing literature on the relationship between remittances and politics in developing countries by studying how remittances fill a welfare gap in austere, market-oriented systems and how the welfare effects of remittances reduce economic grievances and contribute to political stability in various regions of the developing world.

Another key contribution of this book is to debates about the political effects of globalization and market reform in developing countries and the impact of non-state welfare on political outcomes. For years, scholars have asked how the governments of newly-democratic developing countries can cut spending on subsidies and social welfare benefits without succumbing to popular resistance and punishment at the ballot box.[65] This question has become increasingly important in an era when voters' attachments to traditional political parties are weakening and economic crises are becoming more common due to the effects of climate change and global economic interdependence.[66] Some existing explanations for political stability in new democracies include the willingness of politicians to follow shifts in public opinion or focus on issues where there is little disagreement; the propensity of voters to prioritize certain economic conditions more than others; the ways in which power is structured and accumulated after democratic transitions; and how certain political systems and institutional arrangements lend themselves to stability.[67] This book adds a new explanation to debates about political behavior and political stability in developing democracies that focuses on the welfare effects of remittances. The impact of remittances on political stability and electoral outcomes should not be overlooked or underestimated, as large segments of the population in many developing countries receive remittances at least occasionally.

A third contribution of this book is to our understanding of the relationship between remittances and economic development. Researchers have tended to view the relationship between remittances and economic development through three lenses. The pessimistic view is that remittances do not contribute to economic development in any meaningful way. Remittances are overwhelmingly spent on daily consumption rather than saved and invested, therefore their effects on growth are minimal. Remittances may even stunt economic growth if they invite moral hazard, discourage innovation, or cause people to withdraw from the labor market.[68] Two perspectives are more optimistic. One argues that remittances contribute to economic growth through multiplier effects. Whether they are used to purchase food, buy medicine, build a home, or pay for a wedding, remittances stimulate new spending that can jump-start poor economies and create new jobs.[69] Another perspective argues that remittances have the ability to lift families out of poverty traps, allowing them to make investments that contribute to economic development in the long run. If remittances help satisfy basic consumption needs, in other words, families find themselves in a better position to make long-term investments in things like education, healthcare, land, agricultural technologies, and small businesses.[70]

This book adds a fourth perspective. Remittances, like social spending, contribute to the political and social stability needed for development. Food riots, populists, and political upheaval scare off investors and bring commerce to a standstill. Civil unrest creates more poverty, which may lead to more civil unrest. Remittances can help break this cycle, or at least reduce its severity. This is why remittances are so critical. They not only help individuals cope with austerity and the vicissitudes of global capitalism but also help entire societies cope with and adjust to an austere economic environment where markets and states frequently fail, much as welfare state expansion did in many developed countries after the Great Depression and World War II. This could be a good thing if, by fostering political stability, remittances allow politicians to make difficult choices that are economically beneficial in the long run when any number of pressures and constraints limit welfare expenditures. The risk, however, is that remittances also reinforce and perpetuate poverty to some degree by allowing politicians to neglect the development needs of poor communities that have high rates of emigration.

A LOOK AHEAD

The structure of this book follows the logic of the argument I laid out in Figure 1.4, exploring first how remittances substitute for welfare benefits through periods of austerity (chapter 2); then how remittances reduce economic grievances, reduce demand for government-provided welfare, and contribute to economic optimism in times of crisis (chapters 3 and 4); and, finally, how remittances enhance voters' assessments of government performance, reduce the risk of civil unrest, and benefit incumbents in elections (chapters 5 and 6).

Chapter 2, "Outsourcing Social Welfare: How Migrants Replaced the State during Mexico's Market Transition," draws on ethnographic field-work I conducted in a coffee-growing village and pork-producing town in rural Mexico. In this chapter I explain how people living in agrarian communities used remittances to cope with economic shocks associated with Mexico's transition to a more market-oriented economy in the 1990s. I argue that austerity caused the welfare burden to shift increasingly from the state to Mexicans living in the United States, and that counting on emi-grants to send money home became Mexico's de facto social policy in rural areas. In chapter 3, "How Remittances Prevent Social Unrest: Evidence from the Mexican Countryside," I argue that remittances have contributed to economic security and social stability in rural Mexican communities during periods of destabilizing economic change. In this chapter, I ana-lyze data from a survey of 768 households that I conducted in Michoacán, Mexico during the 2007–2008 food crisis. This chapter shows that, despite the high levels of poverty and economic risk that people in these com-munities faced at the time of the survey, remittance recipients were less economically aggrieved and weathered the food crisis with greater opti-mism than neighbors who did not receive remittances. They were also less likely to lobby government officials for economic assistance. Smallholder farmers, remittance recipients, and government officials I interviewed suggest that there would have been great social and political upheaval in the Mexican countryside had remittances not been there to help families cope with austerity and survive economic shocks.

In the second part of the book I look beyond Mexico. Chapter 4, "Optimism in Times of Crisis: Remittances and Economic Security in Africa, the Caribbean, Latin America, and the Middle East," examines emigration and remittance trends in fifty countries. In this chapter, I argue that remittances played an important role in reducing economic griev-ances during the global food and financial crises that shocked economies and exacerbated poverty during the period 2008–2011. This economic security effect, I explain, contributed to social and political stability during the food crisis that afflicted many sub-Saharan African countries in 2008. Chapter 5, "They Came Banging Pots and Pans: Remittances and Government Approval in Sub-Saharan Africa during the Food Crisis," shows that remittance recipients in sub-Saharan Africa were generally less likely than other citizens to experience hunger during the 2008 food crisis and also less likely to disapprove of government economic performance despite widespread suffering and rioting. This chapter also shows that these more positive assessments of the economy and government performance translated into higher levels of support for incumbents during the crisis. Remittance recipients in democratic sub-Saharan African countries, for instance, were up to 15 percent more likely than non-recipients to say they would support the incumbent party in a hypothetical election.

Chapter 6, "No Left Turn: Remittances and Incumbent Support in Mexico's Closely Contested 2006 Presidential Election," provides an example of how the link between remittances and improved assessments of government performance can tip a close election in the incumbent's favor. The 2006 Mexican presidential election was a heated race between Felipe Calderón, the right-of-center candidate from the incumbent party, and Andrés Manuel López Obrador, a left-wing populist who challenged Mexico's austere economic system and pro-market political establishment. I argue that, because they were less economically aggrieved, remittance recipients were less receptive to the populist appeals of López Obrador, and thus less likely to vote for him in the election. Remittance recipients made up a significant share of the Mexican electorate in 2006 and, as my analyses show, they were likely decisive in López Obrador's defeat.

The last chapter concludes and discusses the implications of remittances for democracy and development in an era when citizens are increasingly exposed to economic crises and governments are often unwilling or unable to invest in robust social welfare systems. I close the book with a discussion of some best practices for managing emigration and leveraging the benefits of remittances.

Outsourcing Social Welfare

How Migrants Replaced the State
during Mexico's Market Transition

What does it mean to say that austerity has caused the burden for providing social welfare to shift from governments to international migrants? How does this shift occur in practice? To sketch out some the processes behind this idea, this chapter examines how residents of the Mexican countryside used remittances to cope with dramatic changes that followed from a shift in the Mexican government's relationship to its rural economy.

By 1982, it had become clear to Mexican policymakers that the large amounts of money that the Mexican government was spending on subsidies, social welfare benefits, and state-owned enterprises was no longer sustainable. Decades of undisciplined spending not only resulted in massive debts that could not be repaid but also contributed to the inefficiency, stagnation, and inflation that would plague the Mexican economy throughout the 1980s and 1990s. In an attempt to cure these economic ills, the Mexican government—like the governments of many developing countries at the time—adopted neoliberal reforms. These reforms stressed the advantages of a leaner state, one that practiced fiscal discipline and left market outcomes to be determined more by the invisible hand than by policymakers. In the years that followed, Mexico eliminated longstanding tariff barriers, indirect subsidies, price supports, and other forms of market-distorting assistance that had insulated producers and industries from market volatility and foreign competition.

Austerity and foreign competition caused great suffering for Mexico's rural agrarian poor. In an effort to cope, millions of rural citizens emigrated to the United States and sent home hundreds of billions of dollars in remittances to support those left behind. These growing sums of money systematically filled a welfare gap left in the wake of the Mexican state's fiscal retrenchment. Families improvised new strategies for seeking and providing social insurance during this destabilizing period. In doing so, they changed the countryside in a number of ways. Importantly, remittances raised standards of living and reduced economic suffering for millions of households, which, as I will discuss in chapter 3, created islands of economic stability in regions that were otherwise forced to endure painful economic shocks. This economic stability contributed to political and social stability.

This chapter is based on interviews and observations I conducted in more than a dozen high-emigration communities in the Mexican states of San Luis Potosí, Morelos, and Michoacán between 2005 and 2008. I focus on the experiences of two communities in particular—a coffee-growing village in San Luis Potosí called La Victoria and a pork-producing town in Michoacán called Huandacareo—which I believe are representative of the experiences of hundreds of other communities in the Mexican countryside.[1] Before turning to these examples and discussing how the burden of providing social insurance shifted from the government to migrants, I will first give an overview of the Mexican state's relationship to the rural economy before neoliberal reforms and discuss how that relationship changed in the 1980s and 1990s.

LIBERALIZATION, AUSTERITY, AND THE DECLINE
OF RURAL INCOMES

By the late 1980s, rural Mexican households had come to depend heavily on state intervention in agricultural markets. The Mexican government used public funds to shield agrarian households from market competition and compensate them for their inability to compete in the market.[2] The government kept the price of inputs like gasoline, diesel, fertilizer, and seeds low and the price of harvested crops high so that farmers took more money home at harvest. The state furthermore provided low-interest loans to poor farmers who did not have enough capital to purchase land, tractors, seeds, gasoline, fertilizer, and pesticides. Mexico did this by subsidizing farmers indirectly through a series of state-owned companies. Companies like Mexican Fertilizers (known by its Spanish acronym, FERTIMEX) and the National Seed Producer (PRONASE) sold cheap government-subsidized fertilizer and seed to farmers. Government agencies like the National Bank of Rural Credit (BANRURAL) and the National Insurance Agency for Agriculture and Livestock (ANAGSA) offered low-interest credit and affordable crop insurance to farmers. State enterprises like the National Company for Popular Subsistence (CONASUPO) and the Mexican Coffee Institute (INMECAFÉ) bought harvested crops directly from farmers at prices two to three times the international market value. Then CONASUPO sold those products in government-owned grocery stores at discount prices. This meant that the government was subsidizing the poor twice: first, when it bought crops at above-market prices; and again when it sold food to the poor at below-market prices. Guaranteed producer prices took some of the risk out of farming and allowed small farmers to plan for the future. Mexico's agricultural policy functioned as a social policy that not only helped poor farmers survive but also helped to maintain social stability and foster loyalty to the Institutional Revolutionary Party (PRI), which had held power in Mexico since 1929.[3]

Mexico paid for agricultural subsidies and state-owned companies with loans from foreign lenders, which it serviced with oil revenues during an especially high period of spending in the 1970s. When oil prices declined in the early 1980s, however, Mexico informed the United States that it could no longer make payments on its external debt. To avoid defaulting, Mexico's finance minister Jesús Silva Herzog negotiated a bailout from the United States and the International Monetary Fund (IMF). Under pressure from the IMF, President Miguel de la Madrid slashed spending in a number of areas to reduce Mexico's budget deficit, which included cuts to spending on agricultural subsidies at a rate of 13 percent per year between 1982 and 1988. Retrenchment and high inflation led to a dramatic increase in the price of basic agricultural inputs. In 1987, for instance, 43 percent of Mexican corn farmers sold their corn for less than what it had cost them to grow it. A year later in 1988, this number had increased to 65 percent.[4] The agricultural sector faced further challenges after 1989 when Mexico dismantled, reorganized, or privatized most of the state-owned companies that bought crops from farmers and provided them with production support, credit, and insurance. BANRURAL, for instance, instituted stricter lending requirements that most smallholder farmers would have trouble meeting. At the same time, ANAGSA, the government crop insurer, was shut down. INMECAFÉ, the organization that provided production support to coffee farmers and bought their harvests, was dismantled between 1989 and 1993. The country's largest buyer of crops, CONASUPO, was also dismantled in three major phases between 1991 and 1999.[5] Finally, FERTIMEX was privatized in 1992, resulting in a steep increase in the price of fertilizer. Guaranteed prices, production support, indirect subsidies, cheap credit, and crop insurance would soon be a thing of the past. Small farmers across Mexico looked on while prices of inputs surged and middlemen paid below-market prices for crops that the government previously bought at two or three times above the market rate.[6]

Many farmers I interviewed remembered the old system of PRI patronage fondly for how automatic it was. "From the time of President Manuel Ávila Camacho"—Mexico's president from 1940 to 1946—"until Ernesto Zedillo Ponce de Léon," a corn farmer in his sixties named Cristobal Briseño told me, "in every community and every town, there was support for the countryside. There was an agrarian bank. There was support for farmers there. Local leaders did their best to get us fertilizer and give to the farmers. And they helped us with money. Now there is nothing." Cristobal's friend, Rafael Castellanos, a corn farmer about the same age, interrupted: "The government gave us everything. You went to fill out the application: 'How many hectares do you have?' 'What are you going to grow?' 'Okay, take your seeds, your fertilizer.' Then sometimes at harvest, there was an inspector and they reimbursed you. Everything was insured."

Guaranteed prices, indirect subsidies, and crop insurance took some of the risk out of being a small farmer. The government set prices that farmers could count on, and the state-owned crop insurance agency would compensate if the harvest was poor. Instead of selling on the market, farmers could sell to CONASUPO at prices that usually exceeded the international market price. As another corn farmer, who told me his age was seventy, described it: "There was a time when ten or fifteen days before harvest, the government would say, 'Corn will be worth so much,' and that's the price the buyers had to pay. But the government was buying at the prices it set in the CONASUPO stores. Any other buyer had to then pay at least what the government was paying. But now the government says, 'There are no funds.'" He continued, "They started closing down the CONASUPO stores. They shut them because the country was in crisis. Now the buyers pay whatever they want."

With the government out of the business of setting producer prices, small Mexican farmers, with their antiquated technologies and low yields, were suddenly forced to compete in the market. But they were not just competing with one another. Rather, at the same time that Mexico stopped subsidizing its farmers, it also began opening its economy up to cheaper American food imports. The opening began in 1986 when De la Madrid entered Mexico into the General Agreement on Tariffs and Trade (GATT). President Carlos Salinas de Gortari doubled down on De la Madrid's integration into the global economy in 1994 when he entered Mexico into the North American Free Trade Agreement (NAFTA). With only a few exceptions, NAFTA would lift tariffs on goods flowing between Mexico, Canada, and the United States by 2008.

International trade always creates winners and losers, and workers in vulnerable industries on both sides of the border were understandably anxious about what NAFTA and its competitive pressures would mean for them. Blue-collar workers in the United States, of course, worried about manufacturers moving to Mexico to take advantage of cheaper labor costs—what American billionaire and presidential candidate Ross Perot referred to in 1992 as the "giant sucking sound" of jobs going south of the border. These concerns remain alive and well. Twenty-three years after Perot, populist presidential candidates Donald Trump and Bernie Sanders rose in the polls during their parties' primary competitions in large part due to their anti-NAFTA, anti-trade positions.

While blue-collar workers in the United States worried that they would lose jobs to lower-paid workers in Mexico, Mexico's smallholder farmers worried that they would be driven out of the market by big U.S. agribusinesses. This was of particular concern since the Mexican government had withdrawn so much production support in the decade leading up to NAFTA.[7] As Mexican farmworker advocate Victor Quintana put it in his testimony to the U.S. Congress just weeks before NAFTA was ratified, "From 1982, Mexican agriculture has been in the worst crisis of its history. This has affected the life conditions of our Mexican people, and it cannot be separated from the structural adjustment measures in the economy at large. What President Salinas is doing is to deepen these measures, to broaden them, and to crown them with the NAFTA proposal."[8] Mexican farmers' horse-drawn plows, fifty-year-old tractors, and small plots of rain-fed land, in other words, would be no match for the high-tech, irrigated, highly subsidized mega-farms of the United States.

Because small Mexican farmers were indeed so vulnerable to foreign competition, NAFTA mandated that tariffs on agricultural goods be lifted gradually between 1994 and 2008 so that millions of smallholder farmers would have time to shift production from grains to more lucrative crops. Tariff-rate quotas were set to limit the volume of tariff-free food imports coming from the United States. For any amount over the quota, Mexico was allowed to add a tariff to make its own crops more competitive in domestic markets. The Mexican government, however, often failed to enforce tariff-rate quotas.[9] This was especially true in the case of corn, a staple of the Mexican diet that holds great symbolic and political value in the countryside. Imports of American-grown corn increased fourfold between 1990 and 2008.[10] The effects on Mexico's small corn farmers— already a vulnerable group when subsidized—were catastrophic. The United States spends ten times more on corn subsidies than the Mexican government spends on its entire agricultural sector. American farmers are therefore able to sell their highly subsidized corn well below what it costs Mexican farmers to produce their unsubsidized corn. As a result, corn prices in Mexico plunged by 70 percent between 1994 and 2001 and priced many small Mexican farmers out of local markets.[11] As a small farmer I interviewed in San Luis Potosí put it, "If you invest 1,000 pesos to grow corn, you don't make that 1,000 pesos back. You don't make back your investment. Because there's no return—not like the old days."[12]

Although corn and grain farmers were hit hardest by U.S. competition, other farmers also felt the pain of declining producer prices. Even more competitive crops, like strawberries, were declining in value due to U.S. imports. As Javier García, a strawberry farmer from Irimbo, Michoacán, explained: "Before so much was imported from [the United States], the buyers would come here looking for strawberries, and we could sell at a good price. Now they barely pay anything because of all the strawberries entering from [the United States]."[13] Overall, the prices Mexican farmers received for their goods fell an average of one-half to two-thirds between 1990 and 2008.[14]

Many in the Mexican countryside blame U.S. agricultural subsidies and the Mexican state's retrenchment for their misery. "If the farmers here could get the same amount of money, then that would be something fair," Artemio Díaz Figueroa, a mayoral candidate in Huandacareo, Michoacán, protested. "But it doesn't happen."[15] Crop insurance was another major theme in my interviews. Mexican farmers complained about the lack of crop insurance in Mexico while expressing envy at how little risk American farmers seem to face in comparison. "If you have a bad harvest [in the United States], there's insurance," Rafael Castellanos declared. "They pay you. Here, if you have a bad harvest, nobody pays you anything! Not the government, not anybody!" Some farmers, like Agustín Cisnero Rincón, have seen with their own eyes the scale of safety nets in the United States. "I worked for a season in Idaho," he said, "and they have good government benefits. For example, if they have a bad harvest, they are insured— the insurance companies or the government—they reimburse them for some of what they invested. And here, if you lose [your harvest], you lose everything. There isn't anyone who gives you a hand. Here, there's nothing . . . for this reason, who here is going to be able to compete?"[16]

In interviews, however, government officials emphasized that the Mexican government had not retrenched from the countryside entirely.[17] In fact, the Mexican government developed two major social programs to compensate somewhat for the loss of subsidies and the threat of U.S. competition. First, in 1993, the Salinas administration established the Program for Direct Support to Farmers, commonly known as PROCAMPO, its acronym in Spanish. For most of its more than twenty-year existence, PROCAMPO was a direct cash transfer to agricultural households that owned or rented land. Payments were quite small, ranging from about seventy to one hundred dollars per hectare per year. In theory, PROCAMPO was supposed to help Mexican grain farmers build up capital to invest in producing crops that could fetch higher prices in international markets, such as mangoes and avocados. But at less than ten dollars per hectare per month, the stipends were a pittance—nothing close to the subsidies U.S. farmers received. They were certainly not large enough to help farmers make the costly transition from corn to other crops.[18] Furthermore, most small farmers had neither the technical knowledge nor the arable land to make the transition from grains to more lucrative fruits. Instead, many continued growing grains and used PROCAMPO funds to subsidize daily consumption.

In addition to PROCAMPO, Salinas's successors Ernesto Zedillo and Vicente Fox developed a social insurance program that has had many names over the years, but which many people still know as the Oportunidades program (the program's name from 2002–2012). Oportunidades is a cash transfer program aimed at Mexico's poorest households. In order to receive benefits, families must keep their children in school and make visits to health clinics for preventative care. The objective of the program is thus to attenuate poverty in the immediate term while encouraging families to make long-term investments in health and education. According to a household survey I conducted in early 2008, Oportunidades beneficiaries received about forty-five dollars every two months, plus small scholarships for children and comparable stipends for senior citizens when applicable.[19]

The designs of PROCAMPO and Oportunidades were consistent with the neoliberal model's emphasis on individual responsibility. Unlike indirect subsidies that insured farmers automatically by distorting prices, these programs were direct cash stipends that, in theory, could be saved and used to insure against losses that arise in a competitive market environment. This requires beneficiaries, not the state, to monitor market conditions and decide how to allocate capital.[20] Cash transfers furthermore differ from indirect subsidies in that they demand more effort on the part of households to seek out funding and meet eligibility requirements. As a result, many households never apply for or receive benefits, whereas just about anyone buying seeds or fertilizer under the old patronage system was subsidized automatically as long as they demonstrated loyalty to the PRI. Finally, cash benefits are marginal, vary by household, and often require beneficiaries to meet some set of conditions.[21] So, although they may have insulated households from market forces somewhat, these programs were consistent with the larger objective of neoliberal reform, which was to discourage dependence on government to solve economic problems.[22]

Even with PROCAMPO and Oportunidades, farmers and community leaders I interviewed stated time and again that they felt abandoned by the Mexican government. "We're forgotten by the political system," strawberry farmer Javier García told me. "If you ask the local officials, they say there are no subsidies." Artemio Diáz Figueroa echoed García's point: "Our officials in the city don't tell about all the programs we have in the government. They only talk about them to their closest friends or relatives." Confusing applications and bureaucratic hurdles also seem to limit the rural poor's access to government support. Javier Cerna Villanueva,

a hardware store owner from Pajacuarán, Michoacán, described the difficulty as such: "A person applying for government support must get all of
the paperwork together and spend five hundred pesos on a bus ticket to
the capital. When he arrives to the government offices, he is told that he
is missing a document. So he must then return home to fix the problem.
Then he must spend another five hundred pesos, which he cannot afford,
to return to the state capital."[23]

Officials I interviewed at some of Mexico's agricultural and rural development ministries did not dispute that social benefits often do not reach
those who need them most. One official explained that the government's
outreach efforts are modest because program budgets are so modest.[24]
Another official admitted that the applications are sometimes too complicated for the bureaucrats who administer the programs to understand.[25]
But I found that even PROCAMPO, Mexico's best-known and easiest-to-
obtain subsidy, was bypassing those who needed it most. For example,
when Agustín Cisnero Rincón told me that small farmers like him had
been forgotten by the government, I countered by pointing out that the
Mexican government spends a great deal of money on PROCAMPO. He
chuckled. When I asked why he was laughing, he told me that it is often
the case that poor people who rent land do not receive PROCAMPO
funds. The man who owns the land that Agustín was renting received
PROCAMPO funds, but Agustín, the renter, received no government
support.

Some real numbers show how the loss of input subsidies, guaranteed
prices, and low-cost credit and crop insurance, combined with competition from U.S. farms, made small-scale agriculture far riskier and less
profitable for agrarian households in Mexico. Consider, for instance, that
a smallholder Mexican farmer might use a hundred kilograms of urea
(a basic fertilizer) per hectare to produce three metric tons per hectare
of corn. Assuming that this farmer bought urea from FERTIMEX and
sold corn to CONASUPO in 1990, he spent forty-six pesos per hectare
and earned 6,000 pesos per hectare. In 2007, however, the same farmer
spent 340 pesos per hectare and earned 3,600 pesos per hectare for the
same three metric tons of corn.[26] His profit, in other words, decreased by

45 percent due to the loss of guaranteed prices and indirect subsidies. It is important to note that this example only takes into account the loss of subsidized fertilizer and guaranteed producer prices due to the absence of historical data on other inputs. But certainly the loss of other types of production support, such as seeds, fuel, pesticides, and cheap credit and crop insurance, have further diminished profits and left Mexican farmers without a safety net during particularly difficult growing seasons. Benefits from cash transfer programs may insulate agrarian households from adverse market conditions somewhat. But even if our smallholder farmer received PROCAMPO benefits worth 250 pesos per hectare per season and Oportunidades benefits worth 625 pesos per season, he would still be earning significantly less than he did when the state subsidized prices. Again, these figures do not take into account expenses related to seeds, pesticides, fuel, interest, or crop insurance, the costs of which also increased with the loss of government subsidies. But even this simple comparison of potential pre-reform and post-reform incomes indicates that peasant farmers were adversely affected by the loss of indirect support despite the Mexican government's efforts to provide some direct compensation. Neoliberal reforms, in other words, left behind a significant welfare gap that poor households had to find a way to fill on their own.

NEOLIBERALISM AND THE RISE OF REMITTANCES

La Victoria, a small village located atop a mountain in northeastern Mexico, was one of the thousands of rural communities that suffered as a result of the Mexican government's austerity measures. The only way to La Victoria is in the back of one of the old pickup trucks that occasionally taxi people up the mountain from the two-lane highway that connects the towns of Xilitla and Jalpan de Serra. The old pickups crawl up the mountain as they rattle and bounce on roads that in many sections are a mix of rock, dirt, and crumbling concrete. Those who make this trek often are accustomed to sharing the road with donkeys hauling supplies and elderly women inching up the mountain on foot with large bundles of tree branches on their backs. The old pickup trucks are like time machines that transport anyone in them to a forgotten way of life. There are many communities here where homes still have dirt floors and walls made of sticks; where families speak indigenous languages like Nahuatl and Teenek; where men cut grass with machetes; where chickens roam in and out of homes as they please; and where thick corn tortillas are made by hand on stoves fueled by the tree branches that women, young and old, spend so much of their time collecting.

For decades, the residents of this isolated, largely indigenous community of about one hundred households survived by growing and selling coffee. Almost every family in La Victoria once had a small plot of land with coffee trees on the side of the mountain. They cut their coffee and sold it in town for a profit. Then they would use some of what they earned to pay young men to help out in the fields. They had done it this way for as long as most senior members of the community could remember.[27] It was a modest living, but no one complained because coffee income was a steady income, and it paid better than corn.

Coffee income was so stable because it was regulated by a government company that I mentioned earlier called INMECAFÉ. The Mexican government created INMECAFÉ in 1958 during a time of great volatility in global coffee markets. Although INMECAFÉ's original beneficiaries were large growers, the institute became more oriented to smallholder farmers in the early 1970s under President Luis Echeverría. Coordinating with other state-owned companies, INMECAFÉ provided technical assistance and subsidized pesticides, fertilizer, and seeds to growers in La Victoria and other villages. The institute also offered low-cost credit to peasant farmers and bought their coffee at above-market, guaranteed prices—a welcome alternative to the expensive credit and low, unpredictable prices offered by middlemen. For years, INMECAFÉ ensured that, however meager, predictable coffee revenues kept the families of La Victoria and other coffee-growing communities clothed, fed, and sheltered.[28]

The Mexican government began dismantling INMECAFÉ in 1989 as part of the market reforms discussed earlier. It stopped buying coffee immediately. Input subsidies and production support were phased out between 1989 and 1993. With government subsidies slashed and inflation already high after peaking at 200 percent in 1987, production costs sky-rocketed. With the loss of guaranteed prices from INMECAFÉ, small producers were forced to sell to middlemen at much lower prices. The timing of INMECAFÉ's dismantlement was particularly problematic for producers because it occurred the same year that the global market price of coffee dropped by 50 percent due to the collapse of the International Coffee Organization.[29] Small Mexican coffee growers saw their incomes fall by 70 percent between 1989 and 1993.[30] Prices never recovered. Before the crash, Juan González, a resident of La Victoria, sold his coffee for twenty-five to thirty pesos per kilogram. By 2005, when I first met him, he was receiving just eight pesos per kilo—a 97 percent decrease after inflation. "Many coffee growers lost everything," Juan told me.[31]

There were no jobs in the village besides farming and no safety nets to help families keep food on the table during the crisis.[32] In search of relief, some people left La Victoria to look for work in large Mexican cities. Migrating to the cities, however, did not help much. "If you work in Mexico City," Juan explained, "the rent is so expensive [relative to wages]. You don't save anything. Same in Monterrey—you don't save any money." The objective, in other words, was not to leave La Victoria permanently but to save enough money to support family members through the crisis. To this end, some members of the village proposed that they travel 700 kilometers north to the United States. Juan and a handful of other men were able to cross the lightly patrolled U.S.-Mexico border with ease in the early 1990s, work for awhile, return home to be with their families, then do it all over again. Sometimes they entered on temporary visas—"We flew through Houston one time," Juan told me. Other times they entered illegally, their feet full of blisters after days of walking through vast expanses of Texas ranch land.

The first group of migrants from La Victoria found work on a tobacco farm in Indiana, then in landscaping in Tennessee. Another time they picked tomatoes in Florida. Juan and his friends saved and sent money back to La Victoria. Their remittances allowed spouses back home to buy food for the family. Sometimes earnings in the United States were so good they could save enough to buy cinderblocks and concrete. On return visits to La Victoria, they built new homes to replace their wooden, dirt-floor shacks. Some people replaced their wood-burning stoves with gas ranges and electric toaster ovens. They bought Ford and Chevy trucks in Indiana and Texas and drove them back to La Victoria. They never changed the license plates.

Seeing that working in the United States was not only a good way to deal with the coffee crisis but also a way to boost one's standard of living—to build a nicer house, buy some better clothes, and get a pickup truck—others in La Victoria started following in the footsteps of Juan and other trailblazers. Many stopped growing coffee for good—"Many people said, 'What's the point?'" Juan quipped. The little agricultural production that still takes place in the community is subsidized with remittances. Remittances pay for the seeds, the land, the fertilizer, and the wages of the farmhands.

Just like Juan and the first leavers did, a new generation of migrants saved and sent money back to La Victoria. They returned to the village to build their houses and visit with their families. Then when their savings dried up, they traveled north again. They went to Colorado to scrub the bathrooms of ski resorts. They went to Oklahoma to mow lawns and plant flowers. They went to Alabama to wash cars and pick vegetables. Many children who grew up in La Victoria after the coffee crisis were raised without fathers (and sometimes without mothers), and when they turned fourteen or fifteen, they aspired to join relatives in the United States in what has become a rite of passage. Few people in La Victoria grow up anymore thinking they will make a living working in the fields. For anyone born around or after the coffee crash, the model for success has been to emigrate. In La Victoria, a culture of migration has replaced a culture of coffee farming. And for good reason: most families in the village are far better off economically now than they had been before the coffee crisis.

It could be argued that the outflow of migrants and the inflow of remittances to La Victoria was an economic phenomenon followed by a social one. Coffee prices dropped and livelihoods were threatened, which caused people to seek work elsewhere. This then gave way to a social process that perpetuated future emigration flows from the village by lowering the costs of moving to the United States and instilling a culture of migration in the community. My argument, however, is different. I view the flow of remittances to La Victoria as a fundamentally political phenomenon rooted in the Mexican state's retrenchment from the agricultural sector. Broader political decisions around austerity during the 1980s (and, specifically, the dismantlement of INMECAFÉ) preceded the decrease in global coffee prices and contributed to creating a welfare gap that migrants filled by sending remittances when prices began to plummet.

Economic crises happen all the time, and most do not send people moving hundreds or thousands of miles. Many governments provide a safety net to soften the blow of economic downturns. In the Mexican countryside, the opposite happened. Instead of expanding the social safety net when global coffee prices started falling, the Mexican government continued a broader adjustment program to eliminate it. The loss of the domestic safety net in combination with the drop in global coffee prices made it necessary for most families in La Victoria to spread themselves out geographically so that members abroad could support and insure those at home. By emigrating to the United States and sending back remittances, Juan and dozens of other migrants assumed a social welfare burden that had for decades been the domain of INMECAFÉ. In this respect, austerity caused the burden of providing social welfare to shift from the Mexican government to Mexicans who had emigrated to the United States. The responsibility to produce social welfare and provide it to the Mexican countryside, in other words, was "outsourced" to citizens abroad.

This transfer of responsibility from the state to the transnational family is entirely consistent with the neoliberal model's emphasis on individual solutions. It also suggests that the surge in migration from Mexico to the United States during the 1990s and 2000s was not a purely economic phenomenon—say, a response to poverty in Mexico and prosperity in the United States, as neoclassical migration theorists would argue—but also a phenomenon driven by political decisions.[33] Austerity—not just a bad economy—triggered the movement of disaffected farmers in search of social insurance (remittances) to send to their families. Some have argued that the Mexican government could only get away with such rapid and austere economic reforms because it was able to count on millions of Mexicans to go to the United States and send billions of dollars home.[34] This perspective, which has been applied to other cases such as the Philippines and Honduras, argues that remittances are essential to the functioning of market-oriented economic systems because they contribute to economic security in the absence of adequate social spending by the state.[35] I will return to this argument and discuss its implications for political stability in later chapters.

Coffee growers in northeastern Mexico were by no means the only people using remittances to cope with austerity and economic shocks. Huandacareo, Michoacán, for instance, is a town of about seven thousand people located in southwestern Mexico. Many people I met in Huandacareo told me with great pride about how their town used to be the second-biggest producer of pork in the state of Michoacán. José Refugio Manríquez Díaz, the town's municipal president (mayor), explained to me that about one in every five households in Huandacareo raised pigs prior to NAFTA.[36] As Agustín Cisnero Rincón told me, "Anyone in this town with money had a pig farm, and they would employ twenty or thirty people to take care of the pigs." Pork created jobs, and the cash that flowed into the community from the sale of pork created more jobs when profits and wages were spent at local businesses. In one way or another, most people in Huandacareo depended on the pork industry for their survival.

The glory days of the Huandacareo pork industry have long since passed. It is difficult these days to find anyone in town who still raises pigs. After asking around, I finally found a farm with a dozen or so pigs near the center of town. The farm was owned by a local entrepreneur who also owns a hat-making business. He confirmed that he was among the last pork producers in town.[37] Another pig farmer I located was a young mother who kept about six pigs in a pen behind her home. Pork sales, however, were not enough to sustain her family. The woman told me that her business was being subsidized by the money her husband sent home from the United States. Without any subsidies from the government, remittances paid for production costs like feed. If her husband returned from the United States, the woman told me, they would have to stop raising pigs.

When I asked people in Huandacareo when and why the local pork industry began to fail, I always received the same answer. "From my perspective, it started with the North American Free Trade Agreement," Manríquez Díaz told me. "The pig farmers could no longer compete." Artemio Díaz Figueroa, who ran against Manríquez Díaz for municipal president, agreed: "Free trade allowed all the meat from the U.S. to come into Mexico. And then the small farmers, or small producers, they couldn't compete with that."

Why were pork farmers from Michoacán so unable to compete? One reason is the imbalance of government subsidies between Mexico and the United States. Like the young mother I interviewed, Mexican pork farm ers are unsubsidized and have much higher production costs than their competition in the United States. An unsubsidized Mexican pork farmer, for instance, spends about five times more to raise a pig than her subsidized counterpart in the American Midwest.[38] The influx of American pork after NAFTA contributed to a 50 percent decrease in pork prices in Mexico between 1990 and 2005.[39] This left many small Mexican farms unable to cover their expenses. Unlike U.S. farmers, who can apply for government assistance when they incur losses due to foreign competition, the Mexican farms did not have access to a government safety net.

Just like the coffee farmers in La Victoria, many pig farmers in Huandacareo closed their businesses and migrated to the United States. The Mexican government found that 25 percent of households in Huandacareo received remittances in 2000.[40] In a survey of 353 randomly selected households that I conducted in Huandacareo, I found that this figure increased to 32 percent of families by 2007.[41] Remittances have become a critical safety net and lifeline in Huandacareo. The young mother with the pig farm is the exceptional case of someone who uses her remittances to subsidize agricultural production directly. As Figure 2.1 shows, most households in Huandacareo spend remittances primarily on items like food, health services, medicine, education, electricity, and gas. Huandacareo residents also use remittances to save, pay debts, and build better homes. Huandacareo residents furthermore pointed out that remittances create new employment opportunities.[42] When people find work

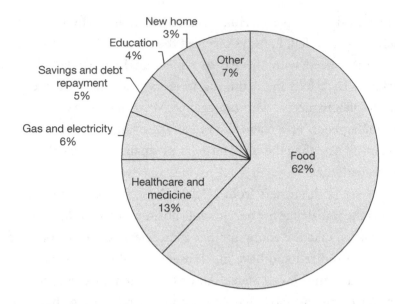

Figure 2.1 Primary uses of remittances in Huandacareo, Michoacán.
SOURCE: Household survey conducted by the author, January 2008. Responses from 116
remittance-receiving households out of a total of 353 randomly selected households
surveyed in the municipality of Huandacareo. Question asked respondents to name their
household's primary use of remittances.

as farmhands, the money they are paid is often money that was earned in
the United States.[43] Everyday spending by remittance recipients makes it
possible for people who do not receive remittances to make money as restaurant owners, shopkeepers, and vendors at weekly markets called *tian-
gis*.[44] Remittances have thus stimulated local economies in ways that have
allowed people in agrarian communities to transition away from agricultural activities and do other kinds of work. As Alejo Froylán Guzmán, a
return migrant and former local government official in Huandacareo, put
it, "Remittances are the wheel that rotates and moves everything else."[45]

The competitive pressures brought about by NAFTA extended well
beyond pork. Javier García, the strawberry farmer from Irimbo, Michoacán
I mentioned earlier, explained to me how migrating and remitting became
his family's best insurance strategy beginning in the 1990s after U.S. competition drove down the price of strawberries and the Mexican government eliminated guaranteed prices, low interest loans, and crop insurance.

Javier invests between sixty and seventy thousand pesos to plant a hectare of strawberries. In the past, the government offered a guaranteed price for his harvest that made up for any difference between the amount he spent to grow his strawberries and what the market would pay him after they were harvested. With that option no longer available, Javier is left with a large debt to repay anytime he has a bad harvest or his production costs exceed revenue. Losses like these have forced Javier to migrate on four occasions to Atlanta, Georgia for periods of twelve to eighteen months at a time. There he works long hours in the kitchen of a restaurant. He saves most of the money he earns and sends it back to Mexico to support his wife and children and to pay back the expensive loans he took out to grow his crops in the first place. Remittances—not government subsidies—are what fill the gap in Javier's community when free markets and the Mexican state fail to guarantee social welfare.[46]

A pronounced exodus from the Mexican countryside took place as agrarian communities were battered first by rising prices tied to the economic crises of the 1980s and 1990s and then the withdrawal of government support and new foreign competition that accompanied market reforms. Between 1991 and 2008, the number of people employed in Mexico's agricultural sector decreased by 2.1 million while the total number of people living in rural communities increased slightly.[47]

Transnational social networks and a relatively open U.S. border (at least until about the mid-2000s) helped make the shift in the welfare burden from state to migrants a fluid one. Transnational social networks play a key role in reducing the costs and difficulty of migrating.[48] Friends, neighbors, and relatives who are already abroad can provide lessons from their own migration experiences to those back home who are contemplating a move. They know which routes to take, which visas to apply for, and which labor recruiters and human smugglers to work with. Conationals abroad also frequently gift or lend money to friends and family members to pay for travel expenses and the fees charged by human smugglers, which can run in the thousands of dollars. At the destination, conationals can provide a place to sleep, a system of social support, information about employment opportunities, and access to forged or authentic labor documents.

As transnational networks grow over time, the costs of emigrating may decrease to a point where migration between two locales becomes fluid and self-perpetuating.

For example, driven from the Mexican pork industry in the 1990s, thousands of residents from Villachuato, Michoacán—a town just to the west of Huandacareo—moved to a meatpacking town in Iowa called Marshalltown. Marshalltown offered not only jobs but also a network of a few dozen Villachuato residents who had moved to Marshalltown in the early 1980s and had obtained legal permanent resident status through 1986 legislation that legalized three million undocumented immigrants. Villachuato residents who had settled in Marshalltown in the 1980s became a valuable source of social capital to friends and relatives displaced by NAFTA. They offered newcomers loans to pay for human smugglers, a place to stay when they arrived in Iowa, and access to jobs at local meatpacking plants.[49] As the network in Marshalltown grew, those back in Villachuato accumulated more social capital, which made it less risky and less costly for them to head north. These social processes perpetuated flows that were set into motion by economic and political shocks. Marshalltown's Latino population increased from less than 1 percent of the overall population in 1990 to more than 15 percent in 2010 as social networks created a cumulative migration effect.[50]

Economic shocks and transnational social networks have similarly perpetuated emigration flows between thousands of other Mexican and U.S. communities. Figure 2.2 shows that the annual flow of Mexican migrants to the United States more than doubled during the 1990s. In each of the three years before NAFTA, an estimated 370,000 to 400,000 Mexicans per year set off to work in the United States. With the passage of NAFTA in January 1994 and the capital flight that followed a pronounced devaluation of the Mexican peso in December 1994, emigration levels rose to more than 500,000 per year. In the years that followed, the competitive pressures of NAFTA took hold, the peso crisis deepened, state-owned enterprises like CONASUPO were eliminated, and the consolidation of transnational social networks continued to lower the costs of emigration. As a result, the number of Mexicans heading to the United States each year peaked at 770,000 by the end of the decade.[51]

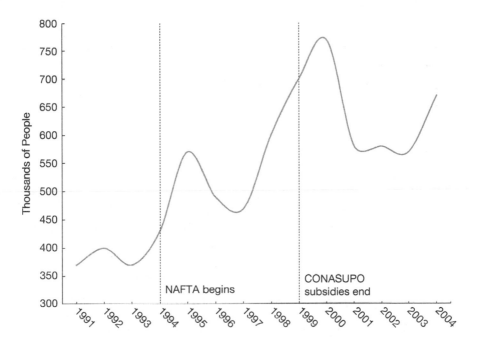

Figure 2.2 Estimated number of Mexicans entering the United States annually, 1991–2004.
SOURCE: Jeffrey Passel, D'Vera Cohn, and Ana Gonzalez-Barrera, "Net Migration from Mexico Falls to Zero—and Perhaps Less," Pew Research Center (April 23, 2012): Table A2.

Figure 2.3 shows that the flow of remittances to Mexico surged during the 1990s and 2000s as more people emigrated and settled indefinitely in the United States. The trend toward permanent settlement was an unintended consequence of U.S. immigration policies during this period that made it increasingly difficult for Mexicans to come and go between the two countries as they had in previous decades.[52] Overall, official remittances to Mexico increased by nearly 750 percent during the fourteen-year implementation of NAFTA, from $3.3 billion in 1993 to $25 billion in 2008.[53] Remittances only began to decline with the onset of the U.S. housing crisis in 2007–2008, which left many Mexicans in the construction industry without jobs. As the crisis spread and the U.S. economy contracted, remittances to Mexico dropped further and eventually recovered to 2008 levels in 2015 with the full recovery of the U.S. economy.

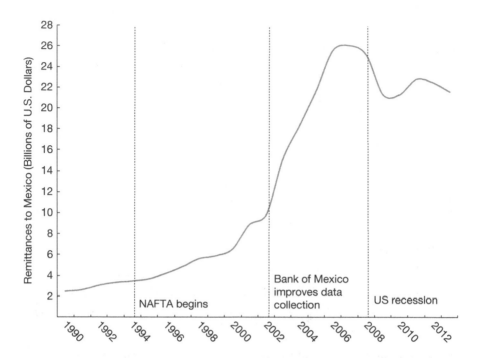

Figure 2.3 Annual remittance flows to Mexico, 1990–2013.
SOURCE: Consejo Nacional de Población, México, International Migration Series,
Table 8.1.1. Data available at http://www.conapo.gob.mx/en/OMI/Series_de_Migracion_
Internacional.

Nevertheless, the growth in remittances to Mexico during the 1990s and
2000s was significant and unprecedented. This money transformed the
Mexican countryside in particular. As more people from the Mexican
countryside emigrated in response to economic shocks and settled in
the United States indefinitely, agrarian communities like La Victoria and
Huandacareo increasingly traded their dependence on the state and its
subsidies for dependence on migrants and their remittances. Figure 2.4
shows that the percentage of households in rural Mexican communities
that received remittances increased steadily during the time of the market
transition. In 1992, two years before NAFTA, 6.2 percent of households
in rural communities received remittances. By 2006, the share of rural
Mexican households receiving remittances had increased to 14.8 percent.[54]
In some of the rural communities where I conducted fieldwork, the share

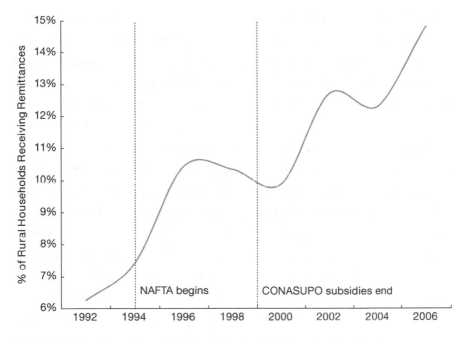

Figure 2.4 Percentage of rural Mexican households that received remittances, 1992–2006.
SOURCE: Consejo Nacional de Población, México, International Migration Series, Table 8.2.2. Data available at http://www.conapo.gob.mx/en/OMI/Series_de_Migracion_Internacional.

of households that receive remittances is as high as 25 to 50 percent.[55] Remittance recipients in Mexico became disproportionately rural over this period as agrarian communities that had been abandoned by the state came increasingly to seek out and depend on remittances to compensate themselves for economic shocks and insure themselves against risk.

REMITTANCES AS DE FACTO SOCIAL POLICY

How do citizens and states cope with the ravages of global capitalism, especially when their governments are cutting, not expanding, social welfare provision? Austere economic policies since the 1980s were devastating for Mexico's rural poor. Livelihoods were lost as a result of austerity measures and U.S. competition. During this time, millions of Mexicans emigrated and sent remittances to support family and friends who were unable or unwilling to leave. Remittances filled a critical welfare gap in rural Mexican communities undergoing destabilizing transitions. In town after town, village after village, Mexicans in the United States assumed a greater social welfare burden as the Mexican government's role in providing social welfare contracted. What the rural areas lost in terms of government protection and support, they gained in the form of remittances. In many cases, Mexico's rural poor traded one type of dependence (dependence on the state) for another (dependence on migrants). In this respect, waiting for people to emigrate from the countryside and send remittances became Mexico's de facto social policy during the 1990s and 2000s. Mexico's proximity to the United States and the booming U.S. economy's insatiable demand for workers assured the Mexican government that this shift in dependence would occur quickly and fluidly. By implementing market-oriented reforms while also pulling the safety net out from under the rural poor, the Mexican government counted on millions of migrants to secure employment in the United States and send money home to help their relatives and communities cope with the bumpy market transition. In this sense, it could be said that the Mexican government outsourced welfare provision to citizens abroad. By leaving the rural poor with few options, the Mexican government essentially forced households to improvise their own strategies for coping and adjusting to Mexico's integration into the global economy. Emigrating to remit became the most effective coping strategy for many families in light of the state's retrenchment.

How Remittances
Prevent Social Unrest

Evidence from the Mexican Countryside

Politicians, even the most committed advocates of austerity and fiscal discipline, know that it is difficult to cut social spending.[1] Citizens who are at risk of losing government benefits inevitably notice, organize, and fight to protect what they believe to be theirs.[2] Sometimes the backlash grows violent if budget cuts cause prices on basic goods to rise and drive angry citizens into the streets in protest. The potential for civil unrest was particularly high in many developing countries during the 1980s and 1990s because governments were cutting spending at the same time that they were opening their economies to competition from abroad. Trade liberalization creates concentrated groups of economic losers who have compelling incentives to organize and pressure the state to adopt more protectionist policies.[3] Many political scientists have argued that Western democracies increased social spending after World War II precisely to avoid this kind of pressure. Proponents of this argument, sometimes called the compensation hypothesis, argue that governments used public funds to "compensate" workers in vulnerable industries or sectors for challenges associated with the establishment of more open, market-oriented systems.[4] Safety nets like unemployment compensation and trade adjustment assistance became tools for absorbing some of the dislocations caused by capitalism and fostering social and political stability.[5] John Ruggie called this the "embedded liberal compromise," an implicit pact between postwar Western states and their publics to use government spending to minimize backlash against open-economy policies that, although good for aggregate growth, create concentrated groups of economic losers.[6] Peter Katzenstein similarly called welfare state expansion an "adjustment strategy" that helped to temper political opposition from the losers of economic globalization.[7]

Instead of expanding safety nets to compensate citizens for the risks and dislocations that come with global market integration, however, many governments in the developing world were eliminating them or scaling them back at the precise moment that they were establishing more open, market-oriented systems. The combination of liberalization and austerity has fueled backlash against neoliberalism throughout the developing world.[8]

One of the most famous instances occurred in southern Mexico in the early hours of January 1, 1994—not coincidentally, the day the North American Free Trade Agreement (NAFTA) began to go into effect. That morning, a group of three thousand armed guerrillas emerged from the countryside in one of Mexico's poorest regions, occupied seven towns, and declared war on the Mexican government. Over the next twelve days, the group, which called itself the Zapatista Army of National Liberation, used violence to protest Mexico's integration into the global economy and continued marginalization of indigenous people. "We have nothing, absolutely nothing. Not a dignified roof, nor work, nor land, nor health care, nor education," one rebel leader said in justifying the uprising.[9] "The struggle is for people to have a better life," another explained. The rebels were largely indigenous people who depended on the small-scale cultivation of coffee and corn. Their livelihoods had been battered by the dismantlement of the Mexican Coffee Institute (INMECAFÉ), falling producer prices, rising input prices, and declining access to credit. They rose up in opposition to neoliberal policies and fear that NAFTA would exacerbate their poverty. As a rebel leader told reporters: "The free trade agreement is a death certificate for the Indian peoples of Mexico."[10]

What some find surprising about the Zapatista insurgency is not that it happened, but that it and other instances of resistance to neoliberalism failed to gain national traction.[11] Mexico in the late 1980s and early 1990s appeared ripe for what Jeffrey Sachs called a "populist cycle."[12] The cycle begins with an economic crisis caused by overspending and market distortions. The crisis leads to the rise of pro-market politicians who promise to liberate markets and cut spending. But market reforms and austerity create economic losers. According to this argument, the pain of austerity and the economic dislocations that come with market reforms should give rise to populists who promise protectionism and exorbitant public spending. The concentrated losses experienced by these farmers made backlash against pro-market parties seem inevitable.

This leftward shift, however, did not occur in Mexico. Rather, as we saw in the last chapter, globalization and austerity gave way to another kind of cycle in many parts of the Mexican countryside. Instead of protesting neoliberal policies, millions in the Mexican countryside voted with their feet. Remittances rose and family members in Mexico were able to weather the economic storm. The result, as I will attempt to show in this chapter, was a marked reduction in economic grievances and demand for government-provided welfare. With some opposition to neoliberalism tempered by remittances, the Mexican government was able to manage backlash against its austere economic policies. The notion that the Mexican government was consciously counting on migrants to absorb shocks associated with neoliberal policies was raised in testimony to the U.S. House of Representatives three weeks before it voted to ratify NAFTA in November 1993. There, a group of researchers and Mexican farmworker advocates argued that millions of agrarian families would abandon their land in response to shocks caused by austerity and foreign competition. They would cope by migrating illegally to the United States. That these families could reliably self-insure by emigrating and sending back remittances meant that the Mexican government got a pass on having to compensate its citizens for dislocations associated with the market transition.

Compare La Victoria, for example, the coffee-growing village we visited in the last chapter, to the communities that were the strongholds of the Zapatista insurgency. The similarities between these two areas are striking in many respects. Both areas are populated primarily by people of indigenous origin. Their residents depended largely on coffee and corn cultivation for their survival. Both areas are isolated in the mountains, impoverished, and cut off from the fruits of Mexico's modernization. Due to their reliance on coffee and corn, the dissolution of institutions like INMECAFÉ and CONASUPO exacerbated poverty and economic anxiety in both areas.

Where La Victoria and coffee-growing villages in Chiapas differ most, however, is in their distance from the United States border. Located in northeast Mexico just a few hours' drive from the border with Texas, the residents of La Victoria had relatively easy access to the U.S. labor market in the early 1990s. A few people emigrated in the early phases of the coffee crisis. Through that process, social networks between La Victoria and the United States were established. These networks and the social capital they brought with them made the costs of emigrating from La Victoria to the United States sufficiently low such that almost every young male and many young females from the village made the trek at least once. Located along Mexico's southern border with Guatemala, on the other hand, the villages in Chiapas where the Zapatista uprising originated are 1,500 kilometers or more from the U.S. border. The barriers to emigrating were extremely high in comparison to those faced in La Victoria. More money was needed for travel, and there was more risk of getting lost or running out of money along the way. As a result, transnational networks were far less developed and far fewer people emigrated and sent money home.

These differences are reflected in the data on remittances sent to both areas. In 1995, a year after the Zapatista uprising and the earliest date state-level data on remittances to Mexico is available, remittances to the state of

Chiapas were only $5.50 per capita. This amount was among the lowest in Mexico—well below the national average of $42.29 per capita in 1995. Struggling coffee farmers from La Victoria, on the other hand, were able to compensate themselves for losses tied to INMECAFÉ's dismantlement relatively quickly and fluidly by migrating to the United States and sending money home. Remittances to San Luis Potosí, the state where La Victoria is located, were $54.49 per capita in 1995—slightly more than the national average and about ten times more than per capita remittances to Chiapas. It is therefore plausible that grievances among poor coffee and corn farmers in La Victoria were less intense than economic grievances in Chiapas because—despite these areas' many similarities—the poor in La Victoria had access to a relatively reliable and significant safety net. The people of Chiapas, on the other hand, were disconnected from the U.S. labor market and forced to manage INMECAFÉ's dismantlement and the coffee crisis without a safety net. Chiapas became a pressure cooker of economic discontent.

The rebellion in Chiapas came and went. The Mexican army had no problem driving the Zapatistas—a ragtag militia made up mostly of poor farmers with no military experience—into the jungle. Although the uprising gave the Mexican government pause and signified that there was strong resistance to neoliberalism, it did not significantly alter the course of Mexico's economic policy. If anything, the Mexican government deepened its commitment to free markets after entering NAFTA in 1994, and the rural poor largely continued to be left behind by Mexico's modernization.

Once it became clear to the rural poor of Chiapas that the uprising would not lead to the policy changes the Zapatistas had taken up arms for, they increasingly mitigated circumstances in the same way that people in other parts of Mexico had: they emigrated en masse to the United States and sent back growing sums of money to support family members back in Mexico. The flow of remittances to Chiapas, in fact, grew faster than remittance flows to any other Mexican state in the years following the Zapatista uprising—from just $5.50 per capita in 1995 to $111 per capita in 2003 to $214.55 per capita in 2007. Figure 3.1 shows the massive increase in remittances per capita to Chiapas compared to other Mexican states and the nation as a whole.

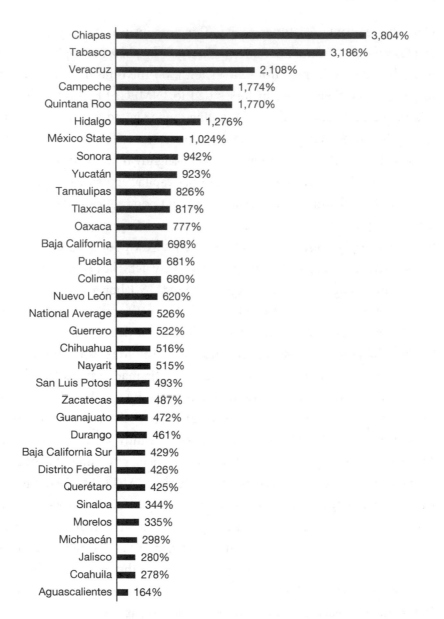

Figure 3.1 Percentage increase in remittances per capita to each Mexican state, 1995–2007.
Author's calculations based on state-level remittance data from Consejo Nacional de Población, México, International Migration Series, Table 8.1.2; and census data from the Instituto Nacional de Estadística y Geografía (INEGI) Censos de Población y Vivienda, 1895–2010.

LIFTING THE MOOD

In La Victoria and many other high-emigration Mexican communities, economic insecurity was minimized in the neoliberal era because the shift in dependence from state to migrants occurred fluidly. In interviews I conducted over the years in La Victoria, I have observed a great appreciation for the United States and the wealth that has flowed back to the community combined with ambivalence about the performance and responsibilities of the Mexican government. For example, on one visit to La Victoria, I asked Juan González what he thought the government could do to help his community considering that coffee prices still had not recovered almost twenty years after the crash. I expected him to reply with a list of demands. Instead, he thought about my question for a few moments and said he did not have any proposals. To be clear, Juan is a very sharp man who is intimately engaged with the affairs of the community. My colleague Juan Carlos Duarte Escalante, who was present for the interview, pressed Juan: "Nothing that the government could do?" he asked. Juan reflected for a few more moments and replied that perhaps the government could help them with funds to raise sheep and goats. That was all. I left the conversation wondering how many proposals Juan would have offered had the community not been able to so reliably depend on remittances.

How might Mexico's market transition have gone in the absence of remittances? Would people like Juan have been angrier at the government for its retrenchment from the countryside? Would there have been more violent uprisings like the one we saw in Chiapas in 1994? Would Mexico have been plagued by more grievance-fueled unrest? Agustín Cisnero Rincón, one of the corn farmers we met in the last chapter, imagined that, without remittances, the situation would have been much different in his town, Huandacareo, after the crash of the pork market in the 1990s. "Remittances are what sustain the people here," he said as we stood in his field. "If money wasn't coming in from the United States, maybe . . . I don't know, people would have to find a way [to survive]. Do like they did in the past: Start another revolution? This is why the government wants us to migrate. You look for a way to survive. It's between killing each other or leaving. And this is what people are doing: leaving the country."

Javier Cerna Villanueva, a business owner and community leader in Michoacán, made a similar point. Lamenting the fact that the economy in his town was particularly bad and that many people were suffering—going hungry, even—he added that remittances "lift the mood here a little bit." The mood is lifted because people feel more secure and less anxious, and the money has multiplier effects that help to support those who do not receive remittances themselves. This security translates into optimism about one's financial future.

Mexican officials I interviewed at a variety of agencies that serve the rural poor agreed that the optimism that remittances engender relieves their offices of pressure. For instance, when I asked a high-ranking official at the Ministry of Rural Development in Michoacán, Mexico what he thinks would happen if the flow of remittances suddenly stopped, he was candid. "It would be a very complicated situation for us," he told me. He knows, in other words, that the countryside would be in far worse shape than it already is and that his office and other government offices would be inundated with more requests for aid than they could handle considering their limited resources—or worse, that there would be more uprisings like the one that took place in Chiapas. Moreover, an official I interviewed at the Michoacán office of the Ministry of Agriculture, Livestock, Rural Development, Fishing, and Nutrition called remittances a "respite for the country."[13] They alone are not the solution, in other words, but they help mitigate suffering in times of crisis. Overall, these and other government officials I interviewed seemed to understand that remittances relieve the government of pressure to guarantee a minimum standard of living.

On one hand, remittances may be "lifting the mood," as Javier Cerna Villanueva described it—reducing economic grievances and making people more optimistic about their own financial circumstances and less angry about the poor economic conditions around them. The result here will be less pressure on the state because people are more economically secure, less aggrieved, and thus less compelled to punish politicians or use political channels in their search for economic relief. At the same time, remittances may promote political disengagement by giving the poor a better non-state option for relief. The result could be that people with family members in the United States have fewer incentives to hold elected officials accountable.[14]

The possibility that remittance recipients exit domestic political life without leaving the geographical bounds of the state came up in a conversation with Alejo Froylán Guzmán, a return migrant and former local government official in Huandacareo. We were talking about political participation and protest when I asked Alejo why more Huandacareo residents had not risen up in protest after NAFTA wiped out the local pork industry. Alejo began responding to my question by describing people in his town as "very laid back." I attribute the "laid back" disposition he was describing at least in part to the calming effect remittances have when they reduce economic grievances. Then Alejo paused, thought about my question for a moment, and added another explanation. "Perhaps this is what's going on," he said. "We don't really depend on the government. We depend more directly on our brothers in the U.S. So we aren't so concerned with what the people in the government do or don't do."[15] His point? Remittance recipients do not bother to hold their politicians' feet to the fire because it is far more effective to place a phone call or send a text message, email, or Facebook message to ask a relative in the United States for help in times of economic need. And for many families, the flow of remittances is so automatic that they do not even need to ask.

REMITTANCES, ECONOMIC GRIEVANCES, AND DEMAND FOR GOVERNMENT-PROVIDED WELFARE IN RURAL MICHOACÁN

Is there anything systematic about these observations? Do remittances promote economic security and reduce economic grievances? Do they reduce public anger during bad economic times and reduce pressure on public officials? Of course it is impossible to know if the Zapatista uprising would or would not have happened had the rural poor in Chiapas been flush with remittances (I do not think it would have), but we can gain some insight into whether remittances systematically reduce economic grievances by looking at how remittance recipients and non-recipients differ in their responses to survey questions about economic issues. To this end, I conducted a face-to-face survey of 768 randomly selected households in ten communities in rural Mexico. Notes on the design of this study can be found in Appendix I.

The communities I worked in are located in the northern part of the state of Michoacán—an area known for having very high rates of emigration to the United States.[16] The communities ranged from small hamlets with between two hundred and six hundred residents, slightly larger communities with anywhere from one thousand to three thousand residents, and small towns with between seven thousand and ten thousand residents. The smallest communities are not quite backwoods villages like La Victoria, but they are sleepy and rural. Roads are often unpaved, and the only buildings are residences, small elementary schools, and little bodegas that sell soft drinks, beer, and packaged snacks. There are usually not any services or businesses apart from bodegas. The larger towns, on the other hand, have well-defined central plazas with large churches, markets, a few schools, a health clinic or two, and basic shops that sell food, farming supplies, hardware, and clothing. Roads tend to be paved in the center of town and a mix of paved and unpaved roads and large fields on the outskirts. The mid-sized communities share a mix of qualities found in the larger and smaller communities: they do not have large churches or markets in the center, but roads tend to be a mix of paved and unpaved and there are some businesses here and there. Most of the homes—even in the smallest and poorest communities—are made of concrete. Occasionally one comes across a relatively large two-story house with slanted roof that mimics the style of homes in the suburban United States.[17] Most homes, however, are very simple two- or three-room one-story houses with flat roofs.

Overall, 34.2 percent of households that I surveyed received remittances. Average annual income for remittance-receiving households was $3,770 per year before remittances and $5,896 per year with the addition of remittances. Average annual income for non-recipient households, on the other hand, was $5,177, or 12 percent less per year than remittance-receiving households. These numbers, however, understate the extent to which remittance recipients are better off. Remittance recipients typically have smaller households because some members are living abroad. More money is therefore spread out over fewer people. Calculating average income per person per day, I find that people in remittance-receiving households live on an average of $4.05 per day, whereas people from households that do not receive remittances live on an average of $3.16 per day. The average non-recipient therefore lives on 22 percent less per day than the average remittance recipient.

Poverty in these areas is exacerbated by high levels of income volatility. Three-quarters of households reported that they consider their income to be either "somewhat unstable" or "very unstable." This instability arises from the fact that half of households rely on small-scale agriculture as their primary income source. Ninety percent of farmers produce grains—usually corn—on an average of seven acres of rain-fed land. Their yields are low and their technologies antiquated. Some farmers still plow fields with the help of horses. Many seed their land by hand or, if they are lucky, with the aid of a small tractor. It is rare to find irrigated land in these communities, although occasionally one will see irrigation canals. Small landholdings, poor technologies, reliance on grains, and lack of irrigation leave farmers in these communities vulnerable to shocks caused by foreign competition, bad weather, and poor harvests. Many who do not own land work as day laborers on farms. The going wage for this kind of work is less than ten dollars a day, and it is far from consistent. When I asked a farmer why the pay is so low, he said, matter-of-factly, "Because the crops aren't worth anything!"

People who do other kinds of work are often no better off. In one of the smallest communities we surveyed, some families survive by making roof tiles by hand. Men shovel muddy clay into wheelbarrows until they are overflowing. They push the wheelbarrows up to an old shack and load the clay into molds. Then they lay the molded clay pieces on the floor to dry and later cook them in a wood burning oven. They sell their roof tiles to construction supply stores for a few cents each. If each man is able to make 150 tiles in the span of a day, he can go home with about twelve dollars. But it is getting harder to make even that much. As big-box construction supply stores like Home Depot and Construrama have opened all over Mexico, more consumers prefer to buy higher-quality roof tiles made in factories. Armando Mora, a return migrant living in one of the communities we surveyed, compared a factory-made tile to one of the tiles he makes by hand. He admires the quality of the factory-made tile. He knocks his fist on the surface of it and hears a *ting-ting* sound. If he did the same to his handmade tile, it might crack. He tells me he wishes he could buy a machine to compete with the companies that make their tiles in big factories, but he says he would need about three hundred thousand dollars—an unimaginable sum.

In another community, a group of six women work in a small sewing business. With the help of a government program that supports small cooperatives run by women from rural areas, they were able to purchase a handful of sewing machines, which they use to make school uniforms in a little brick shack in an arid part of Michoacán. Their tiny community is nearly deserted. They say that although their situation is better than most people's, their business hardly brings in enough money to feel worth the effort. Other people make money working at small workshops sewing palm hats or clothing, selling handcrafted goods at local markets, and working at bodegas that sell soft drinks and snacks.

The economic anxiety people in these communities are normally forced to manage was more intense than usual at the time I collected data in January 2008. First, food prices—particularly prices on tortillas, a staple of the Mexican diet—had been increasing steeply throughout the country for two years.[18] Anxiety over rising prices and anger toward the government for its handling of the crisis were recurring themes in interviews I conducted with farmers and community leaders in the communities I surveyed. In addition to the food crisis, people in the communities I surveyed expressed concern over how their economic situations would be impacted by the final phase of NAFTA's implementation. The agreement lifted tariffs in a series of phases between 1994 and 2008. January 1,

2008—the day before we started collecting data—marked the day in which tariffs on all goods would be lifted. In the weeks leading up to January 1, Mexican newspapers were full of stories about how the complete opening of the Mexican economy to U.S. competition would cripple the countryside. The cover of the January 2008 edition of *El Chamuco*, a satirical magazine, summed up the anxiety.[19] On the cover is a sketch of a peasant farmer in a big traditional hat. He is using a hoe to till a plot of land that contains just a single stalk of corn. As the farmer goes about his work, an ear of corn about three times his size points down at him from above. The giant ear of corn looks very much like a missile—a missile that happens to have an American flag on it. Next to the giant ear of corn, it says, "THIS YEAR IS GOING TO BE THE BOMB."

Are Remittance Recipients Less Aggrieved?

In the midst of an ongoing food crisis and the impending doom of NAFTA's full implementation in a countryside that had already been ravaged by austerity and foreign competition, we would expect respondents to have been feeling particularly aggrieved and worried about their financial situation when data was collected in early 2008. The question I am interested in is whether remittances played any role in reducing economic grievances and tempering economic anxiety.

I begin by looking at the relationship between remittances and respondents' perceptions of the stability of their economic situation. Relative to neighbors who do not receive remittances, do people who receive remittances feel like their financial situation is more stable? To measure respondents' perceptions of economic stability, the survey asked the following question: "Income is considered stable if you can trust that it will be the same or nearly the same month-to-month or year-to-year. Income is considered unstable if it changes frequently and is difficult to predict month-to-month or year-to-year. Would you consider this household's income to be very unstable, somewhat unstable, neither stable nor unstable, somewhat stable, or very stable?"

The remittances variable is an index I created in an effort to measure variation not only between remittance recipients and non-recipients, but also among remittance recipients. People who receive remittances receive different amounts more or less consistently and for various periods of time. To attempt to measure variation among remittance recipients, the survey asked the following three questions to people who said they receive remittances. The first question asked respondents if remittances were a small, medium, or large source of income compared to their income overall. The second question asked respondents how many months or years they had received remittances on a regular basis. The third question asked respondents to state how reliably they received remittances in times of need: always received in times of need, almost always received in times of need, or just sometimes received in times of need. The Methodological Appendix describes the rationale for measuring remittances in this way and describes specifically how scores on these questions were used to create a continuous "remittances index" variable whose aim is to measure the extent to which remittances are a significant, reliable, and enduring safety net to the household. The index ranges from 0 to 1. Respondents with a score of 0 do not receive remittances. Respondents with scores closer to 1 could be said to have highly reliable, significant, and enduring remittance incomes.

Figure 3.2 shows the predicted effect of remittances on income instability among households we surveyed in Michoacán. The dependent variable in this analysis is a dummy variable that identifies respondents who said they consider their income to be "stable" or "very stable," and the key independent variable is the remittances index. The model controls for household income from local economic activities; whether the household has access to public health insurance; whether the household relies on farming for income (a particularly unstable occupation in these areas); major assets such as land and cattle (if any); and the age, gender, and education level of the respondent. Holding control variables at their means, Figure 3.2 shows that the probability respondents said they consider their income to be stable or very stable increases (y-axis) as the remittances index increases (x-axis). This probability is represented by the solid line.

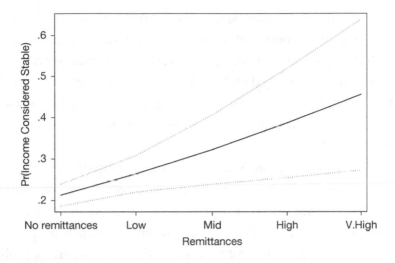

Figure 3.2 Remittance recipients are more likely to say their income is stable.
Figure shows predicted probabilities (solid line) simulated from a binomial logistic regression (dotted lines are 90% confidence intervals). The dependent variable equals 1 in cases where respondents said their income was "stable" or "very stable." All independent variables are held at their means, except the remittances variable. The relationship is statistically significant (p = 0.012). N = 749 respondents.

The dotted lines above and below the solid line are 90 percent confidence intervals, which represent the range of uncertainty in the model's estimates. The positive association between remittances and economic stability is statistically significant. Note that coefficient estimates and standard errors for this and all subsequent statistical models are located in Appendix II at the back of the book.

Figure 3.2 indicates that people in rural areas of Michoacán with substantial, reliable, and enduring remittance incomes were about twice as likely to describe their economic circumstances as "stable" or "very stable" compared to those who did not receive remittances. Starting on the left-hand side of the x-axis, we can see that respondents who did not receive remittances at the time of the survey had a relatively low probability of .21 of saying that they consider their income to be somewhat or very stable. Moving to the right along the x-axis, we see that this probability increases measurably as remittances become a more significant, reliable, and enduring source of income to the household. People with mid-range values on the remittances variable, for instance, had a probability of .32 of reporting that their income is somewhat or very stable overall. Even more impressive is that people with very high scores on the remittances variable had a probability of .45 of saying their income was somewhat or very stable. This result suggests that remittances are a highly effective way to manage the economic risk and instability that are inherent to life in the communities we surveyed.

Does being insulated somewhat from economic instability make remittance recipients less likely to express economic grievances? I analyze this question in two ways. First, I develop a statistical model that analyzes whether there is any association between receiving remittances and naming an economic issue when asked to state "the most important problem confronting Mexico today." I expect that if remittance recipients are less economically aggrieved, they will be less likely to have complaints about the economy and thus less likely to respond to this question by naming an economic issue. Overall, 63 percent of people who participated in the survey cited an economic issue like unemployment, poverty, or inflation when asked to name the most important problem facing Mexico. In second place, 18 percent of respondents cited some domestic security issue like organized crime, drug cartel violence, or kidnappings as Mexico's biggest problem. Other problems people cited include corruption, bad governance, education, health, and pollution.

Figure 3.3 shows the probability that respondents named an economic problem when asked to identify the most important problem facing Mexico. Again, the key independent variable is the remittances index. Like before, all control variables, which include a number of economic and demographic attributes, were held at their means and the remittances variable was varied from its minimum to maximum values. Moving from left to right along the x-axis, we can see that the probability of naming an economic problem drops significantly for respondents with more significant, reliable, and enduring remittance incomes. Respondents who did not receive remittances at the time of the survey had a probability of .67 of naming an economic problem. This probability drops to .53 for respondents with mid-range values on the remittances variable and down to .39

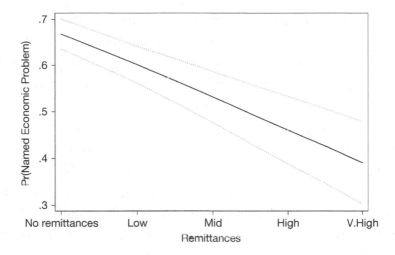

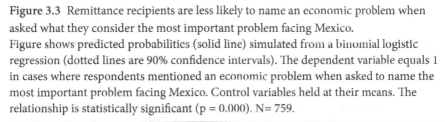

Figure 3.3 Remittance recipients are less likely to name an economic problem when asked what they consider the most important problem facing Mexico.
Figure shows predicted probabilities (solid line) simulated from a binomial logistic regression (dotted lines are 90% confidence intervals). The dependent variable equals 1 in cases where respondents mentioned an economic problem when asked to name the most important problem facing Mexico. Control variables held at their means. The relationship is statistically significant (p = 0.000). N= 759.

for respondents with very high values. The probability that one will name an economic problem, in other words, decreases by 42 percent when people who do not receive remittances are compared to people who can count on remittances to be a highly significant, reliable, and enduring safety net. The suggestion here is that remittance recipients are less economically aggrieved and thus less likely to point to an economic problem when asked to name the biggest challenges confronting the country. Unlike neighbors who cannot count on a reliable social safety net from family members abroad, remittance recipients are relatively insulated from economic adversity. They are therefore less likely to have economic problems on their mind.

A second way to examine whether remittances reduce economic grievances is through an analysis of pocketbook and sociotropic assessments. Pocketbook assessments are citizens' assessments of their own financial situation. Have things been going well, economically speaking? How optimistic or pessimistic is one about the future of his or her financial situation? Sociotropic assessments are assessments of the health of the national economy as a whole. Has the country been going in the right direction, economically speaking? Do you expect the country's economic situation to get better or worse in the months ahead? Some of the most obvious factors affecting citizens' pocketbook and sociotropic assessments include whether one is able to find work, whether earnings are enough to cover household needs, and whether earnings are stable or unstable. The loss of a job, the absence of good jobs, rising prices, stagnant wages, economic volatility, and pessimism about what the future might hold may all contribute to economic dissatisfaction and even anger toward the government.[20]

The survey measured respondents' economic assessments by asking them to report whether they expect their personal economic situation and the national economy to greatly worsen, worsen somewhat, stay the same, improve somewhat, or improve greatly over the next five years. Figure 3.4a shows the probability that respondents said they expect their situation to worsen greatly or somewhat. Respondents who did not receive remittances at the time of the survey had a probability of .28 of saying that they expected their personal economic situation to deteriorate over the next five years. Respondents with significant, reliable, and enduring remittance incomes, on the other hand, were far less likely to make a pessimistic prediction. Respondents with mid-range values on the remittances variable, for instance, had a probability of .17 of saying they expect their personal economic situation to deteriorate in the coming years. Those with very high scores on the remittances variable furthermore had a probability of .09 of saying that they expect their personal economic situation to deteriorate over the next five years. Respondents with highly significant, reliable, and enduring remittance incomes, in other words, were about a third as likely to make a pessimistic prediction about their personal financial situation compared to people who did not receive remittances at the time of the survey. Again, this result suggests strong support for the idea that remittances reduce economic grievances.

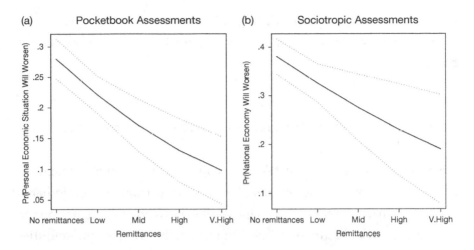

Figures 3.4a and 3.4b Remittance recipients are less likely to predict that their personal economic situation (a) and the economic situation of the country (b) will deteriorate over the next five years.
Figures show predicted probabilities (solid lines) simulated from binomial logistic regressions (dotted lines are 90% confidence intervals). The dependent variable equals 1 in cases where respondents said they expected their personal economic situation or the economic situation of the country to "worsen somewhat" or "greatly worsen." Control variables held at their means. Relationships are statistically significant. Figure 3.4a: N = 681; p = 0.002. Figure 3.4b: N = 668 p = 0.041.

Figure 3.4b shows that the effects of remittances on respondents' assessments of the national economy go in the same direction. Respondents who did not receive remittances had a .38 probability of predicting that the national economy would greatly worsen over the next five years compared to a .27 probability and a .18 probability for those with values in the middle and high ranges of the remittances variable.[21] People in the Mexican countryside who have significant, reliable, and enduring remittance incomes, in other words, are about half as likely to express a pessimistic view of the Mexican economy. The decreases we see in Figures 3.4a and 3.4b are particularly striking when viewed in the context of the adverse economic reality that respondents were confronting at the time of the survey in terms of food prices and NAFTA. These results do not imply that remittance recipients were completely immune to hardship. They were, on the other hand, less likely to express grievances during this difficult economic period. As Javier Cerna Villanueva put it, remittances help "lift the mood" in bad times.

Do Remittances Reduce Demand for Government-Provided Welfare?

Do remittances reduce the state's welfare burden by reducing demand for government-provided welfare benefits? Insulated from economic hardship somewhat, are remittance recipients less likely to make claims on the government in bad economic times? In the small towns and communities where we conducted this survey, as in many other areas of rural Mexico, it is common to see townspeople—particularly farmers, mothers, and the elderly—lining up at municipal, state, and federal government buildings to ask government officials for economic assistance. I was curious to know whether remittance recipients, who are presumably more economically secure because they have access to another kind of safety net, are less likely to turn to the government in times of need.

I asked the following question to measure demand for government-provided welfare: "In order to resolve an economic problem, have you ever asked for aid, funds, or cooperation from the government?" Figure 3.5 provides some evidence to support the argument that remittances reduce the Mexican government's welfare burden by reducing the likelihood that citizens will turn to government officials for economic assistance. Starting on the left side of the x-axis, Figure 3.5 shows that respondents who did not receive remittances had a .22 probability of saying yes when asked if they resolve economic problems by petitioning government officials for aid, funds, or cooperation. The probability of saying yes to this question decreases significantly as respondents' values on the remittances variable increase. Those with mid-range scores on the remittances variable had a probability of .14 of saying yes to this question. Respondents with very high scores on the remittances variable furthermore had a probability of .08 of saying they turn to government officials in times of need. In sum, people with very significant, reliable, and enduring remittance incomes

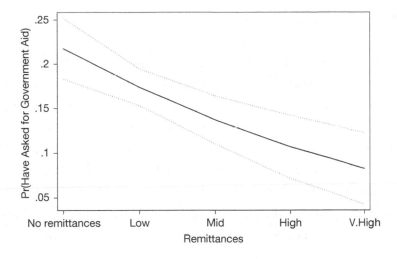

Figure 3.5 Remittance recipients are less likely to ask government officials for economic assistance.
Figure shows predicted probabilities (solid line) simulated from a binomial logistic regression (dotted lines are 90% confidence intervals). The dependent variable equals 1 in cases where respondents said they had tried to resolve an economic problem by asking a government official for aid or funds. Control variables held at their means. The relationship is statistically significant (p = 0.004). N = 757.

were about a third as likely as people who do not receive remittances to say they turn to the government for economic assistance.

These findings suggest some support for the argument that remittances reduce demands on government officials to guarantee social welfare. As the official at the Ministry of Rural Development implied earlier, remittances reduce the complexity of his work by reducing the number of people clamoring for his office's limited resources. There are likely two dynamics occurring here. First, as we have seen throughout this chapter, people who receive remittances reliably are less likely to have economic grievances. They therefore have fewer economic problems that need resolving. At the same time, they have access to a more efficient source of social insurance in their family members abroad. As studies by Gary Goodman and Jonathan Hiskey, Faisal Ahmed, and Yasser Abdih and colleagues have argued, access to non-state welfare may cause people to engage less with state actors and reduce citizens' incentives to hold officials accountable.[22]

CONCLUSION

Whether natural or man-made, economic disasters create demand for social insurance that many governments in the developing world are unable or unwilling to provide. This has been particularly true in the neoliberal era. The poor are more exposed to the vicissitudes of global markets, and governments prioritize austerity and balanced budgets over the development of robust, universal social welfare systems. Remittances have emerged to become an invaluable safety net in many developing countries where public safety nets are weak or in decline. But do they work to reduce economic grievances and public anger in bad economic times?

We have made a first effort toward answering this question by looking at some cases in rural Mexico. I began this chapter with a counterfactual. Would the 1994 uprising in Chiapas have occurred had poor coffee and corn farmers been flush with remittances? Obviously, there is no way to know, but I think the Zapatista uprising in southern Mexico is an interesting example of the kind of resistance that could have been more common had households in other parts of the country not been able to count on such reliable support from family members abroad. There are a number of striking similarities between the villages that were at the center of the Zapatista uprising and La Victoria, the coffee-growing village in northeastern Mexico we visited in the last chapter. The most glaring difference between these areas, I argued, was their access to remittances. The flow of remittances into struggling communities like La Victoria, I believe, played an important role in reducing the likelihood of other violent uprisings like the one that occurred in Chiapas. To explore this idea at the individual level, I analyzed survey data collected in low-income, high-emigration areas of Michoacán. There I found that remittance recipients are significantly more likely to view their economic circumstances as stable and significantly less likely to express economic grievances. They also appear to have less demand for government-provided social assistance.

In the remaining chapters, I will look beyond the Mexican countryside to explore the effects of remittances on economic grievances and assessments of government performance in more than fifty developing countries in the Middle East, North Africa, sub-Saharan Africa, Latin America, and the Caribbean. I will then return to Mexico to explore the effects of remittances on voting behavior.

Optimism in Times of Crisis

Remittances and Economic Security in Africa,

the Caribbean, Latin America, and the Middle East

W
e saw in the last chapter that remittance recipients in rural Mexico had a more optimistic economic outlook during the food crisis compared to non-recipients. To explore whether these findings generalize to other regions and other datasets, this chapter analyzes survey data collected from 120,000 individuals in fifty developing countries. Most of this data was collected during the food and financial crises that affected the global economy between 2008 and 2011. The data come from three well-known public opinion surveys: Afrobarometer, Arab Barometer, and the Latin American Public Opinion Project (LAPOP). In 2008, Afrobarometer conducted nationally representative public opinion surveys in twenty sub-Saharan African countries.[1] In addition to asking a core set of public opinion questions, the 2008 questionnaire asked the following about remittances: "How often, if at all, do you receive money remittances from friends or relatives outside of the country?" Possible responses were, "Never," "Less than once a year," "At least once a year," "At least every 6 months," "At least every 3 months," and "At least once a month."[2] In 2010–2011, Arab Barometer conducted nationally representative public opinion surveys in nine Middle Eastern and North African countries.[3] That survey asked the following question about remittances: "Does your family receive remittances from someone living abroad?" Possible responses were "We do not receive anything," "Yes, once a year," "Yes, a few times a year," and "Yes, monthly." Finally, LAPOP conducted nationally representative public opinion surveys throughout Latin America and the Caribbean between 2004 and 2014.[4] The LAPOP survey asked the following question about remittances in all countries surveyed in the 2008 and 2010 rounds and in a handful of countries in the 2004 and 2006 rounds: "To what extent does the income of this household depend on remittances from abroad?" Possible responses were "nothing," "little," "some," and "a lot."[5] Before moving onto the analyses, I will briefly discuss trends in the flow of remittances to these three regions.

TRENDS IN MIGRATION AND REMITTANCE FLOWS

Latin America and the Caribbean

An estimated 32.5 million people from Latin America and the Caribbean lived outside their country of birth in 2013.[6] More than a third of Latin American migrants are Mexicans living in the United States. The Mexican immigrant population in the United States peaked in 2007 at about 12.5 million people, but has plateaued since due to the U.S. recession and an aggressive deportation campaign that has largely targeted immigrants from Mexico.[7] Although Mexican migration to the United States has slowed in recent years, migration from Central America to the United States has been on the rise, possibly by as much as 500 percent between 2009 and 2014.[8] More than three million people from Central America were living in the United States in 2014—the vast majority from El Salvador, Guatemala, Honduras, and, to a lesser extent, Nicaragua. The outflow of people from these small impoverished countries peaked in mid-2014 when tens of thousands of families and unaccompanied children turned themselves in to U.S. border officials in Texas to apply for asylum. This phenomenon was years in the making and continues to be driven by drought, poverty, gang violence, and a desire on the part of many young Central Americans to reunite with parents who have lived illegally in the United States for many years. Some labor migration also occurs within Central America, particularly from Guatemala to Mexico and from Nicaragua to Costa Rica.

The Caribbean is also a major migrant-sending region. An estimated four million Caribbean immigrants lived in the United States in 2014, more than half of whom came from Cuba and the Dominican Republic.[9] Unlike migration from Mexico and Central America, Dominican and Cuban migration to the United States tends to occur through legal channels since American foreign policy welcomed immigrants from these countries during the Cold War. Many Cubans and Dominicans with permanent resident or citizenship status have gone on to sponsor the visas of relatives back home. At the same time that the Dominican Republic is a major sending country of emigrants to the United States, it is home to about six hundred thousand migrants from Haiti.[10] A roughly equal number of Haitians live in the United States.[11] Many settle in Miami, Florida and Brooklyn, New York near migrants from other Caribbean nations like Jamaica, Guyana, and Trinidad and Tobago. Caribbean migrants have also settled outside of the Western Hemisphere in significant numbers. In the mid-twentieth century, for instance, large numbers of Jamaicans, Barbadians, and Trinidadians migrated to the United Kingdom as British colonial subjects.[12] There have also been significant migration flows from Dutch-speaking Caribbean countries like Aruba and Suriname to the Netherlands, and from French-speaking Caribbean countries, such as Guadeloupe and Martinique, to France.

South American migration falls into three main patterns: migration to the United States, migration to Spain, and migration between countries on the continent. Colombia sends the most migrants from the region and fits all three patterns. The United Nations estimates that 2.7 million Colombians were living abroad in 2017, with the vast majority in the United States, Spain, and Venezuela.[13] Other South

American countries that send large numbers of migrants to the United States and Spain include Peru, Ecuador, and Brazil. Within the continent, key migration routes include the movement of Peruvians to Chile, Paraguayans and Peruvians to Brazil, and Paraguayans and Bolivians to Argentina.[14]

Migrants from Latin American and Caribbean countries sent home an estimated $67.2 billion in 2015, up from $56.8 billion in 2006.[15] More than 75 percent of this money was earned and sent by immigrants living in the United States.[16] Spain is the next leading source of remittances to Latin America and the Caribbean, accounting for 8 percent of flows. Much of what remains flows within Latin America.[17] In absolute dollar amounts, Mexico receives the most remittances in the region. In 2015, Mexico received an estimated $26.2 billion from citizens abroad— 98 percent of whom were sending money from the United States. With slightly more than a tenth of Mexico's population, Guatemala's remittance income was about $6.6 billion in 2015. Other major remittance-receiving countries in Latin America include the Dominican Republic ($5.2 billion in 2015), Colombia ($4.7 billion), El Salvador ($4.3 billion), and Honduras ($3.7 billion). Remittances are also significant in many small Latin American and Caribbean countries. In Haiti, for example, remittances were equivalent to 24.7 percent of gross domestic product (GDP) in 2015. Other countries where remittance income is large relative to the overall size of the economy include Honduras (18.2 percent of GDP), Jamaica (16.9 percent of GDP), El Salvador (16.6 percent of GDP), Guatemala (10.3 percent of GDP), and Guyana (9.3 percent of GDP).[18]

Figure 4.1 shows the percentage of respondents to the 2010 Latin American Public Opinion Project survey who said they depend on remittances at least "a little." This figure demonstrates that dependence on remittances varies considerably throughout the region. The countries that are least dependent on remittances are, not surprisingly, wealthier South American countries like Argentina, Uruguay, Chile, and Brazil. The South American countries with the highest proportions of remittance recipients include lower-income countries like Peru, Bolivia, Ecuador, and Paraguay.

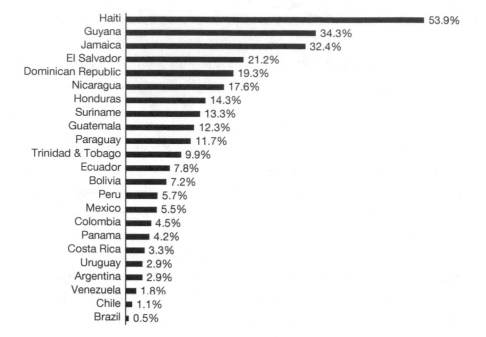

Figure 4.1 Percentage of the population that depends on remittances at least "a little," Latin America and the Caribbean (2010).

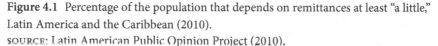

SOURCE: Latin American Public Opinion Project (2010).

Small impoverished countries in Central America and the Caribbean are highly dependent on remittances. About 20 percent of respondents in the Dominican Republic and El Salvador samples, for instance, were remittance recipients, and more than 30 percent of respondents in Haiti, Guyana, and Jamaica received remittances in 2010.

The Middle East and North Africa

An estimated 23.9 million people from developing countries in the Middle East and North Africa were living outside their country of birth in 2013. These countries include Algeria, Djibouti, Egypt, Iran, Iraq, Jordan, Lebanon, Libya, Morocco, Syria, Tunisia, Palestine (West Bank and Gaza), and Yemen.[19] Emigration from these countries typically falls into three general patterns. First, there are significant migration and refugee flows between developing Arab countries. An estimated 4.9 million Syrian refugees, for instance, settled in neighboring countries such as Turkey, Lebanon, Jordan, Iraq, and Egypt between 2011 and 2017 as a result of the Syrian civil war.[20] Other significant flows of people between developing countries in the region include the movement of Palestinian refugees to Jordan and the movement of Iraqis to Jordan, Lebanon, and Egypt.

A second pattern includes the movement of people from developing countries in the region to nearby oil-producing countries to work temporary jobs in the construction and oil industries. Saudi Arabia, in fact, is the world's second-largest recipient of migrants and second-largest sender of remittances after the United States. Furthermore, 72 percent of the population of Kuwait is foreign-born and 90 percent of the populations of Qatar and the United Arab Emirates (UAE) are foreign-born.[21] Although many foreign-born workers in Saudi Arabia, Kuwait, Qatar, and the UAE come from South Asian countries like Pakistan, the Philippines, Bangladesh, and India, many also come from neighboring countries, such as Egypt, Jordan, Lebanon, Syria, and Yemen.

The third general pattern is of migration from developing Middle Eastern and North African countries to wealthy countries in Europe and North America. Some of these flows are highly concentrated due to geography, language, and colonial legacies. Algerians, for example, have settled largely in France. Moroccans emigrate primarily to Spain and France. Others in the region go to a wide variety of countries. People from Lebanon, for instance, have settled in many parts of the world, including the United States, Saudi Arabia, France, Australia, Germany, and Canada.

The World Bank estimates that migrants sent $51.7 billion to developing countries in the Middle East and North Africa in 2015. This is about double the amount they sent through formal channels in 2006.[22] In absolute dollar amounts, Egypt is the largest recipient of remittances in the region with an estimated $18.3 billion recorded in 2015. Other important remittance-receiving countries include Lebanon with $7.5 billion recorded in 2015 and Morocco with $6.9 billion recorded in 2015. Measuring remittances as a percentage of GDP, the most significant remittance-receiving countries in

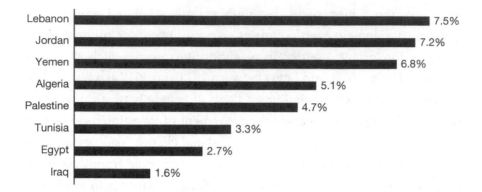

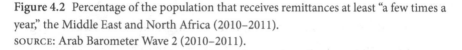

Figure 4.2 Percentage of the population that receives remittances at least "a few times a year," the Middle East and North Africa (2010–2011).
SOURCE: Arab Barometer Wave 2 (2010–2011).

the region in 2015 were Lebanon (15.9 percent of GDP), Jordan (14.3 percent of GDP), and Palestine (13.2 percent of GDP).[23] Figure 4.2 shows the percentage of respondents to the 2010–2011 Arab Barometer survey who reported that they receive remittances at least a few times a year. We can see from this figure that remittance recipients made up between 6.8 percent and 7.5 percent of the population in Yemen, Jordan, and Lebanon. Remittance recipients furthermore made up about 5 percent of the population in Algeria and Palestine.

Sub-Saharan Africa

Remittances are also an increasingly important source of income in sub-Saharan Africa. An estimated 23.2 million people from sub-Saharan Africa lived outside their country of birth in 2013. Two-thirds of these migrants resided in another sub-Saharan African country.[24] In some cases, these intracontinental migrants are refugees fleeing violence and oppression. Examples include people who move from countries like Eritrea, Somalia, and the Democratic Republic of the Congo to neighboring countries like Chad and Kenya. Employment and earnings prospects are generally grim for migrants fleeing violence and oppression within Africa. Although violence is one major driver of migration within sub-Saharan Africa, millions also migrate within the continent for labor purposes. Migrants from Mali and Burkina Faso, for example, seek out labor opportunities in nearby Côte d'Ivoire. Workers from Chad and Niger tend to go to Nigeria. Tanzania is an important destination for economic migrants from Zambia to the south and Burundi to the west, while neighboring Kenya is a key destination for Tanzanians. South Africa is a leading destination for job seekers from neighboring countries like Botswana, Zimbabwe, and Mozambique, as well as from Lesotho, which is bordered by South Africa on all sides.

The third of sub-Saharan African migrants who leave the continent go largely to the United States, Western Europe, and oil-producing countries in the Middle East. Those who are able to enter the United States and Europe tend to be wealthier and more educated than migrants who stay on the African continent or go to the Middle East. One reason is that poverty constrains movement to faraway destinations like the United States. The cost of a plane ticket alone is prohibitive for the very poor. Another reason is that the immigration policies of North American and Western European countries prioritize well-educated, highly skilled immigrants. Other sub-Saharan Africans, however, enter Western countries as refugees, as sponsored family members, and as winners of the U.S. diversity visa lottery, a program that offers legal permanent residency to people from countries whose nationalities are underrepresented in the United States.[25] Furthermore, unauthorized migration from Africa to Europe has been on the rise in recent years. Many people, particularly from wartorn or repressive countries in East Africa, make the journey on overcrowded rafts and rickety boats that travel the Mediterranean Sea from the coast of Libya bound for Italy. Once on Italian shores, many apply for asylum or attempt to travel to other European countries where job prospects and public benefits are more generous than in Italy. Others remain stuck in Italy. But those who make it to Europe are the lucky ones. Thousands of migrants have died in recent years trying to cross the Mediterranean Sea.

Remittances to sub-Saharan African countries were estimated to be $38.4 billion in 2015.[26] This was up from just under $5 billion in 2000. The official numbers reported by the World Bank and other institutions, however, underestimate the true volume of remittances flowing into sub-Saharan African economies. What are likely billions of dollars flowing to Zimbabwe, Somalia, Chad, the Central African Republic, and Mauritania, for example, simply go unrecorded (or at least are unreported) by those countries' governments. Even when record-keeping and reporting systems are in place, remittances go uncounted when they are sent through the mail, transferred through informal hawala networks, or carried back with returnees. This is particularly true for remittances sent within Africa. A recent World Bank survey found, for instance, that only 14 percent of migrants sending money to Burkina Faso from other African countries used formal channels like Western Union, MoneyGram, banks, or money orders. Similarly, only 23 percent of remittances to Ghana from other African countries was transferred formally. In Senegal, this number was higher at 37 percent, but the majority of remittances to Senegal from other African countries were nevertheless unrecordable.[27] Due to high levels of informality, official data grossly underestimate the flow of remittances to and within sub-Saharan Africa.

Figure 4.3 presents data from the 2008 wave of the Afrobarometer survey. Here we see the percentage of respondents who reported that they receive remittances at least every six months. Nearly one in three people in the small island nation of Cabo Verde and one in five people living in Senegal, Zimbabwe, and Lesotho received remittances at least twice a year in 2008. Remittance recipients make up a significant share of the population in many other sub-Saharan African countries. About one in ten people in Liberia, Mali, Ghana, South Africa, and Nigeria and one in twenty in Kenya, Mozambique, Benin, and Malawi received some support from a family member abroad in 2008.

The social insurance and welfare effects of remittances are well documented in sub-Saharan Africa. One of the first studies on the social insurance function of remittances noted that remittances to Botswanan farmers tended to increase after droughts.[28] Other studies in Ghana, Mali, Ethiopia, and Senegal reveal that remittances tend to increase during droughts, famines, and other economic shocks, making remittances among the most stable sources of social insurance on the continent.[29]

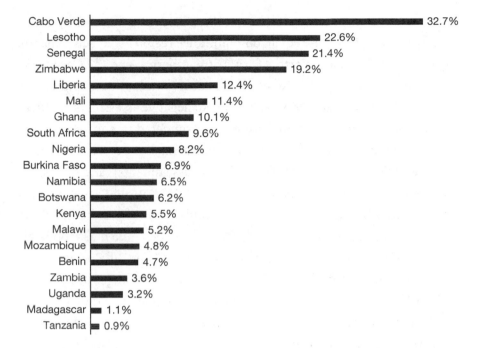

Cabo Verde — 32.7%
Lesotho — 22.6%
Senegal — 21.4%
Zimbabwe — 19.2%
Liberia — 12.4%
Mali — 11.4%
Ghana — 10.1%
South Africa — 9.6%
Nigeria — 8.2%
Burkina Faso — 6.9%
Namibia — 6.5%
Botswana — 6.2%
Kenya — 5.5%
Malawi — 5.2%
Mozambique — 4.8%
Benin — 4.7%
Zambia — 3.6%
Uganda — 3.2%
Madagascar — 1.1%
Tanzania — 0.9%

Figure 4.3 Percentage of the population that receives remittances at least "every 6 months," sub-Saharan Africa (2008).
SOURCE: Afrobarometer (Round 4, 2008).

Anecdotally, Ghanaian economists Peter Quartey and Theresa Blankson write that "[i]t is general knowledge in Ghana that families with migrant workers, particularly those in developed countries, are able to withstand shocks to income and threats to household welfare."[30]

REMITTANCES AND ECONOMIC ASSESSMENTS

Data on Economic Assessments

We saw in the last chapter that even during the 2007–2008 food crisis, respondents from rural areas of Michoacán, Mexico were more economically secure and less likely to make pessimistic assessments of their personal financial situation and the state of the Mexican economy. To what

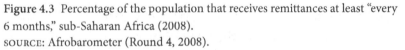

extent do these patterns generalize to other regions and countries in the developing world? All else equal, do remittance recipients in sub-Saharan Africa, the Middle East, North Africa, Latin America, and the Caribbean tend to be less aggrieved? Like our Mexican respondents, are remittance recipients in these regions less likely to make negative assessments of their financial situations and national economies compared to non-recipients?

Afrobarometer and LAPOP asked respondents both to describe their personal economic situation (pocketbook assessments) and to assess the overall health of their national economy (sociotropic assessments), whereas Arab Barometer only asked respondents to assess the health of their national economy. Specifically, Afrobarometer asked respondents to "[d]escribe your own present living conditions" and "the present economic condition of this country." Possible responses ranged from "very bad" to "very good." Afrobarometer also asked respondents if they expect "economic conditions in this country in twelve months' time . . . to be better or worse" and if they expect their "living conditions in twelve months' time . . . to be better or worse". Possible responses ranged from "much worse" to "much better." Similarly, the LAPOP surveys asked respondents to "describe your overall economic situation" and "the country's economic situation." Possible responses ranged from "very bad" to "very good." The LAPOP surveys also asked, "Do you think that in 12 months your economic situation will be better than, the same as, or worse than it is now?" and "Do you think that in 12 months the economic situation of the country will be better than, the same, or worse than it is now?"[31] Finally, the Arab Barometer survey asked, "How would you evaluate the current economic situation in your country?" with possible responses ranging from "very bad" to "very good"; and it also asked, "What do you think will be the economic situation in your country during the next few years compared to the current situation?" with possible responses ranging from "much worse" to "much better."

I used these data to explore statistical relationships between remittances and economic assessments in fifty developing countries. Just as in the last chapter, the line graphs in this chapter show predicted probabilities simulated from my statistical models. In each, the dependent variable identifies respondents who made a negative or pessimistic assessment when asked to rate their personal economic situation and the economic situation of the country. When I say they made a negative assessment, I am referring to responses like "very bad," "bad," and "fairly bad." When I say they made a pessimistic assessment, I am referring to responses such as "worse" and "much worse." My assumption here is that people who are less aggrieved will be less likely to make negative or pessimistic economic assessments.

Depending on which dataset we are analyzing, the key explanatory variable measures the degree to which respondents depend on remittances or how frequently they receive remittances. Control variables include respondents' gender, age, education, and income.[32] All statistical models in this chapter and the next chapter also include country fixed effects to mitigate the effects of omitted variable bias and control for country-specific factors, such as the effects of political institutions and economic structure.[33] I will first discuss my findings with reference to overall trends within each region. Then I will drill down to explore patterns in specific countries.

Regional Trends

The analyses of overall trends in Latin America and the Caribbean are based on data collected from up to 83,692 respondents in twenty-two countries in 2004, 2006, 2008, and 2010. Analyses of overall trends in sub-Saharan Africa are based on data collected from up to 26,881 respondents in twenty countries in 2008–2009. Analyses of overall trends in the Middle East and North Africa are based on data collected from up to 8,591 respondents in eight countries in 2010–2011. Table 4.1 lists the countries included in each regional sample.

Analyses from all three regions indicate that there is a strong association between receiving remittances and having fewer economic grievances. Remittance recipients throughout the developing world, in other words, are less pessimistic about their own financial circumstances and less

TABLE 4.1   CASES ANALYZED

LAPOP cases		
Argentina	Ecuador	Nicaragua
Belize	El Salvador	Panama
Bolivia	Guatemala	Paraguay
Brazil	Guyana	Peru
Chile	Haiti	Uruguay
Colombia	Honduras	Venezuela
Costa Rica	Jamaica	
Dominican Republic	Mexico	
Afrobarometer cases		
Benin	Liberia	Senegal
Botswana	Madagascar	South Africa
Burkina Faso	Malawi	Tanzania
Cabo Verde	Mali	Uganda
Ghana	Mozambique	Zambia
Kenya	Namibia	Zimbabwe
Lesotho	Nigeria	
Arab Barometer cases		
Algeria	Lebanon	
Egypt	Palestine	
Iraq	Sudan	
Jordan	Yemen	

pessimistic about the state of their national economies. The optimism that is associated with remittances even reveals itself during major economic crises, such as the global food and financial crises that were occurring when much of this survey data was collected. In fact, of the ninety-two survey datasets I draw upon in this chapter, seventy-two of the surveys were conducted between 2008 and 2011. During that time, people in many of the developing countries studied here were forced to manage a steep rise in food and fuel prices in 2007–2008, the devastating effects of the global financial crisis in 2008–2010, and another spike in food and fuel prices in 2010–2011. As we will see, remittance recipients were less pessimistic even during those painful economic crises.

Let's begin by looking at the results for pocketbook assessments. Figure 4.4a shows the probability that a respondent in the Latin American and Caribbean sample reported that her personal economic situation is "bad" or "very bad." All control variables are held at their means. The only variable whose value changes is the variable for remittances. The far-left side of the x-axis represents respondents who reported that they did not receive remittances at the time of the survey. I find that respondents in this group had a .28 probability of saying their economic situation is bad or very bad. The likelihood that respondents state that their economic conditions are bad or very bad decreases as values on the remittances variable increase. As we move to the right along the x-axis, the relative significance of remittances increases from nothing to a lot. Respondents who said they depend on remittances "some" were 10 percent less likely to describe their economic situation as bad or very bad compared to respondents who said they do not receive remittances. Those who depend on remittances "a lot" were 14 percent less likely to describe their economic situation as bad or very bad.

The effects of remittances were slightly larger in the sample of sub-Saharan African countries. This, however, is not an apples-to-apples comparison because the LAPOP and Afrobarometer surveys measured remittances differently—LAPOP in terms of level of dependence and Afrobarometer in terms of frequency. Figure 4.4b shows that as the frequency of receiving remittances increases, respondents in the sub-Saharan African sample were less likely to say their economic situation is "fairly bad" or "very bad." Respondents who said they never receive remittances had a probability of .51 of reporting that their economic situation is fairly bad or very bad. Moving to the right along the x-axis, we observe that respondents who said they receive remittances at least once every three months were 17.6 percent less likely to describe their economic situation

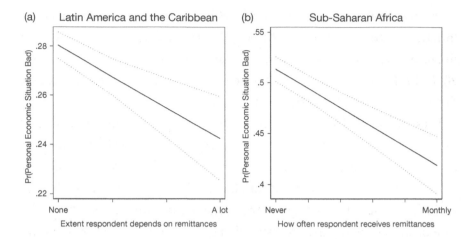

Figures 4.4a and 4.4b Remittance recipients in Latin America, the Caribbean, and sub-Saharan Africa are less likely to say their economic situation is "bad" or "very bad." Figures show predicted probabilities (solid lines) simulated from binomial logistic regressions (dotted lines are 90% confidence intervals). The dependent variable equals 1 in cases where respondents described their economic situations as "bad" or "very bad." Control variables held at their means. Relationships are statistically significant. Figure 4.4a: N = 83,692; p = 0.001. Figure 4.4b: N = 26,833; p = 0.000.

as fairly bad or very bad. Those who said they receive remittances at least once a month were 20 percent less likely than non-recipients to describe their economic situation as fairly bad or very bad. In sum, remittance recipients in Latin America, sub-Saharan Africa, and the Caribbean are up to 14 and 20 percent less likely to express economic grievances on pocketbook issues compared to people who do not receive remittances.

We see a similar pattern when people were asked to predict whether their financial situation would worsen or improve in the near future. People who said they receive remittances were far less likely to make a pessimistic prediction. In the Latin American and Caribbean sample, people who reported that they do not receive remittances had a .19 probability of saying that their personal economic situation would be worse in twelve months. Those who reported that they depend on remittances a lot, on the other hand, were 15 percent less likely to predict that their economic situation would worsen (Figure 4.5a). Respondents to the Afrobarometer survey had a .21 probability of predicting that their economic situation

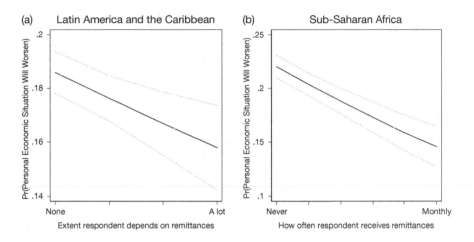

Figures 4.5a and 4.5b Remittance recipients in Latin America, the Caribbean, and sub-Saharan Africa are less likely to say their economic situation will worsen over next twelve months.
Figures show predicted probabilities (solid lines) simulated from binomial logistic regressions (dotted lines are 90% confidence intervals). The dependent variable equals 1 in cases where respondents reported that they think their economic situation will get worse or much worse over the next twelve months. Control variables held at their means. Relationships are statistically significant. Figure 4.5a: N = 25,406; p = 0.005. Figure 4.5b: N = 23,152; p = 0.000.

would be worse or much worse in twelve months' time. This probability also decreases as remittances increase: Respondents who reported receiving remittances at least once a month were 38 percent less likely to say that they expected their economic situation to be worse or much worse in twelve months (Figure 4.5b). Access to remittances appears to make people—even very poor people—far more optimistic about what their economic future might hold. This safety net removes some uncertainty about how poor economic conditions might affect them and softens the pain of economic adversity when it strikes.

We observe similar patterns when examining the effect of remittances on respondents' assessments of the health of the economy overall. For these tests, I was able to add cases from the Middle East and North Africa. In Figure 4.6a, we see that respondents in Middle Eastern and North African countries who did not receive remittances had a probability of

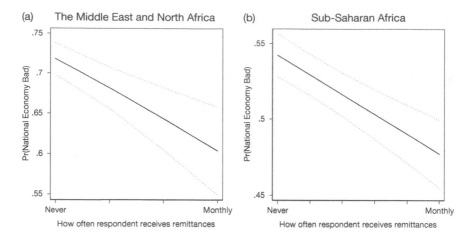

Figures 4.6a and 4.6b Remittance recipients in Africa and the Middle East are less likely to say their country's economic situation is bad or very bad.
Figures show predicted probabilities (solid lines) simulated from binomial logistic regressions (dotted lines are 90% confidence intervals). The dependent variable equals 1 in cases where respondents described their country's economic situation as bad, fairly bad, or very bad. Control variables held at their means. Relationships are statistically significant. Figure 4.6a: N = 8,591; p = 0.000. Figure 4.6b: N = 26,453; p = 0.000.

.72 of describing their country's economic situation as bad or very bad. This probability decreases with the frequency of receiving remittances. Respondents who said they receive remittances a few times a year were 11 percent less likely than non-recipients to make a negative assessment of the economy. Respondents who said they receive remittances monthly were 16 percent less likely than non-recipients to make a negative assessment.

This pattern holds in the sample of sub-Saharan African countries. Respondents in sub-Saharan Africa who did not receive remittances had a probability of .54 of saying that economic conditions in their country are fairly bad or very bad. Again, grim outlooks become less common among those who receive remittances regularly. Figure 4.6b shows that respondents who said they receive remittances at least once a month were 14 percent less likely than non-recipients to describe their country's economic conditions as fairly bad or very bad.

   Remittance-receiving respondents in the Middle East and North
African and sub-Saharan African samples were also more optimistic than
non-recipients about the direction of their respective countries' economies. Figure 4.7a shows that in the sample of Middle Eastern and North
African countries, respondents who said they never receive remittances
had a probability of .37 of saying that they expect economic conditions in
their country to deteriorate over the next few years. Moving to the right
along the x-axis we can see that this probability drops by 26 percent in
the case of respondents who said they receive remittances a few times
a year and by 38 percent for respondents who said they receive remittances monthly. Figure 4.7b shows that in the sample of sub-Saharan
African countries, non-recipients had a probability of .26 of predicting
that the economic conditions of their country would deteriorate over the
next twelve months. Moving to the right along the x-axis, we see that this
probability drops by 11.5 percent in the case of respondents who receive

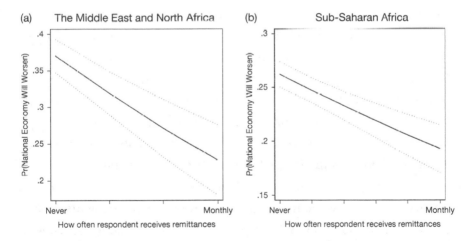

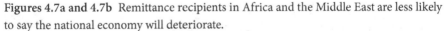

Figures 4.7a and 4.7b Remittance recipients in Africa and the Middle East are less likely
to say the national economy will deteriorate.
Figures show predicted probabilities (solid lines) simulated from binomial logistic
regressions (dotted lines are 90% confidence intervals). The dependent variable equals
1 in cases where respondents reported that they think their country's economic situation will get worse or much worse. Control variables held at their means. Relationships
are statistically significant. Figure 4.7a: N = 8,303; p = 0.000. Figure 4.7b: N = 23,047;
p = 0.000.

remittances about once every six months and by 26 percent in the case of respondents who receive remittances at least once a month.

The impact of remittances on sociotropic assessments was not nearly as strong in the sample of Latin American and Caribbean countries. Remittances, in fact, did not have a statistically significant effect on respondents' assessments of their countries' present or future economic situation. The coefficient on the remittances variable was negative in both cases, however, which suggests a pattern that is consistent with the patterns we observed in the sub-Saharan African and the Middle Eastern samples.

Summarizing Regional Trends

The upshot of these analyses is that remittances are strongly associated with feelings of economic security and optimism throughout the developing world. Remittance recipients in Latin America and the Caribbean were up to 14 percent less likely than non-recipients to describe their personal economic situation as bad or very bad and up to 15 percent less likely to say they expect their personal economic situation to be worse in a year's time. The effects of remittances on pocketbook assessments were even more pronounced in sub-Saharan Africa. There, remittance recipients were up to 20 percent less likely than non-recipients to describe their personal economic situation as fairly bad or very bad and up to 38 percent less likely to say they expect their personal economic situation to be worse or much worse in a year's time. Remittance recipients in sub-Saharan Africa were also up to 14 percent less likely than non-recipients to describe their country's economic situation as fairly bad or very bad and up to 26 percent less likely to predict that their country's economic situation will be worse or much worse in a year's time. Finally, remittance recipients in the Middle East and North Africa were up to 16 percent less likely than non-recipients to say that their country's economic situation was bad or very bad and up to 38 percent less likely to say that they expect their county's economic situation to be worse in a year's time.

Country-Level Trends

It is interesting to drill down into the various country samples to explore the effects of remittances on economic grievances in particular national contexts. Figures 4.8 and 4.9 show probabilities that respondents in Ghana, Mali, Senegal, and Haiti reported that their personal economic situation was fairly bad or very bad, depending on how frequently they received remittances (in the African cases) or how dependent they are on remittance income (in the case of Haiti).

Food and fuel prices were rising rapidly at the time of the 2008 Afrobarometer survey. West Africa was hit particularly hard by this crisis. However, as they did during Mexico's food crisis of 2007–2008, remittances appear to have helped insulate some respondents from the full pain of the crisis. In Ghana, for example, the probability that a respondent described her economic situation as fairly bad or very bad decreases from .50 to .31 as the frequency of receiving remittances increases from never to at least once a month. In other words, Ghanaians who reported receiving remittances regularly were about 40 percent less likely to describe their living conditions as fairly bad or very bad compared to non-recipients (Figure 4.8a). We observe a similar pattern in Mali. Malian respondents who did not receive remittances had a .61 probability of describing their economic situation as fairly bad or very bad. This number again dropped by 44 percent to .34 for respondents who received remittances at least once a month (Figure 4.8b). Likewise, in Senegal remittances helped temper citizens' overwhelmingly negative assessments of their living conditions. The probability a Senegalese respondent described his living conditions as fairly bad or very bad is .72 among those who said they do not receive remittances. This number drops to a more manageable .54 among respondents who said they receive remittances at least once a month (Figure 4.8c). Put differently, about three-quarters of the Senegalese population was economically aggrieved at the time of the survey. However, zooming in on just the population of people who received remittances regularly at the time of the survey, only about half were economically aggrieved, presumably because added remittance income offset the impact of rising food prices. In the

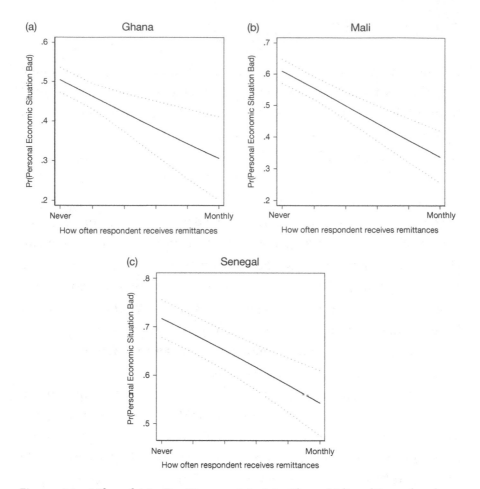

Figures 4.8a, 4.8b, and 4.8c Remittance recipients in Ghana, Mali, and Senegal are less likely to say their personal economic situation is bad.
Figures show predicted probabilities (solid lines) simulated from binomial logistic regressions (dotted lines are 90% confidence intervals). The dependent variable equals 1 in cases where respondents described their economic situations as fairly bad or very bad. Control variables held at their means. Relationships are statistically significant. Figure 4.8a: N = 1,151; p = 0.008. Figure 4.8b: N = 1,214; p = 0.000. Figure 4.8c: N = 1,130; p = 0.000.

next chapter, I will explore how greater economic security among remittance recipients affected political preferences and assessments of government performance in Senegal and other sub-Saharan African countries during the 2008 food crisis.

The effects of remittances on pocketbook assessments were also particularly notable in Haiti in 2006 and 2008. Haiti is the poorest country
in the Western Hemisphere and profoundly dependent on remittances,
which are equivalent to at least 20 percent of the country's gross domestic
product. The impact of remittances on people's pocketbook assessments is
substantively very large. Respondents in the 2006 and 2008 Haiti samples
who did not receive remittances had, respectively, .72 and .81 probabilities of viewing their overall economic situations as "bad" or "very bad."
These are among the highest probabilities in any of the country samples,
next only to Senegal during the food crisis. These probabilities, however,
decrease in a big way as the remittances variable increases. In the 2006
sample, the probability of making a negative assessment of one's economic
situation dropped from .72 to .53 in the case of respondents who said they
depend on remittances "some," and down to .43 in the case of Haitians who
said they depend on remittances "a lot" (Figure 4.9a). This is a 40 percent
decrease compared to non-recipients. In the 2008 sample, the probability

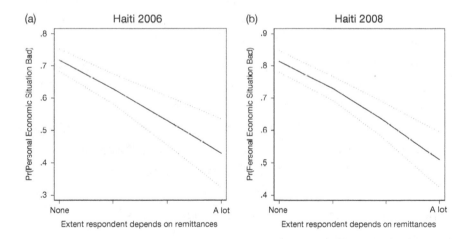

Figures 4.9a and 4.9b Remittance recipients in Haiti are less likely to say their personal
economic situation is bad.
Figures show predicted probabilities (solid lines) simulated from binomial logistic
regressions (dotted lines are 90% confidence intervals). The dependent variable equals
1 in cases where respondents described their economic situations as bad or very
bad. Control variables held at their means. Relationships are statistically significant.
Figure 4.9a: N = 932; p = 0.000. Figure 4.9b: N = 1,151; p = 0.000.

of making a negative pocketbook assessment went from .81 to .63 in the case of respondents who said they depend on remittances "some," and down to .51 in the case of those who said they depend on remittances "a lot"—a 37 percent decrease (Figure 4.9b). Put differently, eight out of every ten Haitians who did not receive remittances said they were dissatisfied with their economic situation, whereas five out of ten Haitians who counted remittances as a significant source of income expressed dissatisfaction with their economic situation.

Compared to non-recipients, remittance recipients in Zambia and Algeria were far less likely to complain about their countries' economic situations. Copper exports had driven economic growth in Zambia during the 2000s. When data was collected in June 2009, however, copper prices were falling due to the spread of the global economic crisis. This precipitated an economic slowdown and decrease in tax revenue, which limited the Zambian government's ability to spend on safety nets and economic stimulus programs. Understandably, Zambians had a negative outlook when asked about the state of the national economy at the time of the survey. Remittances, however, were able to temper this generally negative outlook. Zambians who reported that they did not receive remittances had a probability of .73 of saying that economic conditions in the country were bad, whereas those who said they receive remittances at least once a month had a probability of .51 of saying economic conditions were bad (Figure 4.10a). Likewise, the Algerian public was on the heels of a steep spike in food prices and months of unrest when Arab Barometer collected data in April and May 2011. The suffering is reflected in how respondents described their countries' economic conditions. Figure 4.10b shows that respondents who said they never receive remittances had a probability of .69 of saying that economic conditions in the country were bad. This probability, however, drops by 31 percent to .48 among respondents who said they receive remittances at least once a month.

The relationship between remittances and economic grievances holds when respondents were asked to predict future economic conditions. In Uganda, for example, I find that the probability of predicting that one's financial situation will deteriorate drops by 67 percent—from .33 to

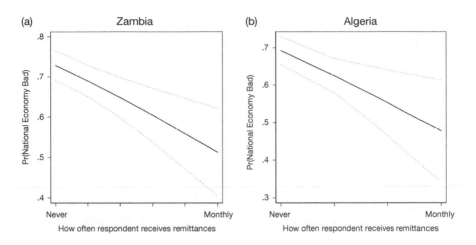

Figures 4.10a and 4.10b Remittance recipients in Zambia and Algeria are less likely to say the national economy is bad.
Figures show predicted probabilities (solid lines) simulated from binomial logistic regressions (dotted lines are 90% confidence intervals). The dependent variable equals 1 in cases where respondents described their country's economic situation as bad, fairly bad, or very bad. Control variables held at their means. Relationships are statistically significant. Figure 4.10a: N = 1,172; p = 0.001. Figure 4.10b: N = 1,119; p = 0.014.

.11—as the frequency of receiving remittances increases from never to at least once a month (Figure 4.11a). Furthermore, in Jamaica, respondents who did not receive remittances at the time of the survey had a .35 probability of predicting that their economic situation would worsen over the next twelve months. Respondents who considered remittances a significant source of income, on the other hand, had a smaller .21 probability of predicting that their economic situation would deteriorate—a decrease of 40 percent (Figure 4.11b). Finally, in Guyana, respondents who did not receive remittances had a .17 probability of predicting that their economic situation would be worse in twelve months' time. Pessimism was reduced significantly with remittances. The probability that respondents in Guyana who depended on remittances a lot would make a pessimistic prediction decreased by 40 percent to .10 (Figure 4.11c).

Remittance recipients are also less pessimistic about the future of their countries' economies. A couple cases stand out. Figure 4.12a shows, for instance, that remittances were associated with less pessimism about the

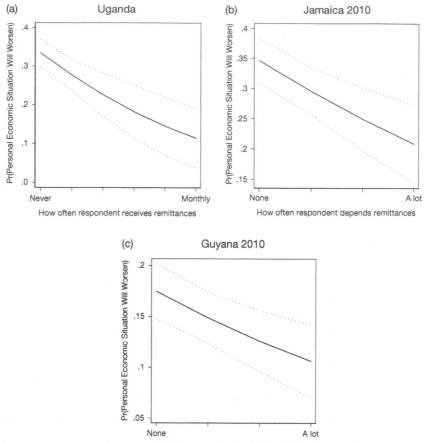

Figures 4.11a, 4.11b, and 4.11c Remittance recipients in Uganda, Jamaica, and Guyana are less likely to say their personal economic situation will deteriorate.
Figures show predicted probabilities (solid lines) simulated from binomial logistic regressions (dotted lines are 90% confidence intervals). The dependent variable equals 1 in cases where respondents reported that they think their economic situation will get worse or much worse over the next twelve months. Control variables held at their means. Relationships are statistically significant. Figure 4.11a: N = 2,092; p = 0.004. Figure 4.11b: N = 968; p = 0.003. Figure 4.11c: N = 951; p = 0.011.

economy in Lebanon when data was collected in April 2011 in the wake of the Arab Spring and in the early days of the Syrian civil war. This figure shows that respondents who did not receive remittances had a probability of .70 of saying that economic conditions in Lebanon would get worse in the next few years compared to a probability of .43 among respondents

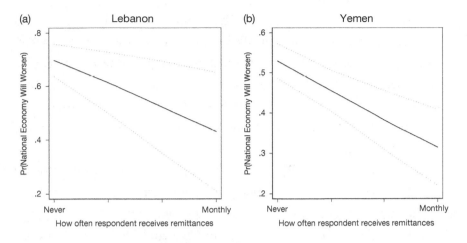

Figures 4.12a and 4.12b Remittance recipients in Lebanon and Yemen are less likely to say their country's economic situation will deteriorate.

Figures show predicted probabilities (solid lines) simulated from binomial logistic regressions (dotted lines are 90% confidence intervals). The dependent variable equals 1 in cases where respondents reported that they think their country's economic situation will get worse or much worse in the next few years. Control variables held at their means. Relationships are statistically significant. Figure 4.12a: N= 1,337; p = 0.006. Figure 4.12b: N = 1,044; p = 0.001.

who said they receive remittances monthly. Similarly, remittance recipients in Yemen were more optimistic despite the political and economic turmoil associated with demonstrations against President Ali Abdullah Saleh and his government's violent response in the first weeks of 2011. Figure 4.12b shows that respondents in Yemen who did not receive remittances had a probability of .53 of predicting that the national economy would be worse off in the next few years. People who received remittances on at least a monthly basis, on the other hand, had a probability of .31 of predicting that the national economy would be worse off in the next few years—a decrease of 41.5 percent.

CONCLUSION

This chapter presented evidence from about 120,000 individuals living in fifty countries in the Middle East, North Africa, sub-Saharan Africa,

Latin America, and the Caribbean. The results indicate that people who receive remittances are systematically less likely to express economic grievances. In many cases, I found that remittance recipients were between 20 and 40 percent less likely to say that their economic situation was bad, that they felt like the economic situation of the country was bad, or that they expected their economic situation or the economic situation of the country to worsen in the near future.

The optimism associated with remittances is striking because most of these surveys were conducted during the painful food and financial crises that rippled throughout the global economy between 2008 and 2011. Remittances appear to have helped ordinary people stay relatively optimistic despite the pain these crises were inflicting on their pocketbooks and economies. Economic grievances fuel political and social instability. People who are angry about the economy are more likely to support measures to overturn the established political order, whether at the ballot box or through riots and conflict. But can remittances operate as a stabilizing force? In other words, are remittance recipients less angry at their governments and less likely to punish incumbents for bad economic times? I explore this question in the next two chapters.

They Came Banging Pots and Pans

Remittances and Government Approval in
Sub-Saharan Africa during the Food Crisis

R ising food prices are an increasingly potent threat to social and political stability in developing countries and the cause of frequent bouts of rioting and unrest.[1] In 2007 and 2008, for instance, riots and protests tore at the social fabric of as many as thirty countries when the price of staple foods doubled or tripled due to speculation in commodity markets, low agricultural production, climate change, and increased biofuel production. In Haiti, Senegal, Somalia, Cameroon, Mexico, Côte d'Ivoire, Mozambique, Mauritania, Yemen, Peru, South Africa, Burkina Faso, Niger, and Sudan, thousands of people poured into the streets to voice their grievances. Some demonstrations turned deadly, and many governments faced intense pressure from their citizens.

Sub-Saharan Africa was hit hardest by the crisis. In Senegal, for instance, the price of rice—a staple of the Senegalese diet—doubled between

January 2007 and October 2008. At least five major protests occurred in opposition to President Abdoulaye Wade's handling of the situation. The suffering and anger reached a boiling point in March and April 2008 when protesters jammed the streets of Dakar. Under immense pressure from the media, trade unions, opposition parties, consumer groups, and ordinary citizens, Wade finally acted to suspend tariffs on imported rice, approve new consumer subsidies, and roll out a new agriculture plan. Desperate for a scapegoat, Wade blamed the Food and Agriculture Organization of the United Nations, which he called "a bottomless pit of money largely spent on its own functioning with very little effective operations on the ground."[2]

Anger over food prices and other economic problems turned violent in many African countries during 2007 and 2008. In Burkina Faso, citizens burned government offices. Aggrieved citizens in South Africa directed anger not only at the government but also at the country's immigrant population. Dozens of immigrants were killed and immigrant neighborhoods burned when anger over food prices and employment prospects turned violent and migrant workers were scapegoated.[3] Food riots furthermore killed at least a hundred people in Mozambique, Mauritania, and Cameroon.[4] Even when the suffering did not lead to rioting, governments came under pressure. In Ghana, for instance, the price of kerosene nearly doubled between September 2007 and May 2008. Many Ghanaians believed that the party in power, the New Patriotic Party (NPP), had the ability to reduce fuel prices but that it hesitated to act. Support for the NPP slipped during the latter half of 2008, and it fell short of a majority in the first round of voting in the presidential election on December 8, 2008. It was only after the first round that the NPP moved to reduce fuel prices, but by then it was too late. The NPP lost the runoff election (and the presidency) three weeks later.[5]

ASSESSMENTS OF GOVERNMENT PERFORMANCE DURING THE CRISIS

Was the suffering and anger in sub-Saharan Africa during the 2007–2008 food and fuel crisis mitigated by the safety net provided by family members and friends working abroad? Most remittances are spent on food and other basics, and as we saw in the last chapter, this economic cushion can reduce grievances in times of economic crisis. Did the economic security effect of remittances result in less anger toward the government for its handling of the economy? To explore if remittances reduce anger toward governments during economic crises, I will focus on the twenty African countries discussed in the last chapter. That the Afrobarometer survey data was collected during the height of the food crisis provides an interesting opportunity to explore whether and by how much remittances reduce the likelihood that citizens blame and oppose their governments during economic crises. Ideally, we would explore this question by observing whether remittance recipients are more or less likely than other citizens to participate in food riots. Unfortunately, there are no surveys that I am aware of that offer detailed data on who participated in the food riots that swept sub-Saharan Africa in 2008, much less data that identifies remittance-receiving participants from the rest of the population.[6] Afrobarometer did, however, collect data that helps us measure respondents' level of support for—or anger toward—their governments during the food crisis by asking them to assess government performance in a number of areas. Four areas are of particular interest considering that the survey was conducted during a period when food and fuel prices were spiking. First, the survey asked respondents to rate how well or how badly their government was doing at "keeping prices down." Second, the survey asked respondents to rate how well or how badly the government was doing to "ensure everyone has enough to eat." Third, and more generally, the survey asked respondents to rate how well or how badly the government was doing at "improving the living standards of the poor." Finally, the survey asked respondents to assess how well the government was doing to "narrow the gap between rich and poor."

With prices on everyday goods and services rising so quickly and so steeply, it is not surprising that most respondents were critical of government performance in each of these areas. As food expenditure—already about half of household expenditure in many sub-Saharan African countries—became an increasingly larger share of total household expenditure, people went hungry, the living conditions of the poor deteriorated, and the gap between rich and poor grew.

Remittance recipients, however, had a safety net to help them adjust to the surge in food and fuel prices, which I have argued should make them less critical of government performance. Focusing in on the four key areas of government economic performance listed above—keeping prices down, making sure everyone has enough to eat, improving living standards for the poor, and narrowing the gap between rich and poor—I explore remittance recipients' assessments of government performance. My statistical models control for respondents' age, level of education, gender, employment status, socioeconomic status, interest in politics, and whether they live in a rural or urban area.[7] I also include a dummy variable that identifies respondents who, at the end of the interview, said they believed the survey was sponsored by the government. The assumption is that these respondents have an incentive to express more positive assessments of government performance out of fear of reprisal or because doing so seems socially desirable.[8] Finally, the models include country fixed effects in an effort to mitigate omitted variable bias and control for country-specific factors such as political institutions, party systems, and economic conditions.

Keeping Prices Down

High prices were on most people's minds during the food crisis. Not only were food prices increasing to unprecedented levels, but so too were prices on items like cooking fuel and fertilizer. African governments were largely slow to act. In fact, in most cases, steps to subsidize prices, increase domestic agricultural production, or lift tariffs were a reaction to the food riots. When asked to rate their governments' efforts at keeping prices down, most respondents to the Afrobarometer survey gave their leaders low marks. As Figure 5.1a shows, the vast majority of respondents said their government was doing a fairly bad or very bad job of keeping prices down. On the left side of the x-axis are people who reported that they did

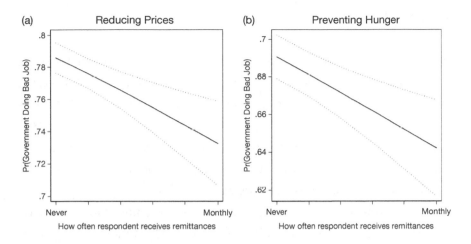

Figures 5.1a and 5.1b Remittance recipients in sub-Saharan Africa were less likely to say their government was doing a bad job at keeping prices down (a) and preventing hunger (b) during the food crisis.
Figures show predicted probabilities (solid lines) simulated from binomial logistic regressions (dotted lines are 90% confidence intervals). The dependent variable equals 1 in cases where respondents described government performance as fairly bad or very bad. Control variables held at their means. Relationships are statistically significant. Figure 5.1a: N = 25,882; p = 0.001. Figure 5.1b: N = 25,638; p = 0.001.

not receive remittances at the time of the survey. These respondents had a probability of .79 of stating that their government was doing a fairly bad or very bad job of managing the price increase. Figure 5.1a also shows, however, that the probability of making a critical assessment of government performance declines as the frequency of receiving remittances increases. Respondents who said they receive remittances at least once a month had a probability of .73 of disapproving of their government's efforts to keep prices down—a 7 percent decrease compared to people who did not receive remittances at the time of the survey.

A plausible explanation for this difference is that remittance recipients were less affected by rising prices and thus less angry. We already saw in the last chapter that remittance recipients were indeed less likely to describe their economic conditions and those of the country negatively. Exonerating the government for its handling of prices, even if only slightly, would appear to stem from having fewer economic grievances in general.

Preventing Hunger

Next, we look at responses to the question of how well governments were doing in efforts to make sure everyone had enough to eat. The food crisis was causing tangible suffering in many countries at the time of the survey. In Lesotho, for instance, a spike in the price of maize meal caused an estimated fifth of the population to face food shortages.[9] In Liberia and Senegal, rising food prices meant that households were consuming significantly fewer calories, less protein, and less nutrient-rich foods.[10] In Mozambique and Mauritania, where the average household dedicates more than half its budget to food, child malnutrition increased with the price of food.[11] In many African countries, rising prices forced people to sell valuable assets, such as farm animals, in desperate attempts to raise money to buy food.[12]

Figure 5.1b shows that the majority of respondents were understandably critical of their governments on this issue—they largely did not approve of their government's efforts (or lack thereof) to ensure that everyone had enough to eat. Remittance recipients, however, were less likely to criticize their leaders' performance. Respondents who reported that they did not receive remittances at the time of the survey had a probability of .69 of saying that their government was doing a bad or very bad job of ensuring that everyone had enough to eat. Respondents who reported receiving remittances at least once a month, on the other hand, had a .64 probability of saying the government was doing a bad job of ensuring that everyone had enough to eat—a 7.4 percent decrease.

My hypothesis is that remittance recipients were less critical of their governments because they were less likely to experience the kind of anger that follows from going hungry or falling below one's minimum consumption threshold. To test this possibility, I looked at data on a question that asked respondents how often they had experienced hunger during the food crisis. Figure 5.2 shows the probability that a respondent said she had gone without enough food "several times" or more over the past year. The far-left side of the x-axis represents respondents who reported that they did not receive remittances at the time of the survey. On the far

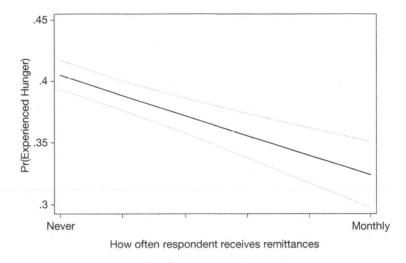

Figure 5.2 Remittance recipients in sub-Saharan Africa were less likely to say they experienced hunger several times or more during the food crisis.
Figure shows predicted probabilities (solid lines) simulated from binomial logistic regressions (dotted lines are 90% confidence intervals). The dependent variable equals 1 in cases where respondents said they had experienced hunger several times or more over past year. Control variables held at their means. The relationship is statistically significant (p = 0.000). N = 26,917.

right of the x-axis are respondents who reported that they received remittances at least once a month. Respondents who reported that they did not receive remittances had a staggering .40 probability of stating that they had gone without enough food at least "several times" over the preceding year. The fact that two out of five non-remittance-receiving respondents went without enough food on such a regular basis underscores just how deep and widespread the food crisis was. Remittances, it appears, provided some significant relief. Moving to the right on the x-axis, we see that respondents became far less likely to report that they had gone without enough food as the frequency of receiving remittances increases. People who said they received remittances at least once a month had a probability of .32 of saying they had gone without enough food at least several times. People who received remittances regularly, in other words, were more than 20 percent less likely to experience extreme hunger during the food crisis compared to people who did not receive remittances.

These results are further evidence that people who received remittances regularly were able to count on a safety net to help them adjust to rising food prices. They were less likely to have had to cut back on the number of calories they consumed or reduce the quality of the food they consumed. Because they could call on a family member abroad to send money home to help them through the crisis, they and their children were less likely to experience hunger and malnutrition. These results suggest that because remittance-receiving respondents suffered less and were less angry, they were somewhat less critical of government performance during the food crisis. In this sense, we can think of remittances as playing a role similar to the food subsidies that some African governments introduced to quell civil unrest fueled by rising prices. First, like a food subsidy, remittances helped people cope with the food crisis by maintaining regular or near-regular consumption levels. Second, by softening the blow of the crisis and reducing economic griev-ances, remittances, like subsidies, may have helped governments survive the crisis and maintain political and social order. Furthermore, because remit-tance recipients have access to a non-governmental safety net, it is possible that they would be somewhat less inclined to believe that it is the govern ment's responsibility to ensure that everyone has enough to eat.[13]

Poverty and Inequality

Now to more general questions about how well or how badly governments were doing to improve the living standards of the poor and narrow the gap between rich and poor. At least one hundred million people, most of whom were living in sub-Saharan Africa, are believed to have been pushed into poverty as a result of the 2008 food crisis.[14] For this reason, it is not surprising that the majority of respondents were again critical of their governments' efforts to fight poverty and inequality. Figure 5.3a shows that respondents who said they never receive remittances had a .66 probability of saying their government was doing a fairly bad or very bad job of improving living standards for the poor. People who said they receive remittances at least once a month, on the other hand, had a .60 probability of saying the government was doing badly or very badly, for a

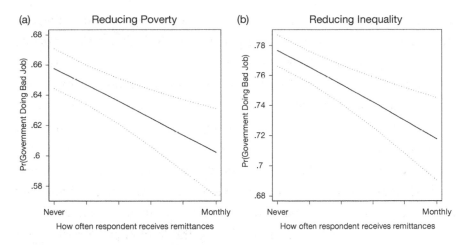

Figures 5.3a and 5.3b Remittance recipients in sub-Saharan Africa were less like to say their government was doing a bad job at reducing poverty (a) and inequality (b) during the food crisis.
Figures show predicted probabilities (solid lines) simulated from binomial logistic regressions (dotted lines are 90% confidence intervals). The dependent variable equals 1 in cases where respondents described government performance as fairly bad or very bad. Control variables held at their means. Relationships are statistically significant. Figure 5.3a: N = 25,851; p = 0.001. Figure 5.3b: N = 25,214; p = 0.000.

decrease of 8.6 percent compared to non-recipients. Finally, on the issue of inequality, Figure 5.3b shows that respondents who did not receive remittances had a probability of .78 of disapproving of the government's job of narrowing the gap between rich and poor, while those who received remittances at least once a month had a probability of .72 of disapproving of government performance. Remittance recipients, in other words, were 7.5 percent less likely to say they disapproved of their governments' efforts to reduce inequality compared to non-recipients.

REMITTANCES AND SUPPORT FOR INCUMBENTS DURING THE CRISIS

We have learned a couple important things about remittance recipients in sub-Saharan Africa during the food crisis. First, we saw in the previous chapter that remittance recipients are more economically secure and less likely to express economic grievances compared to non-recipients. Remittance recipients were up to 38 percent less likely than non-recipients to say their personal economic situations were bad or would deteriorate, and up to 26 percent less likely to say that national economic conditions were bad or would deteriorate, even during a time of profound economic crisis. Second, as we learned in this chapter, remittance recipients were more than 20 percent less likely than non-recipients to say they experienced extreme hunger during the food crisis, and up to 8.6 percent less likely than non-recipients to disapprove of their governments' economic performance during the food crisis. The vast majority of respondents gave their governments very low marks during the food crisis, especially on issues like rising prices and hunger, but remittance recipients appear to have been somewhat less critical, angry, or aggrieved compared to the general population.

These findings are likely interconnected. When people have access to a safety net—in this case, remittances—they are less likely to experience disruptions to consumption. Higher levels of economic security mean fewer economic grievances and less animus toward government for failing to guarantee social welfare. An important question is whether relatively lower levels of disapproval translate into a more forgiving electorate that is less likely to mobilize against and seek to punish political leaders for a bad economy. The economic voter thesis predicts that incumbents are less likely to come under fire when people are doing better economically. If food prices are rising but my family is able to consume as usual, what incentive do I have to demand the president's ouster or mobilize against the party in power on election day? Clearly, I may not be happy that I am spending more on food. I may not be happy to know that my fellow citizens are suffering. But if the crisis never affects my consumption personally, I will be less motivated to oppose those in power compared to a neighbor who cannot afford food and feels that the government has failed him.

An important empirical question with an imperfect answer is how we actually measure one's act of actively opposing the government. Short of some kind of social experiment (one whose ethics would be highly suspect) or detailed data on the individuals who participated in the 2008 food riots (this data certainly does not exist), it is difficult to measure and test the hypothesis that remittance recipients are less likely to mobilize against and punish incumbents during times of economic crisis. Two potential alternatives would be to look at questions in the Afrobarometer survey on past protest activity and vote choice in the most recent election.[15] These questions are problematic, however, because we do not know if respondents received remittances at the time that they say they protested or at the time of the last election. All we know about respondents' remittances is how frequently they said they received this money at the time of the survey. Looking back at past protest activity or voting behavior in elections is not helpful, in other words, because we do not know if someone who received remittances at the time of the survey also received them at the time that they last protested or last voted.

This leaves us with only one good option. In an attempt to measure support for incumbents and get a sense of the political preferences that may drive political behavior, we can look at how respondents say they would vote in a hypothetical election. In all twenty countries, Afrobarometer asked, "If a presidential election were held tomorrow, which party's candidate would you vote for?" The question was open-ended—respondents were free to name any party. Across the twenty countries surveyed, respondents mentioned 224 political parties. I went through the list of parties mentioned in each country and created a dummy variable that identifies respondents who voiced support for the party that held the presidency at the time of the survey. I thus considered someone a supporter of the party in power if they mentioned that they would vote for the party that was holding the presidency in their country at the time of the survey.[16]

With incumbent support our outcome of interest and frequency of receiving remittances the explanatory variable of interest, the statistical model controls for age, education, gender, employment status, high socioeconomic status, interest in public affairs, being from a rural area, and whether respondents thought the interviewer was sent by the government. The model also includes country fixed effects. Consistent with the logic of economic voting and evidence presented earlier about remittance recipients' assessments of government performance, the model indicates that remittance recipients indeed have a higher likelihood of saying they would support the incumbent party. Starting at the left side of the x-axis in Figure 5.4, we can see that respondents who did not receive remittances had a probability of .43 of saying they would support the incumbent party in a hypothetical election. This probability increases as we move to the right along the x-axis to respondents who said they receive remittances. Respondents who said they receive remittances at least once every three months, for instance, had a probability of .46 of voicing support for the incumbent party. Respondents who said they receive remittances at least once a month voiced the most support for the incumbent party with a probability of .47. In sum, people who receive remittances at least once a month were 9.3 percent more likely to voice support for the incumbent party during the 2008 food and fuel crisis compared to people who said they do not receive remittances.

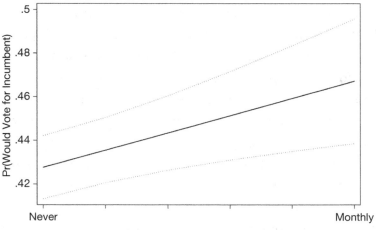

Figure 5.4 Remittance recipients in sub-Saharan Africa were more likely to say they would support the incumbent party in a hypothetical election.
Figure shows predicted probabilities (solid lines) simulated from a binomial logistic regression (dotted lines are 90% confidence intervals). The dependent variable equals 1 in cases where respondents said they would vote for incumbent party. Control variables held at their means. The relationship is statistically significant (p = 0.012). N = 22,800.

Figure 5.5 shows that the effects of remittances on incumbent support are even stronger when we restrict the analysis to respondents living in democratic countries (these respondents made up 65 percent of the Afrobarometer sample).[17] In Figure 5.5a, we can see that the probability of supporting the incumbent in democratic countries increases from .38 for respondents who said they do not receive remittances to .44 for respondents who said they receive remittances at least once a month. Remittance recipients in more democratic systems, in other words, were up to 15 percent more likely to express support for the incumbent compared to people who did not receive remittances. Figure 5.5b shows that remittance recipients in non-democratic countries appear to be slightly less likely than non-recipients to say they would support the incumbent. This relationship, however, is not statistically significant, so we cannot conclude that the difference between remittance recipients and non-recipients is

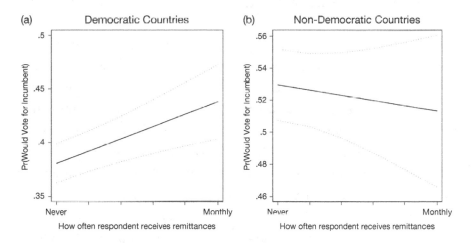

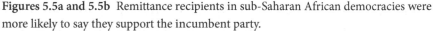

Figures 5.5a and 5.5b Remittance recipients in sub-Saharan African democracies were more likely to say they support the incumbent party.
Figures show predicted probabilities (solid lines) simulated from binomial logistic regressions (dotted lines are 90% confidence intervals). The dependent variable equals 1 in cases where respondents said they would vote for the incumbent party. Control variables held at their means. Relationship shown in 5.5a is statistically significant (p = 0.002). N = 14,455 (Figure 5.5a) and N= 8,345 (Figure 5.5b). Democratic countries, defined as countries with a 2008 Polity IV score of +6 or greater, included Benin, Botswana, Cabo Verde, Ghana, Kenya, Lesotho, Liberia, Madagascar, Malawi, Namibia, Senegal, South Africa, and Zambia.

different from zero. Despite the differences in incumbent support shown in Figures 5.5a and 5.5b, I find in additional statistical tests (not shown) that remittance recipients in both democratic and non-democratic contexts were significantly less likely to say they experienced hunger during the food crisis, less likely to make negative economic assessments, and less likely to say their governments were performing poorly during the crisis, although the effects of remittances on these outcomes were stronger and more consistent in democracies.

Why does the positive relationship between remittances and incumbent support only show up in democracies? I can think of three reasons. First, in terms of measurement, a survey question that asks which party one would support in a hypothetical election may not be a valid or precise instrument for measuring political preferences in non-democratic countries. There may not be any viable alternatives to the incumbent, for instance, and if there are, respondents may fear reprisal if they voice support for an opposition party.

Second, because remittances make the poor less dependent on government benefits, some scholars argue that they raise the price an autocratic or dominant-party regime must pay in order to buy votes or political support.[18] Remittance recipients, according to this argument, are thus freer to support opposition parties than non-recipients.[19] Although I do not observe evidence in these tests that remittance recipients are significantly more likely to support opposition parties, this mechanism may be at work in specific locales, or it may be obscured by the measurement issues I just discussed.

Third, it is plausible that remittance recipients in autocracies would be less supportive of incumbents because many people emigrate from autocracies in direct response to political repression. People who flee repressive regimes have profound and enduring grievances with the political leaders of their home countries. This opposition is likely shared by remittance recipients who, coming from the same family or community, endure threats of repression or violence as well. Remittance recipients in autocracies may furthermore explicitly blame political leaders for actions that caused their loved ones to flee more so than the family members of a typical economic migrant would because the line of causality from government actions to emigration decision is so direct and explicit. Finally, because there is little political turnover in autocracies, opposition to the government is likely an enduring one.

At the same time, however, the results indicate that remittance recipients' opinions of political leaders' performance are softened by the welfare effect of remittances somewhat. Remittance recipients in autocracies, in other words, are probably more opposed to the regime than non-recipients due to the predispositions I just discussed, but they are not as opposed as they would be in the absence of the safety net provided by family members abroad.

IMPLICATIONS

Remittances appear to systematically relieve respondents of grievances and their politicians of pressure during economic crises. A difference of 15 percent in the likelihood of supporting the incumbent could be decisive in a close election in a democratic country where remittances are a significant source of income. In fact, we will explore this possibility in the next chapter using data on voting behavior in Mexico's closely contested 2006 presidential election.

Findings that remittance recipients are less economically aggrieved, less critical of government performance, and, at least in democracies, more likely to voice support for the incumbent party corroborate analyses of macro-level data from Africa by Patrick Regan and Richard Frank.[20] Regan and Frank argue that in times of economic crisis, citizens will make demands on their governments and family members abroad for economic assistance. When the transnational community provides a safety net, economic grievances and pressure on the state to guarantee social welfare are reduced. This reduction in grievances makes it less likely that people will direct anger at and rebel against a poorly-performing government. Using country-level data, Regan and Frank suggest that countries that receive more remittances are at lower risk of experiencing civil conflict during periods of economic crisis. But Regan and Frank's study did not model or provide evidence about individual-level preferences. The preceding findings that remittance recipients are less aggrieved, and less critical of and less likely to oppose their governments during such a profound period of economic crisis, indicate that the dynamics postulated by Regan and Frank may indeed be occurring at the micro-level.

These findings also help us make sense of prior studies that, using aggregate-level data, have revealed associations between remittances and lower levels of spending on social security in developing countries. Yasser Abdih and colleagues and Faisal Ahmed argue that remittances cause disengagement and complacency on the part of the public. This reduces accountability and allows governments to divert funds away from social programs to fund corruption.[21] David Doyle furthermore argues that remittances are associated with lower levels of social spending because remittance recipients are more likely to oppose taxation and thus less likely to support leftist parties.[22] I add another argument. Remittance recipients are less needy, which reduces public demand for social welfare programs for two reasons. First, the income boost from remittances may make some people ineligible for social programs that aim to combat the most extreme forms of poverty. Second, because remittance recipients are more likely to consume at or above their minimum threshold, they have less demand for government-provided welfare and are therefore less motivated to apply for benefits or lobby local officials for assistance, as I found in Michoacán, Mexico (recall Figure 3.5). This is not necessarily a reflection of complacency, disengagement, or lack of interest in politics, but rather a reflection of the fact that remittance recipients are, relatively speaking, more economically secure and satisfied with government performance.

TESTING FOR DISENGAGEMENT

Still, it is not entirely clear if remittance recipients are less critical of and less likely to oppose incumbents because they are more economically secure or because they have chosen to disengage from or tune out political life. What about remittances might cause political disengagement? Gary Goodman and Jonathan Hiskey argue that the process is one of switching from a less effective provider of social welfare (the state) to a more effective provider of social welfare (migrants).[23] As migrants abroad become a more effective provider of social welfare, remittance recipients look more to "transnational linkages to solve problems that historically fell under the domain of the state."[24] They argue that this process causes "citizens in high migration towns to feel that politics matter less in terms of improving their lot in life" and that politics is a less efficacious way to resolve economic problems.[25] That is, although remittance recipients do not vote with their feet by emigrating, they essentially exit the polity because they are able to engage with non-state providers of social welfare.

As evidence that remittances cause political disengagement, Goodman and Hiskey present statistical results that show that citizens from areas of Mexico with higher levels of emigration were less likely to vote in the 2000 Mexican presidential election. Moreover, Jorge Bravo found that remittance recipients were less likely to vote in the 2006 Mexican election—a finding I corroborated in my smaller sample of respondents from Michoacán.[26] Other studies have used country-level data to explore the relationship between remittances and corruption. Abdih and colleagues argue, for instance, that the notion that remittance recipients depend less on the government to provide basic goods and services "reduces the household's incentive to hold the government accountable."[27] Disengagement caused by remittances may therefore mean that governments come under less scrutiny when they divert public money to corruption. In this vein, various studies argue that countries with more remittances tend to also have higher levels of corruption.[28]

Are remittance recipients in sub-Saharan Africa less politically engaged? Because the survey does not tell us whether people received remittances at the time they report engaging in political activities like voting or protest, we are limited to analyzing respondents' self-reported interest in politics and attitudes toward hypothetical political participation. This kind of analysis, of course, is not the same as analyzing actual participation, but it provides at least some insight into how remittance recipients think about political participation and if remittances cause them to make a cognitive exit from political life.

Looking at remittance recipients' self-reported interest in public affairs, their news consumption, and their responses to questions about the efficacy of contacting representatives and voting in hypothetical elections, I do not find evidence that remittances cause outright political disengagement in sub-Saharan Africa. Instead, remittance recipients report that they are more interested in public affairs and more likely to participate. Figure 5.6a shows, for instance, that the likelihood a respondent said she was either somewhat or very interested in public affairs increases as the frequency of receiving remittances increases. The far left of the x-axis in Figure 5.6a represents respondents who reported that they did not receive remittances at the time of the survey. On the far right of the x-axis are respondents who reported that they received remittances at least once a month at the time of the survey. Starting on the left side of the x-axis, notice that respondents who said they did not receive remittances at the time of the survey had a probability of .64 of stating that they were somewhat or very interested in public affairs. Moving to the right on the x-axis, we can see that respondents become increasingly more likely to express interest in public affairs. Among those who said they receive remittances at least once a month, the probability of reporting interest in public affairs rises to .69. Figure 5.6b furthermore shows that remittance recipients were less likely to say they never watch the news. Respondents who said they did not receive remittances at the time of the survey had a probability of .47 of saying they never watch the news. Moving to the right along the x-axis, this number decreases to .38 for respondents who said they receive remittances at least once a month—a decrease of 20 percent.

Remittance recipients in sub-Saharan Africa were also more likely to say they would participate in politics and more likely to say that their efforts at participating would make a difference. Figure 5.6c shows that remittance recipients were more optimistic that they could make their representatives in government listen to their concerns. They also indicated that they would be more likely to vote in a hypothetical presidential election. Figure

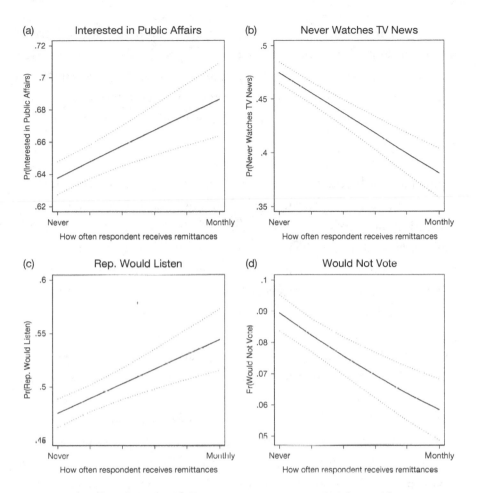

Figures 5.6a, 5.6b, 5.6c, and 5.6d Remittance recipients in sub-Saharan Africa are more likely to be civically engaged.

Figures show predicted probabilities (solid lines) simulated from binomial logistic regressions (dotted lines are 90% confidence intervals). The dependent variable (dv) varies by model: (a) dv=1 if respondent says she is somewhat or very interested in public affairs; (b) dv=1 if respondent says she never watches news on television; (c) dv=1 if respondent believes she could make representative listen to concerns; (d) dv=1 if respondent says she would not vote in hypothetical election. Control variables held at their means. Relationships are statistically significant. Figure 5.6a: N = 26,728; p = 0.000. Figure 5.6b: N = 26,728; p = 0.000. Figure 5.6c: N = 24,839; p = 0.000. Figure 5.6d: N = 24,008; p = 0.000.

5.6d shows that, when asked what party they would vote for if a presidential election were to be held the next day, people who said they never receive remittances had a probability of .09 of saying that they would not vote. People who said they receive remittances at least once a month, on the other hand, had a probability of .06 of saying they would not vote—a decrease of 33 percent.

There are a number of reasons why outright political disengagement may not be the inevitable consequence of receiving remittances. One reason is that remittances are frequently used to fund education. Education augments the development of civic skills, which we know fuels interest and participation in politics.[29] Furthermore, a small fraction of remittance recipients develop civic skills by participating in community groups and projects funded by Hometown Associations (HTAs).[30] HTAs are organizations that pool remittances for community projects in migrants' communities of origin. Some typical HTA projects include funding the construction of new roads, health clinics, wells, and stadiums. Generally, remittance-funded community projects require migrants abroad to coordinate their projects through government officials and family members back home. Community organizations have consequently sprung up in some developing countries to manage projects funded by remittances.[31] Productive experiences working with government officials on remittance-funded community projects may contribute to remittance recipients' interest in politics and sense that their participation matters.

In addition to civic skills, remittance recipients have two things that are known to boost political interest and participation: money and time.[32] Money can be used to fund political activities and support candidates.[33] Rising incomes also attract the attention of local politicians looking to leverage remittances for particular uses. This attention may draw remittance recipients into political life.[34] Remittances may also increase exposure to the news if they are used to purchase TVs and internet access.[35] Finally, remittance recipients may have more time on their hands because remittances sometimes reduce incentives to participate in the labor market.[36] In fact, in the Afrobarometer sample, remittance recipients were less likely to be employed full-time. This extra time may free them to follow the news more and participate more in political and community affairs.

TESTING FOR SELECTION EFFECTS

Although about two-thirds of people who migrate from sub-Saharan African countries go to other sub-Saharan African countries, a significant proportion of remittances sent to sub-Saharan African countries come from migrants who work in Europe and North America. Due to the high costs of leaving the continent and immigration laws that give priority to high-skilled immigrants, Africans who migrate to Europe and North America tend to be better educated and better off than migrants who stay on the continent.[37] It is possible, then, that we have found associations between receiving remittances and being more politically engaged and more economically secure not necessarily because remittances have an independent effect on civic skills and economic security, but because some remittance recipients come from households whose members are relatively better educated and better off to begin with.

I made an effort to account for selection effects when I controlled for respondents' education levels, employment status, and socioeconomic status. As an additional check, I reestimated all models on subsamples of respondents in the top quartile of educational attainment and respondents who had running water inside their home, which, in the Afrobarometer sample, is suggestive of relatively high socioeconomic status. Of course, in the absence of longitudinal data or more detailed household income and education histories, it is impossible to know what causes what. Is it that having more education and income put these respondents' households in a position to send members abroad so that they could receive remittances? Or is it that remittances were used to fund the higher education levels and improved living conditions that put respondents in these subsamples? Education expenses are a key use of remittances, and prior research has shown that remittances are sometimes used by households to fund the pipes and labor needed to connect their homes to public water systems.[38]

So the causal arrows go in both directions, and the strength of one direction or the other likely varies from country-to-country, household-to-household. Still, analyzing these subsamples can provide at least a bit of insight into whether the results are being driven by selection effects.

Analyses on just the high-education and high-socioeconomic subsamples confirm earlier results on the full samples. Remittance recipients in these subsamples were, like remittance recipients in the full sample, less likely to express economic grievances, more likely to support the incumbent party in a hypothetical election, more likely to say they watch the news and are interested in public affairs, and more likely to say they would vote in a hypothetical election.

CONCLUSIONS

The upshot of this chapter is that not only are remittance recipients less aggrieved, as we saw in chapters 3 and 4, but the relative absence of economic grievances appears to translate into less critical evaluations of government performance. Citizens who are less critical of government performance are also more likely to support the political and social status quo, even during a period as trying as the 2008 food crisis.

Remittances now look like social welfare benefits in multiple respects. First, they are countercyclical and, for many recipient households, serve as a safety net. Second, they help families purchase and continue consuming basic goods and services like food and healthcare. Third, they have a consumption-smoothing effect that not only reduces economic grievances but also makes recipients less hostile toward their governments during times of crisis. The relative absence of anger toward the government furthermore reduces the likelihood that remittance recipients will seek to mobilize against and punish those in power. It is therefore plausible that the social insurance effect of remittances helped to reduce the severity of the civil unrest that erupted in many African countries during the food crisis, and it may have prevented unrest altogether in countries where significant numbers of citizens receive remittances.

As we have seen, remittances are not a panacea for governments facing widespread disapproval. However, they do seem to reduce the level of anger directed toward the government at least somewhat. This may alleviate governments of pressure in a variety of ways, with fewer people rioting when prices rise, less punishment on election day, and less backlash from certain constituencies, like those who lose out to free trade policies. This calming effect has the potential to benefit society as a whole. If fewer people are rioting because fewer people are hungry, the impact of riots on the larger functioning of the economy is bound to be smaller. In these respects, remittances act as an important stabilizing force in developing countries that are otherwise undergoing destabilizing economic change.

No Left Turn

*Remittances and Incumbent Support
in Mexico's Closely Contested 2006 Presidential Election*

So far, we have seen that remittances contribute to feelings of economic security in developing countries. They are also associated with more positive assessments of government performance and a preference for incumbent parties. The question that motivates this chapter is whether remittances impact political preferences to the point of influencing how people vote in actual elections. To explore this question, I turn to the only survey dataset that I am aware of that collected data on both remittances and vote choice very soon after a competitive democratic election.[1]

The Mexico 2006 Panel Study collected data on a number of economic and political variables from a national sample of voters just days after Mexico's 2006 presidential election.[2] That election pitted Felipe Calderón of the National Action Party (PAN) against Andrés Manuel López Obrador of the Party of the Democratic Revolution (PRD). The PAN had held power in Mexico since the last presidential election in 2000, when its candidate Vicente Fox ended seventy-one years of dominance by the Institutional Revolutionary Party (PRI). Although the PAN initiated many political and economic reforms during Fox's six-year term, it remained committed to the neoliberal economic approach that originated under the PRI in the 1980s and 1990s. Calderón, the PAN candidate in 2006, represented a continuation of that model. López Obrador, on the other hand, rejected neoliberal orthodoxy. Chief among his campaign slogans were his pledge to reduce inequality and spend more on poverty relief, his desire to reevaluate Mexico's economic relationship with the United States, and his opposition to a proposal to privatize Mexico's state-owned oil company.[3]

López Obrador's fiery brand of left-wing populism resonated with much of Mexico at a time of growing inequality and dissatisfaction with neoliberal policies. Polls in the fall of 2005 showed him with a commanding lead over both the PAN and PRI candidates. By the spring and summer of 2006, however, the PAN had made substantial gains, and shortly after ballots were cast on July 2, 2006, Calderón was declared the victor by less than 1 percent of the vote. Reports of fraud and ballot stuffing left many Mexicans questioning the outcome. López Obrador and his supporters argued that the PAN had tampered with ballots. They called for an investigation and full recount. Mexico's Federal Electoral Institute settled on a partial recount. After the recount, the Institute declared Calderón the winner with 35.89 percent of the vote to 35.31 percent for López Obrador. Roberto Madrazo of the PRI came in third with 22.26 percent of the vote, and the remaining 6.5 percent went to smaller parties, write-ins, and null votes.

As an American living in Mexico at the time, I could not help but draw comparisons between this election and the unusually close contest between George W. Bush and Al Gore in 2000. Although Gore never accused Bush of fraud, he pointed to irregularities that, if investigated, he believed would have demonstrated that he had won the election. A partial recount and controversial Supreme Court ruling, however, ultimately made Bush the winner. The similarities between the two elections end there. Although he disagreed with the Supreme Court ruling, Gore conceded to Bush and went into voluntary exile. López Obrador, on the other hand, only grew more visible and more vocal in the weeks after the Federal Electoral Institute ruling. For weeks, his supporters shut down Mexico City, blocking major thoroughfares and camping out in the streets. López Obrador encouraged the protests and continued to press his claim that the PAN won through fraud. He said again and again that he—not Calderón— was the legitimate winner of the election.

With Calderón's inauguration approaching and no sign that the Federal Electoral Institute would reverse its decision in his favor, López Obrador made an odd move. On November 21, 2006—more than four months after the election—he declared himself the "legitimate president of Mexico" in an unofficial ceremony in Mexico City's central square in front of about a hundred thousand people. At the ceremony's climax, a woman emerged from the side of the stage and donned López Obrador with the same kind of red, white, and green sash draped on Mexican presidents during their inaugurations. After some fumbling, she finally affixed the sash to his dark suit. López Obrador then moved to the podium and held out his right hand. The crowd erupted with cheers of joy.

To his opponents, López Obrador looked delusional. This "inauguration" gave him no formal powers to govern. To López Obrador's supporters, however, it was an important moment—a celebration of how close the left had come to winning the presidency after three decades out of power. The left found it particularly difficult to accept defeat because for most of the campaign the election looked like López Obrador's to lose.[4] López Obrador's calls for a more compassionate state that looked after its poor energized much of the population at a time when many Mexicans were disillusioned with neoliberalism. This "statist mood," as Andy Baker calls it, was sweeping Latin America at the time.[5] Starting with the election of Hugo Chavez in Venezuela in 1998, one Latin American electorate after another demanded more redistribution to counter the instability and inequality associated with neoliberal policies.[6] During the 2000s, leftist presidents were elected, and later reelected, in Chile, Brazil, Argentina, Uruguay, Bolivia, Nicaragua, and Ecuador. Guatemala and El Salvador, once bastions for right-wing military governments, went on to elect leftist presidents in 2008 and 2009. Peru elected a leftist president in 2011, and Costa Rica elected a center-left candidate in 2014. A López Obrador victory in 2006 would have fit the pattern.

Whether or not López Obrador's allegations of fraud have any validity, a number of other factors have been identified to account for Calderón's victory. Among those usually cited are media bias, an effective negative ad campaign by López Obrador's opponents, the PAN's expansion of poverty reduction programs like Oportunidades, and the PAN's incumbency advantage. One factor that has yet to receive much attention is how, by contributing to economic security in poor areas that had been adversely affected by neoliberal economic policies, remittances may have made poor voters more forgiving of the PAN and the PRI or less energized by López Obrador's populist, anti-neoliberal rhetoric.

In chapter 2, we saw how coffee farmers in La Victoria and corn, pork, and strawberry farmers in Michoacán responded to market reforms and fiscal austerity by emigrating and sending remittances to fill the welfare gap. These were punctuated economic crises where families had little option but to find a way to compensate themselves for economic losses and insure against future losses. Although the Mexican government compensated somewhat with programs like Oportunidades and PROCAMPO, benefits were not sufficient to make up for what agrarian communities lost when the Mexican government opened the economy to agricultural imports and shut down state-owned enterprises like CONASUPO and INMECAFÉ. To achieve its goal of rapidly establishing a market economy, Mexican politicians outsourced welfare provision to citizens abroad.

In Mexico and many other developing countries, we saw in earlier chapters that remittances are associated with feelings of economic security. In analyses of survey data from rural Mexico, we saw how this economic security may reduce pressure on politicians to guarantee a minimum standard of living by reducing the volume of people who seek government assistance. Moreover, in analyses of data from sub-Saharan Africa, we saw that remittance recipients tend to be less critical of government economic performance and more likely to say they would vote for the incumbent party in an election. Remittances are an important source of income in many areas of Mexico. In fact, at the time of the 2006 presidential election, about 7 percent of Mexican households received remittances, according to government estimates.[7] Did these voters' insulation from a bad economy leave them feeling less critical of the PAN and the PRI or less energized to vote for the bold changes proposed by the PRD candidate?

DID REMITTANCES CONTRIBUTE TO LÓPEZ OBRADOR'S DEFEAT?

I used data from the Mexico 2006 Panel Study to develop a statistical model that investigates whether and how much remittances influenced vote choice in the 2006 Mexican presidential election. The dependent variable in this analysis is how respondents said they voted a few days earlier on July 2. I coded this variable as a choice between the PAN, the PRI, the PRD, or one of the smaller parties who ran candidates that year, such as New Alliance or the Social Democratic and Peasant Alternative Party. To measure remittances, I used a question on the survey that asked respondents if they received money from someone living in the United States, and if so, how often. Possible responses were never, less than every six months, every four to six months, every two or three months, once a month, and more than once a month.

The model controls for demographic characteristics, income, party identification, welfare benefits, economic assessments, and approval of outgoing president Vicente Fox (a member of the PAN).[8] Holding control variables at their means, I calculated the predicted probability of voting for any one candidate based on each score on the remittances variable. Using software developed by Gary King, Michael Tomz, and Jason Wittenberg, I then used these probabilities to simulate one thousand mock presidential elections for each of the six scores on the remittances variable.[9] Figure 6.1 shows the simulated election outcomes. The dots in Figure 6.1 represent the probability that a mock election was won by the PAN, the PRD, or the PRI. The closer a dot is to any of the three vertices, the more likely that

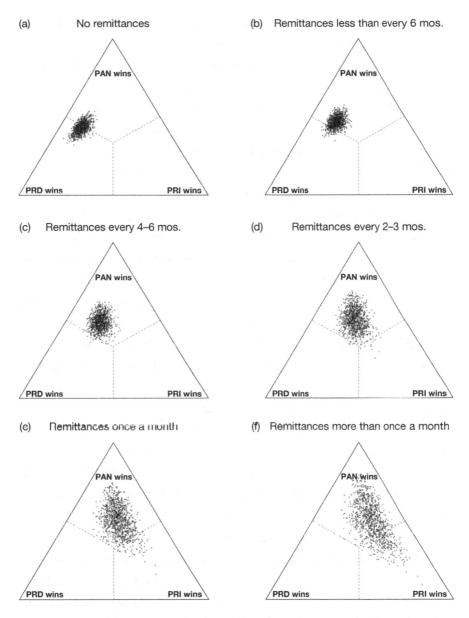

Figure 6.1 Remittance recipients were less likely to vote for López Obrador in the 2006 Mexican Presidential Election (National Sample).

Dots in (a) through (f) represent 1,000 mock election outcomes simulated from a multinomial logistic regression. The dependent variable was respondents' vote choice in the 2006 Mexican presidential election. Control variables held at their means. Statistical models show that remittance recipients were more likely to vote for the PAN over the PRD (p = 0.046) or for the PRI over the PRD (p = 0.001). N = 633.

party was to have won a mock election. For instance, if a dot were to be positioned on the PRI vertex, that would mean that the PRI had a 100 percent chance of winning that particular mock election and the PAN and the PRD had a zero percent chance. A dot at the center of the triangle, on the other hand, tells us that each of the three parties had an equal (33.33 percent) probability of winning. A dot on the line between two parties tells us that those two parties had an equal probability of winning, and depending upon how far away this dot is from the third party, that the third party had a lower probability of victory than the other two.

Figure 6.1a shows the distribution of probabilities of winning one thousand mock elections. Here the simulated condition is one where no respondents receive remittances. All other variables are held at their means. In this scenario, we can see that the dots (that is, the simulated probabilities of winning a mock election) are almost evenly split between the PAN and the PRD. In this scenario, in other words, the PAN and the PRD had nearly equal probabilities of victory, with the PRI in a much weaker position than either of its rivals. This result looks similar to what polling suggested prior to the election — a very close contest between the PAN and the PRD that could have gone either way.

Figure 6.1b shows a different set of probabilities based on another scenario. In this set of simulations, all voters receive remittances once or twice a year. Here we can see that the PRD's probability of victory decreases and the PAN's probability of victory increases as the remittances variable increases. This shift is represented by the movement in the dots away from the PRD vertex toward the PAN's. Although it is difficult to see in Figure 6.1b, the probabilities also shift slightly in the PRI's favor at the same time that they shift away from the PRD and more toward the PAN. Figure 6.1c and 6.1d show that the shift away from the PRD intensifies the more we dial up values on the remittances variable. As remittances flow to more voters more frequently, the PRD's average probability of victory drops to less than 20 percent compared with the PAN, which is 50 percent or higher in most cases. Higher probabilities of victory follow for the PRI as well. The smaller number of survey respondents with data on the upper ends of the remittances variable causes the results to get noisier when we get to scenarios where people receive remittances about once a month (Figure 6.1e) and more than once a month (Figure 6.1f), but the pattern nevertheless follows in the same direction. The more frequently people receive remittances, the less likely they are to vote for the PRD and the more likely they are to vote for the PAN or the PRI.

I interpret these results as follows. Although the consensus is mixed as to how much economic factors determine electoral outcomes in Mexico relative to other factors like campaign effects, media coverage, and candidate traits,[10] a number of studies indicate that Mexicans tend to punish incumbents for poor economic performance, particularly when there is a strong and viable opposition.[11] We have, of course, seen throughout this book that remittance recipients report feeling more economically secure and that they tend to make less critical assessments of incumbent economic performance. So remittance recipients should have been less likely to oppose the PAN. They should have also been less likely to support the PRD. The PAN's big argument against López Obrador was that his brand of left-wing populism threatened to imperil the Mexican economy. They painted López Obrador as another Hugo Chávez—a big-spending, left-wing populist whose lack of fiscal discipline would create an economic crisis like the one Mexico had endured in 1982. Voters therefore had a choice between keeping the status quo or rejecting it for the purportedly riskier approach López Obrador and other leftists in Latin America were advocating. A voter whose livelihood had been destroyed by the PRI's and the PAN's economic policies may have had little to lose and a lot to gain from taking a risk on López Obrador. This is why a lot of poor people, as well as people who believe strongly in norms of social equity, voted for López Obrador. But many voters are motivated more by the fear of losses rather than the prospect of gains.[12] Poor voters who felt like they indeed had something to lose were less enthralled by the idea of a López administration. Moreover, voters who were less economically aggrieved had less incentive to seek to punish the PAN for slow growth and high underemployment and unemployment under President Vicente Fox.

As we dial up the remittances variable in these simulations, it is as if we are leveling the economic playing field, insulating voters from market vicissitudes, making voters feel more economically secure, and giving voters more to lose. The outcome here, as I interpret it, is that as people become more economically secure, they become less critical of the incumbent's performance and less interested in rejecting the status quo. They gravitate toward familiar approaches like those the PAN and the PRI advocated—not the big, seemingly risky changes proposed by López Obrador. Furthermore, a big aspect of López Obrador's appeal was his pledge to use social spending to help the poor. But if households can count on a reliable safety net from family members in the United States, they may be less energized by proposals for more spending. In some cases, they may be opposed to more spending because, as David Doyle argues, they fear that more of their remittances will be eaten up by increasing consumption taxes put in place to raise revenue to pay for new social programs.[13]

Of course, in the real world, only some voters receive remittances, and the frequency and amounts vary. So these graphs do not reflect reality. But they are powerful for how clearly they illustrate that in a national survey conducted just after the election, remittance recipients systematically said they were more likely to have voted for the PAN or the PRI *at the expense of the PRD*. According to official government data, 7 percent of Mexican households received remittances in 2006. Calderón won the election by less than 1 percent of the vote. It is therefore mathematically possible that remittance-receiving voters, who were presumably less critical of the PAN's economic performance or less energized by López Obrador's brand of left-wing populism, tipped the election in the PAN's favor.

As a check on the robustness of this finding, I ran similar tests on other datasets. First, I used the survey data I collected in Michoacán. Although I collected this data eighteen months after the election in January 2008, I asked detailed questions on respondents' income histories that allowed me to know who did and who did not receive remittances in July 2006. The survey also asked respondents how they remember voting in July 2006. My statistical model treats the voting decision as a choice between the three major-party candidates: Calderón of the PAN, López Obrador of the PRD, and Madrazo of the PRI. In this dataset, recall that the remittances variable is a zero-to-one continuous index that measures the extent to which remittances are a substantial, reliable, and enduring source of household income. The model controls for demographic characteristics, income, ideological orientation, and responses to public opinion questions about trade, social spending, and privatization. I used the results of this model to again simulate one thousand mock elections for various values on the remittances variable while holding all other variables constant at their means.

Figure 6.2 shows that the effects of remittances on vote choice are nearly identical to those in the 2006 national sample. In Figure 6.2a, we are looking at a set of simulated elections where no voters receive remittances. Here, again, we find that the probability of winning is more or less split between the PRD and the PAN, with what looks like a slight advantage for the PRD. In a second set of simulated elections shown in Figure 6.2b, on the other hand, I have increased the value on the remittances variable slightly from zero to 0.25. Just like we saw in the national sample, the PAN's probability of victory increases as values on the remittances variable increase. This tendency toward the PAN and the PRI continues for even higher values on the remittances variable.

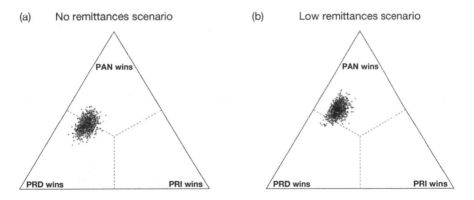

(a)   No remittances scenario   (b)   Low remittances scenario

PAN wins   PAN wins

PRD wins   PRI wins   PRD wins   PRI wins

Figure 6.2a and 6.2b Remittance recipients were less likely to vote for López Obrador in the 2006 Mexican Presidential Election (Michoacán Sample).
Dots in (a) and (b) represent 1,000 mock election outcomes simulated from a multinomial logistic regression. The dependent variable was respondents' vote choice in the 2006 Mexican presidential election. Control variables held at their means. In (a) no respondent receives remittances. In (b), all respondents have a relatively low (0.25) score on the remittances variable. Statistical models show that remittance recipients were more likely to vote for the PAN over the PRD (p = 0.005). N = 411.

The relationship between remittances and support for the incumbent persists in other datasets. In 2008 and 2010, for instance, the Latin American Public Opinion Project asked a national sample of Mexican respondents if they would vote for the incumbent party (which in both years was the PAN) or another party in a hypothetical election. Figure 6.3 shows that households that depended on remittances more were more likely to say they support the incumbent party. In the 2008 sample, respondents who said they did not receive remittances had a probability of .41 of saying they would vote for the PAN. Moving to the right along the x-axis, we see that the probability of voicing support for the PAN rises to .61 for respondents who said they depend on remittances "a lot." By the time of the 2010 survey, Mexico had endured about two years of intense drug cartel violence. Many Mexicans blamed Felipe Calderón's crackdown on the cartels for triggering the violence, and his poll numbers plummeted. In

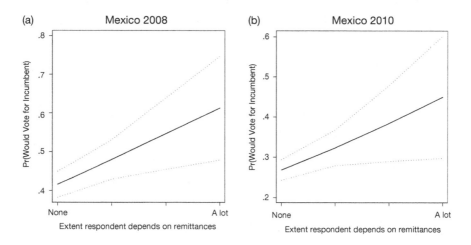

Figures 6.3a and 6.3b Remittance recipients in Mexico were more likely to express support for the incumbent party in 2008 and 2010 (National samples, Latin American Public Opinion Project data).

Figures show predicted probabilities (solid lines) simulated from binomial logistic regressions (dotted lines are 90% confidence intervals). The dependent variable equals 1 in cases where respondents said they would vote for the incumbent party. Control variables held at their means. Relationships are statistically significant. Figure 6.3a: N = 894; p = 0.021. Figure 6.3b: N = 925; p = 0.04.

the 2010 sample, people who did not receive remittances had a probability of .27 of saying they would vote for the PAN in a hypothetical election— down by 34 percent compared to two years earlier. Again, remittance recipients were more loyal to the incumbent. Respondents who said they depend on remittances "a lot" had a probability of .45 of saying they would vote for the PAN.

Taken together, Figures 6.1–6.3 suggest that millions of poor remittance-receiving voters may have helped tip the 2006 election in Calderón's favor by voting more often for the PAN or the PRI over the PRD. The implication is that Mexico's large remittance income in the 2000s may have prevented the country from joining the ranks of leftist governments in Latin America. A population that was insured by millions of family members in the United States was shielded somewhat from the full pain of a bad economy. This, I have argued, made the Mexican poor less likely to seek to punish the PAN and less likely to support leftists who, like López Obrador, called for a more statist approach in place of the neoliberal status quo.

TESTING ALTERNATIVE EXPLANATIONS

The results reveal a clear association between remittances and support for the PAN. We furthermore have seen evidence presented throughout the book to suggest that remittances contribute to economic security and are associated with less critical assessments of government economic performance. This combination of effects, I have argued, should make remittance recipients more likely to vote for incumbents in elections. But there are other plausible explanations for remittance recipients' apparent anti-PRD preference in 2006 and pro-incumbent preference in 2008 and 2010. Before concluding this chapter, I will briefly explore some of these arguments. They include the possibility that the PAN and the PRI targeted remittance recipients more aggressively in get-out-the-vote efforts; that remittance recipients were influenced by family members abroad, who, surveys show, largely supported the PAN; that remittance recipients fit the demographic profile of a PAN voter; and that remittance recipients were more likely to be loyal *panistas* or agree more with the PAN's policy positions.

Targeting

One possibility is that the PAN or the PRI used their resources to target remittance recipients in get-out-the-vote efforts. But how would parties know who is and who is not a remittance recipient? In addition to knowledge from local party operatives who may know which households have relatives abroad, there are many outward signs. In rural areas at least, people who receive remittances tend to have nicer houses and automobiles. Their homes sometimes have distinctively American characteristics, such as carports and slanted roofs.[14] Furthermore, their cars and pickup trucks sometimes still have license plates from states in the United States where they were purchased.[15] These and other signs make it rather easy to drive through any small Mexican town and guess which households receive remittances and which do not. The PAN could have used these markers to target remittance recipients if the party was particularly interested in winning their votes in 2006.

Figure 6.4 shows, however, that there is no evidence in the Mexico 2006 Panel Study data that the PAN or the PRI courted remittance recipients more aggressively than did the PRD. If anything, remittance recipients were slightly more exposed to the PRD's appeals. Notice in Figure 6.4 that among remittance-receiving respondents surveyed by the Mexico 2006 Panel Study, 6.9 percent reported that a representative from the PAN had knocked on their door in the weeks before the election, 6.2 percent said that a PRI representative had knocked on their door, and 7.6 percent said that a PRD representative had knocked on their door. Overall, it appears that all three parties targeted remittance recipients more than non-recipients. Differences between remittance recipients and non-recipients, however, are not statistically significant.

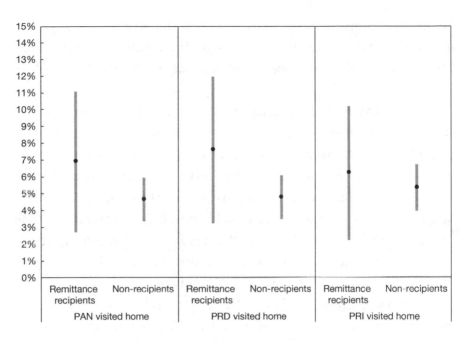

Figure 6.4 Percentage of respondents who were visited by party representatives prior to the 2006 election, by remittance-receiving status.
Bars represent 95% confidence intervals. Differences are not statistically significant.
SOURCE: Mexico 2006 Panel Study.

Social Learning

Clarisa Pérez-Armendáriz and David Crow argue that, in addition to remitting money, international migrants also transmit political values and ideas to those in the homeland.[16] When they live in the United States, Mexican immigrants learn from and adapt to American political life. By communicating with family members back home, Mexicans abroad may knowingly or unknowingly convey what they have learned to those who stay behind.

A survey conducted by the Pew Hispanic Center in the months before the 2006 Mexican presidential election found that Mexicans in the United States said they identified with the PAN over the PRD by a nearly three-to-one ratio.[17] Moreover, the 40,000 Mexicans abroad who voted in the 2006 Mexican presidential election voted for Calderón over López Obrador by nearly two-to-one. It thus appears that if Mexicans in the United States had any influence over their non-emigrating family members' political preferences, this influence would have largely worked to the PAN's advantage.

One could argue that the transnational learning and diffusion process should become more pronounced when remittances are a more substantial, reliable, and enduring source of social insurance. The reason would have little to do with the actual money that is being transferred. Rather, high levels of attentiveness to the origin household's economic needs could be a reflection of stronger transnational bonds. If this were the case, then the remittances variables in our analyses may not be measuring remittances' significance as a form of social insurance. Instead, they may be measuring the strength of transnational bonds between Mexicans abroad and their non-emigrating relatives. Remittance recipients may have been more likely to vote for the PAN, in other words, not because of remittances' economic security effects but because those sending remittances are remitting ideas about politics in addition to money.

To test this alternative hypothesis, I analyze responses to a question asked in the survey I conducted in Michoacán. This survey asked respondents if they ever talk about politics with friends or family members in the United States. Only 8.7 percent of respondents said yes, they sometimes talk to family members in the United States about politics. I developed a statistical model to try to understand the factors that affect whether or not someone talks politics with relatives and friends living in the United States. In particular, I was interested to learn whether people who receive remittances very reliably are more likely to talk politics. Not surprisingly, I find that the propensity to talk about politics with someone in the United States increases with the number of family members one has living abroad and one's education level and interest in public affairs. I do not find, however, a statistically significant association between receiving remittances and talking politics with a family member abroad. This null result suggests that my remittances variables are not acting as a proxy for the transmission of political ideas from Mexicans in the United States to their relatives and friends in Mexico.

Demographic Profile

Do the demographic characteristics of remittance recipients explain some
of the association between remittances and voting for the PAN? I controlled for many demographic variables in my statistical models, but as a
check on this argument, I compared the average age, education, income,
and gender of remittance recipients and non-recipients. Remittance recipients and non-recipients indeed differ on a number of demographic variables. For example, remittance recipients were slightly older on average
($p = .051$), slightly less educated ($p = .001$), and slightly poorer ($p = .09$)
than non-recipients at the time of the 2006 election.[18] I do not, on the
other hand, find a statistically significant difference between recipients
and non-recipients in terms of their gender ($p = .909$).

   Although there are some demographic differences here, they do not suggest an inherent pro-PAN bias. According to exit polls after the election, for
instance, Calderón did particularly well with higher-income voters, better-
educated voters, and younger voters, and better than López Obrador with
female voters. Remittance recipients happen to come from poorer areas, so
although they tend to be better off and better educated compared to their
neighbors, they look poorer, older, less educated, and more rural than the
Mexican population on average. In this respect, remittance recipients fit the
demographic profile not of a PAN voter, but of a PRI voter.[19] A demographic
selection effect may therefore explain some remittance recipients' preference for the PRI in the 2006 election, but this explanation does not tell us
why these voters preferred the PRI over the PRD and not the PAN, why they
tended to support the PAN over the PRD in 2006, or why they voiced support for the PAN over other parties in 2008 and 2010. These specific patterns
seem more convincingly explained by the economic security argument.

Are Remittance Recipients Partisans?

I can think of at least two more alternative explanations for the association between remittances and support for the PAN in Figures 6.1–6.3.

One possible explanation has to do with geography. Mexico's western and north-central regions have been important remittance-receiving regions for decades. A number of populous states in this region—including Jalisco, Guanajuato, Querétaro, and San Luis Potosí—have also been important strongholds of PAN support.[20] Furthermore, outgoing president Vicente Fox—a member of the PAN—was a champion of the expatriate community both as governor of the state of Guanajuato and as president. He frequently referred to migrants as heroes, pushed for overseas voting rights for Mexicans abroad, and made a migration pact with the United States a centerpiece of the first year of his presidency—an effort that was stymied by the terrorist attacks of September 11, 2001.[21] If geography or an affinity for Vicente Fox are confounding factors, we should expect to find a strong association between receiving remittances and considering oneself a loyal follower of the PAN.

We can test the possibility that remittance recipients are more likely to identify with and support the PAN with a question on the Mexico 2006 Panel Study survey that asked respondents if they generally consider themselves *panistas, priistas*, or *perredistas*. These terms are familiar in Mexico and refer to people who considered themselves loyal supporters of one of Mexico's three main political parties in 2006. A *panista*, for instance, is someone who considers herself a loyal supporter of the PAN; a *priista*, a loyal supporter of the PRI; and a *perredista*, a loyal supporter of the PRD. Figure 6.5 shows the percentage of remittance recipients and non-recipients who said they identify as *panistas, perredistas,* and *priistas*. These percentages suggest that remittance recipients did not have stronger loyalties to the PAN. To the contrary, they were somewhat more likely to say they consider themselves *perredistas* and *priistas*. Among remittance recipients, for instance, 26.2 percent said they consider themselves *priistas*, 24.8 percent said they consider themselves *perredistas*, and 21.4 percent said they consider themselves *panistas*. Figure 6.5 furthermore shows that remittance recipients were no more partisan than people who did not receive remittances. This test helps us rule out the explanation that the remittances variables are to some extent measuring party identification rather than the independent effect of remittances on vote choice.

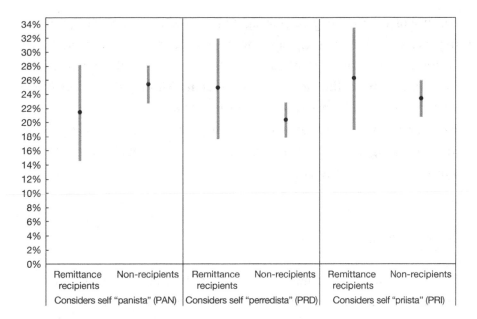

Figure 6.5 Percentage of respondents who identified with each of Mexico's three major political parties prior to the 2006 election, by remittance-receiving status.
Bars represent 95% confidence intervals. Differences are not statistically significant.
SOURCE: Mexico 2006 Panel Study.

Policy Preferences

The last alternative explanation I will examine is the idea that remittance recipients preferred the PAN or the PRI over the PRD because their policy preferences were systematically different from the policy preferences of people who did not receive remittances. On the issue of trade, the Mexico 2006 Panel Study found that most Mexicans were somewhat in favor of increasing trade with the United States. Remittance recipients' opinions on this issue, however, were no different on average than those of non-recipients ($p = .16$). When asked whether they believed the government should privatize Mexico's oil resources or keep them in the hands of the state, remittance recipients were on average somewhat in favor of privatization. But again, differences between remittance recipients and non-recipients were not statistically significant here ($p = .53$). Finally, I consider the possibility that remittance recipients were attracted to Calderón

because of a campaign pledge to fight organized crime and drug trafficking. Were remittance recipients more likely than non-recipients to see
crime as an important issue? To the contrary, when asked to identify what
they thought to be the biggest problem facing Mexico at the time of the
2006 election, remittance recipients were less likely than non-recipients to
name crime, drug trafficking, and other public security issues ($p = .005$).
These tests suggest that the remittances variable is probably not acting as
a proxy for policy preferences.

CONCLUSION

The goal of this chapter has been to explore if remittance recipients vote
differently than non-recipients. We have gone beyond assessments of government performance and party preferences here to examine the effects of
remittances on self-reported voting behavior. Previous chapters indicated
that remittance recipients feel more economically secure and are less critical of incumbent economic performance. We saw in the African context
that remittance recipients in democratic countries prefer incumbents. In
this chapter I focused on a particularly close election between an incumbent who represented a continuation of a status quo neoliberal economic
approach and a populist opposition candidate who rejected neoliberalism
and called for major economic changes. My argument was that the economic security effects of remittances should leave remittance recipients
feeling less critical of the incumbent and less energized by populist rhetoric and proposals for change. As a result, we should find that remittance
recipients voted more for the incumbent. An analysis of national survey
data collected just after the vote showed a clear association between remittances and casting a ballot for the PAN or the PRI over the PRD. These
results held up in three other datasets and demonstrate the kind of pro-
incumbent preference among remittance recipients that we observed in
democratic countries in sub-Saharan Africa.

The implication is that remittance recipients may have played an unwit-
ting role in forestalling a shift to the left in Mexico. One after another,

Latin American publics were electing leftist executives in the late 1990s and 2000s. After years of painful neoliberal policies, Latin American voters revealed a preference for a more active state to help cushion the effects of volatile and competitive markets. Much of the Mexican electorate similarly supported a reevaluation of neoliberal orthodoxy. At the same time, a significant share of the electorate enjoyed the economic security benefits of remittances. I have argued that these economic security benefits made remittance-receiving voters less aggrieved and less likely to punish the incumbent. They may have also been less energized by the leftist candidate's promises to spend more on welfare programs and poverty relief since they already had access to a reliable safety net: friends and family members in the United States. Just as we saw in sub-Saharan Africa, remittance recipients in Mexico exhibited a pro-incumbent bias in 2006—one that may have cost the PRD the election and prevented Mexico from joining the ranks of the Latin American left.

Conclusion

"In twenty days, our poverty will end." This was the promise Olga Guerra made to her family before she left Honduras. For this single mother of three, migrating began to feel like the only option in the months after she took in her three young nephews after their parents were murdered—victims of a wave of gang violence that was plaguing Honduras. Olga's struggle was profound. She told me she needs at least thirty dollars a day "just to get by—to have rice, beans, water to drink, and a cup of milk in the morning" for all six of the kids. The most she could make was ten dollars a day cleaning houses, and the work was not consistent. Olga did not feel like she could count on the Honduran government for support. She and her neighbors complained that they were forced to purchase water after the government neglected to repair a nearby well. They shook their heads at news that the country's social security system was on the brink of collapse in the wake of an embezzlement scheme. Olga did not have a safety net. The only option she could see for filling the gap between what she was able to earn in Honduras and what her family needed to stay fed and healthy was to leave the children in the care of her aging mother, migrate to the United States, and send money home.[1]

I interviewed another mother named Kacie Jesus, a U.S. citizen from Utah, around the time I interviewed Olga. When I met Kacie, she was struggling to support herself and her five children after her husband Ray had been deported to his native Guatemala. Ray had been the Jesus family's sole breadwinner. With Ray gone, Kacie, a stay-at-home mom, had to figure out how to keep the kids fed, healthy, and sheltered. It certainly was not easy for Kacie to support her big family alone, but in contrast to Olga, she was able to supplement her small income with government benefits. All five of her children were insured by Medicaid. She paid for food with the help of a government food assistance program; she used Section 8 housing subsidies to help her pay rent; and she paid for most household expenses with the eight hundred dollars her nine-year-old son drew each month in social security disability payments.[2]

There is much to critique about the state of social spending in the United States and other developed countries. In both Europe and North America, budget cuts and the absence of political will to expand the reach of the welfare state have caused suffering, anger, and civil unrest in recent decades. Anti-austerity protests in Athens and London are evidence of this. But the comparison here between Olga and Kacie shows that even in the United States, one of the more austere systems in the West, there are any number of safety nets available to families experiencing economic shocks that simply do not exist in developing countries like Honduras.

In this book, I have drawn parallels between remittances and social welfare benefits. Like welfare benefits, remittances tend to increase in times of crisis and are used by millions of poor families to fund basic needs like food, clothing, healthcare, cooking fuel, electricity, and education. Unlike social welfare benefits, however, remittances are not public funds, but money sent privately—often altruistically—from one family member to another. This private, transnational safety net has grown in importance in the current era of neoliberal globalization. The poor are increasingly exposed to the vicissitudes of global capitalism, but they generally lack a strong public safety net to help them weather economic crises. In an era when states are unable or unwilling to develop expansive social insurance programs, remittances fill an important welfare gap. They not only help families cope with economic adversity and austerity but also help entire societies adjust. Remittances can, as one man I interviewed in rural Mexico put it, help "lift the mood" when poor people are faced with economic crisis. The economic security effects of remittances leave people feeling more optimistic about the future and less angry at their government for a bad economy. These effects, I have argued, contribute to social and political stability and have the potential to reduce the severity of grievance-fueled unrest.

The work that international migrants do to fill the welfare gap in their home countries is significant. Remittances are at least three times greater than the aid wealthy countries send to the developing world. In many developing countries, remittances are equivalent to between 10 percent and 25 percent of gross domestic product (GDP) and received by between 10 percent and 30 percent of the population. In some developing countries, coverage of the "transnational safety net," as I've called it, is comparable to the coverage of welfare states in some developed countries, which spend 22 percent of GDP on entitlements and welfare on average.[3]

Throughout this book, we have witnessed how remittances are associated with more positive assessments of the economy and more positive assessments of government performance. Interviews I conducted in rural Mexico and analyses of survey data from fifty developing countries showed that remittance recipients are significantly less aggrieved than people who do not receive remittances. They are also less likely to blame their governments for poor economic performance during economic crises. Economic security translates into more political stability. The relative absence of economic grievances—not necessarily disengagement—may mean that remittance recipients place less pressure on their governments to guarantee a minimum standard of living.[4] In extreme situations, the reduction in economic grievances could prevent people from taking up arms and rebelling against their governments.[5]

REMITTANCES, DEMOCRACY, AND DEVELOPMENT

Remittances have important implications for democracy and development in an age of austerity, global market integration, and climate change. Leaders in developing democracies face many challenges in their efforts to maintain economic, political, and social stability. First, they are regularly tasked with managing crises that are beyond their control. Crises are not only caused by shocks and downturns in an increasingly interconnected global economy but also triggered by natural disasters, some of which, such as droughts, floods, and hurricanes, are becoming more frequent and intense due to climate change.[6] At the same time, leaders in developing democracies are limited in their ability to use welfare programs to offset the pain of these crises. For some governments, austerity is self-imposed. For others, limits on spending are due to an absence of resources or the conditions of agreements with the International Monetary Fund and other lenders.[7] Finally, the weakening of partisan attachments in many developing democracies means that economic conditions play a more significant role in the formation of public opinion.[8] They are also an increasingly critical determinant of political stability.[9] An important question, then, is how do leaders avoid backlash and unrest when their ability to spend to offset economic crises is limited?[10]

The answer this book has offered is that leaders themselves do not do much. Rather, millions of families have adjusted to austerity and economic crisis by seeking out their own forms of social insurance. The availability of a reliable, non state welfare option not only reduces citizens' demand for government-provided welfare but also contributes to improved economic well-being. The result is a reduction in economic grievances, and with it, a reduction in the risk of civil unrest and electoral backlash. Politically speaking, the winners of this appear to be incumbents, and the losers, opposition parties—particularly leftist opposition parties. I believe that remittances help incumbents not only by leading to improved assessments of government performance but also by reducing the appeal of left-wing parties that reject market policies and promise more spending. This could be, as David Doyle has argued, due to

a preference for lower taxes or, more generally, less desire on the part
of remittance recipients to support change due to feelings of optimism
under the status quo.[11]

Remittances are a mixed bag for democracy, and I hesitate to say that
they are either always beneficial or always harmful. The reality is probably
that remittances have both positive and negative implications for democracy that operate simultaneously and to varying degrees, depending on
the context. A key implication of the central arguments of this book is
that remittances reinforce democracy when they help stave off threats to
vulnerable democratic institutions during destabilizing periods of crisis.
Economic grievances—whether their underlying causes are natural or
man-made, global or domestic—regularly lead to rioting, unrest, and conflict in developing countries. They are furthermore capitalized upon and
manipulated by populists and demagogues who seize the moment and
promise a better tomorrow.

Kurt Weyland makes a compelling case for the incompatibility of populism and democracy, which he argues is rooted in a tension between the
personalistic nature of populism and the institutions- and process-based
nature of democracy.[12] Populists, in other words, accumulate power through
the strength of their personalities and the force of their personal appeals.
Democratic institutions and checks and balances, on the other hand, place
limits on the power and influence of any single individual. Populism is a
threat to democracy because populists inevitably come to view democratic
institutions and checks and balances as nuisances that must be weakened
or done away with. Weyland is particularly skeptical of left-wing populists
who use government spending to consolidate authoritarian rule and an
inward-looking economic policy to fend off outside pressure.

Remittances are important to this story because, in an era of austerity and
weak welfare states, they may be the only safety net large swaths of a country's population can count on. If remittances reliably contribute to economic
security and reduce the impulse to reflexively blame and punish incumbents in times of crisis, they may play a role in preserving democracy by
diminishing the appeal of populists—particularly left-wing populists—who
seek to upend the political order and undermine democracy in the process.

Remittances furthermore reduce the severity of the suffering and anger that trigger social and political upheaval when markets and states fail. This is critical for development. Economies cannot grow if they are plagued by constant social and political instability. By lifting the mood and contributing to economic security, remittances contribute to the social stability and support for markets that are needed for investment, commerce, and growth.

At the same time that remittances reduce the risk of civil unrest and impede the rise of authoritarian-minded populists, they may also be harmful to democracy and development if they help corrupt or inept leaders hold on to power.[13] While economic conditions are sometimes beyond policymakers' control, leaders should be held accountable when bad economic outcomes stem from government neglect, corruption, and poor performance or when governments do not do everything in their power to insulate citizens from market, environmental, and life course risks. But when remittance recipients are able to resolve economic problems by turning to relatives abroad, they have fewer incentives to participate in politics and demand better performance from their leaders.[14] In a nod to Albert Hirschman's famous framework,[15] Gary Goodman and Jonathan Hiskey call this dynamic "exit without leaving."[16] Hirschman argued that citizens who are unhappy with government performance have the option of voting with their feet or pressuring the state to change. With access to economic relief sent by family members abroad, however, remittance recipients are not forced to choose between exit and voice. Instead, they may make a cognitive exit from political life without making a physical exit from the territory where they live.

If remittance recipients are less politically engaged, political leaders may neglect constituents in areas that benefit from significant inflows of remittances because there is less fear those constituents will hold them accountable. A larger consequence of this neglect is that governments may never fully develop the capacity to deliver social services. Low levels of accountability and low state capacity will be particularly damaging to the even greater numbers of poor households in developing countries that do not receive remittances.[17] And as Faisal Ahmed has argued, deteriorating accountability may mean that remittances provide governments more opportunities to divert public money to corruption, which can perpetuate the survival of weak or repressive governments.[18]

A key question going forward is whether remittance recipients simply disengage from political life or if their improved economic situation makes them less likely to mobilize against their leaders in anger. There appears to be a clear theoretical difference between disengaging and being less aggrieved, but I imagine that these processes are not so distinct in the real world and occur in combination to varying degrees from person to person. Either way, it appears that remittances allow governments to perform badly and shirk on welfare responsibilities with fewer consequences. The implication, then, is that governments can neglect certain populations. On one hand, they may neglect remittance recipients (or communities with high rates of out-migration) specifically because they are less likely to complain about government performance or make claims on the state. On the other hand, they may, more generally, neglect the poor and count on the most aggrieved citizens to emigrate and send money home. Again, the effects of this neglect will be most damning for people living in extreme poverty who cannot afford to move to another country.

As we saw in chapter 5, however, outright political disengagement may not be the inevitable consequence of remittances. Families often use remittances to fund education, and we know that education is essential in helping citizens develop the civic skills needed to sustain a vibrant democracy.[19] Remittances moreover increase citizens' access to media and information, which can stimulate more civic engagement. Remittances are also sometimes used to fund campaigns and other political activities, and some scholars believe that by boosting poor households' income, remittances make it more difficult for authoritarian regimes to buy votes and political support.[20] A number of excellent studies have furthermore shown that remittances lead to new forms of accountability when migrants pool their money and collaborate with their home governments to provide public goods in their home communities.[21] Finally, the existence of non-state social welfare in some locales—in this case, remittances—leaves open the possibility that governments will shift limited resources to needier areas that are not served by non-state welfare providers.[22] How remittances contribute to democracy will thus depend on many factors, such as how people spend remittances; whether migrants and remittance recipients pool remittances to fund community projects; and how governments react to the inflow of remittances in terms of deciding whether to neglect populations, shift resources, or engage with remittance recipients and citizens abroad in the delivery of public goods. The remittances-democracy nexus is therefore mixed, complex, and necessarily context-specific.

Other context-specific variables may have to do with how the characteristics of remittance-receiving households vary from place to place. Remittances do not flow to households at random, but by virtue of the fact that certain people with certain characteristics decide to migrate abroad. In the Mexican context, for instance, emigrants tend to be of lower socioeconomic status than Mexico's population average and near the middle of the education distribution.[23] In sub-Saharan Africa, on the other hand, emigrants (particularly those who go to Europe and North America) tend to be better educated and of higher socioeconomic status than the population average.[24] Remittance recipients may therefore come from households with higher or lower socioeconomic status compared to others in the population, depending on the country context, and these factors may influence political attitudes and behavior apart from the independent effect of remittances. Selection effects like these may explain why remittance recipients in Mexico seem somewhat less politically engaged while the opposite appears to be true in sub-Saharan Africa—at least hypothetically so, according to chapter 5. I attempted to minimize the impact of selection effects by controlling for socioeconomic status and education, and by examining subsamples of wealthier, more educated respondents. It is impossible, however, to rule out the impact of selection effects as I have analyzed the data.

I am less concerned about the impact of selection effects on the core arguments I made in this book about the effects of remittances on economic grievances and assessments of government performance. In fact, the way in which remittance recipients are selected should bias statistical tests against my arguments about remittances' effects on economic assessments and assessments of government performance. Remittance recipients are generally the close relatives of people who emigrate, so we should expect that they, like emigrants, have some economic and political grievances in the absence of remittances. Despite this inherent selection bias, remittance recipients throughout the developing world ultimately appear less economically aggrieved, less critical of government performance, and more likely to support the incumbent. This, I believe, is a testament to the profound impact remittances have on standards of living.

REDUCING COSTS

This book has explored some of the many ways that remittances are beneficial to the families and countries that receive them. But it is important to remember that remittances are far from inevitable and their flow is anything but automatic. Olga, for instance, the Honduran woman whose story I mentioned at the beginning of this chapter, was unfortunately not able to keep her promise to her family. Her family's poverty did not end after twenty days because she was never allowed the opportunity to work in the United States. After spending two weeks traveling through Mexico to the U.S. border, Olga was arrested by the U.S. Border Patrol, detained for three weeks, and ultimately deported back to Honduras. She lost thousands of dollars and more than a month on a dangerous, unsuccessful immigration attempt. She returned to Honduras heartbroken and in more poverty than before she left.

Olga's story is not uncommon. Moving abroad—the first step in the remitting process—requires a large upfront investment in transportation expenses, moving expenses, and the fees charged by labor recruiters or human smugglers. Syrians traveling from Turkey to Germany or Sweden are reported to pay smugglers around ten thousand dollars.[25] People from impoverished areas of Central America similarly pay up to ten thousand dollars to be smuggled to the United States.[26] Even in legal migration situations, labor recruiters may charge exorbitant fees. Bangladeshi migrants, for example, are known to pay labor recruiters three thousand dollars just to secure a temporary construction job in the Middle East—a job that typically pays no more than three thousand dollars per year.[27] Many migrants spend their first months or years abroad working off these fees rather than sending money home to their families.

For those who go abroad without a job, securing employment and earning one's first paycheck can take many weeks or months, leaving new immigrants to rely on high-interest loans, savings, or support from the same non-emigrating relatives they have left home to help out. A household may moreover save and spend great sums to finance a member's journey abroad only to have that member return with news that a labor recruiter's employment offer was fraudulent or an illegal immigration attempt unsuccessful, dealing a devastating financial blow to a household that was counting on a steady stream of remittances.[28] A premature return like Olga's can leave a poor household in a much worse position—facing a mountain of debt or without hard-earned savings—than if the decision to emigrate had never been made.[29]

None of this is to mention the human costs associated with unauthorized migration. The world's poorest migrants often risk their lives crammed in unsafe boats, as in the case of Africans crossing the Mediterranean Sea to Europe, or walking through scorching deserts, as in the case of Mexicans and Central Americans who cross the southern border of the United States. Many thousands die every year in search of a better life, and unknown numbers of migrants lose their freedom to kidnappers and human traffickers who pose as human smugglers, labor recruiters, and legitimate employers.[30] For those who are fortunate enough to make it abroad safely and find a job, significant amounts of the money directed to family members back home may be lost to high money-transfer fees and unfavorable exchange rates.

Countries that depend on remittances count on their citizens having the ability to go abroad, stay abroad, and continue to send money home unencumbered. Governments, non-governmental organizations, and international organizations can (and sometimes do) play an important role in reducing the costs of emigrating and sending money so that more money makes it back to poor families. If governments are to outsource welfare to migrants, then it is imperative that they work to lower the costs of emigrating and remitting. The following areas should be priorities.

Information

Information is one way to reduce the cost of migration. Emigrants who are equipped with reliable information are more likely to make it abroad safely and find work. Reliable information is particularly valuable in light of the misinformation that is frequently thrust upon migrants. In particular, labor recruiters and human smugglers commonly misrepresent conditions abroad, such as employment prospects and the difficulty of crossing a border, to persuade migrants to agree to their fees.[31] In 2014, for example, human smugglers spread rumors in Honduras, Guatemala, and El Salvador that the United States was admitting women and children who requested asylum at the border. The smugglers collected their fees and guided tens of thousands of people like Olga to the U.S. border. When the migrants requested asylum, however, many were detained and later deported. In the worst cases, smugglers and recruiters are actually human traffickers who lure people with the promise of good jobs abroad and then sell them into servitude and slavery.[32]

Governments can help prepare their citizens for the risks, challenges, and realities of migrating. One well-intentioned information campaign that stirred up controversy in the United States was the Mexican government's *Guide for the Mexican Migrant*.[33] Through text and illustrations, this booklet, which was published in 2004, alerted would-be Mexican migrants to the dangers of crossing the U.S.-Mexico border illegally at a time when record numbers of Mexican migrants were dying in the Arizona desert and finding themselves scammed and assaulted by human smugglers. Some conservatives in the United States saw this as a shameless attempt by the Mexican government to solve its economic problems by exporting its people north of the border, while others understood that the booklet's intention was to give people who were going to migrate anyway information to help them survive.

Formal orientation and training programs are another way that governments can provide valuable information to emigrants. The Sri Lankan Bureau of Foreign Employment, for instance, offers predeparture workshops that teach emigrants about social norms in destination countries and how to avoid abuse when working in people's homes.[34] These workshops also impart job skills, which can make a country's citizens more attractive to foreign employers and result in higher wages.[35]

Another form of information is an official account of foreign labor markets. The Philippine Overseas Employment Administration, for example, runs a job search and employment coordination service that allows potential emigrants to search for jobs in locations as diverse as Qatar, Malaysia, and the United Kingdom. Egypt's Ministry of Manpower and Emigration experimented with a similar service called the Integrated Migration Information System.[36] Perhaps most critical in terms of reducing costs to migrants, this type of information gives job seekers an official account of the foreign labor market situation that can be compared to the picture painted by labor recruiters.

Temporary Labor Agreements

Governments can reduce the costs of emigration by establishing temporary labor agreements with key destination countries. Bilateral labor agreements allow migrants to move through legal channels. This is valuable because it eliminates the need for expensive human smugglers and reduces the risk that migrants will be trafficked or exposed to dangerous conditions in transit. Agreements that promote temporary or circular migration are particularly valuable because migrants who go abroad temporarily tend to remain more attentive to the economic needs of their home communities compared to migrants who go abroad on a more permanent basis.[37] Of course, the primary challenge in establishing temporary labor programs is that destination countries must be willing to agree to admit foreign workers. Increasing immigrant admissions can be politically controversial, which explains why such agreements are so difficult to establish and maintain over time. Historical, colonial, military, or linguistic ties, like those Pakistan shares with the United Kingdom and Peru shares with Spain, can increase the likelihood that a developing country's citizens will be able to secure visas and find work abroad.[38]

Diversifying the Remittance Portfolio

Establishing temporary labor agreements with many countries can contribute to a steadier flow of remittances by reducing dependence on economic and political conditions in any one destination country. When
economic conditions are good in destination countries, governments are
usually more willing to import foreign workers and foreign workers earn
more money to send home. In times of economic crisis, on the other hand,
anti-immigrant sentiment increases and destination countries tend to
restrict immigration, as happened in Europe after the 1973 economic crisis and in the United States after the 2008 recession. Recessions also mean
higher unemployment and lower wages for immigrants, which affects the
flow of remittances. At the time of writing, for instance, low oil prices
mean less revenue for Middle Eastern countries like Saudi Arabia, which
means less work for guest workers and lower remittance income for countries like Pakistan and Bangladesh.

For these reasons, it is advantageous for governments to diversify
their countries' remittance portfolios by establishing agreements with
many countries. The Philippines, for example, has labor agreements with
Canada, South Korea, Qatar, Spain, Switzerland, Taiwan, the United Arab
Emirates, and others.[39] This strategy paid dividends during the global
financial crisis—a time when remittances to many developing countries
dropped. Figure 7.1 shows that remittances to the Philippines rose steadily
despite the global financial crisis.[40] This is because Filipinos send remittances from a diverse array of countries. About half is sent from the United
States (47 percent), while the other half comes from Europe (16 percent),
the Middle East (15 percent), Asia (11 percent), and Canada (8 percent).[41]
These countries and regions were affected by the global financial crisis at
different times and to different degrees, so a big downturn in one country
or region did not cause a drop in remittances to the Philippines overall.
Compare the steady flow of remittances to the Philippines in Figure 7.1
to the pronounced drop in remitted income to Mexico during the same
years. Almost all of Mexico's remittances come from migrants living in the

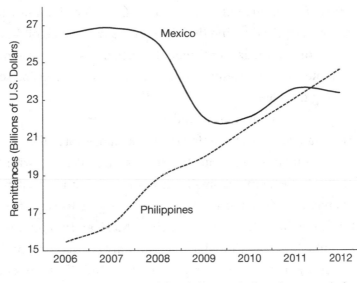

Figure 7.1 Remittances to Mexico and the Philippines before, during, and after the
Global Financial Crisis.
SOURCE: World Bank Migration and Remittances Data (rev. April 2016).

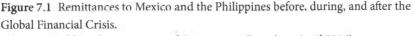

United States, a great many of whom are employed in construction jobs
and other jobs tied to housing. Remittances to Mexico started dropping off
slightly between 2007 and 2008 in the early days of the U.S. housing crisis,
then decreased by 15 percent between 2008 and 2009 as the U.S. recession deepened and spread to other sectors of the economy.[42] Had Mexico's
expatriate population been distributed across more countries and more
regions of the world, the drop in remittances during the financial crisis
likely would not have been so severe.

Regulating Fees

In many developing countries, labor recruiters connect would-be emigrants to jobs abroad. Some labor recruiters, however, misrepresent the
potential for earnings in destination countries (or even misrepresent the
existence of jobs) in efforts to draw emigrants into contracts with high

recruitment fees. Consequently, upon arriving in a destination country, workers may be surprised to find that they must spend much of their time working to pay off an unfair recruitment fee rather than saving and sending money home.[43] Governments can reduce this cost by licensing recruiters and capping their fees.[44]

Once migrants make it abroad and find work, they face more costs. High money-transfer fees and unfavorable exchange rates divert money away from poor families and into the coffers of banks and wire transfer companies. For example, Somali immigrants living in Sweden spent about 13 percent on fees and exchange-rate margins to send two hundred dollars home in early 2016. In contrast, Mexican immigrants sending money home from the United States paid only about 5 percent in fees and exchange-rate margins on average in early 2016.[45] Governments and international organizations like the World Bank can (and do) help reduce the costs of remitting by encouraging competition in the money transfer market.[46] Bilateral agreements are particularly advantageous. Funds wired from U.S. bank accounts to Mexican bank accounts, for instance, are routed through the U.S. Federal Reserve's automated clearinghouse to Mexico's central bank. This direct link means that money can be sent at or near the official exchange rate for a nominal fee. United States banks competing for migrants' business can then pass savings on to their customers.[47]

Matching Remittances

Governments can establish matching funds programs to help migrants capitalize on their remittances and make investments. Mexico's Three for One Program for Migrants is a model in this regard. The name of the program sums up the basic premise: every dollar remitted by migrants through the program to help fund approved community development projects is matched with a dollar from each level of the Mexican government—one dollar from the federal government, one dollar from the migrant's origin state government, and one dollar from the migrant's origin municipal government. Projects funded through this program

range from recreational projects (e.g., building stadiums or beautify-
ing plazas in migrants' hometowns) to projects with more direct devel-
opmental impacts, such as the construction of roads and wells and the
establishment of cooperatives. Furthermore, in 2016, Mexico's National
Housing Commission announced that it would establish a program that
matches remittances sent for the purpose of purchasing a new home in
Mexico.[48]

Maintaining Ties

Migrants tend to remit less as time goes on.[49] Governments can use policies and institutions to maintain ties with citizens abroad and remind
migrants of their home countries' economic needs even as they become
settled members of their new societies. States' attempts to foster stronger
ties with emigrants abroad often begin with expressions of gratitude to
migrants for their economic contributions and declarations of migrants'
value to the homeland. In Mexico, for example, Jesús Martínez-Saldaña
writes that the "construction of the heroic migrant" surfaced in the rhetoric of public officials at the turn of the twenty-first century after a "long
tradition of neglect, disdain, and denial that historically characterized the
policies of the Mexican government towards emigrants and their US-born
descendants."[50]

More concrete efforts to strengthen migrants' relationships with the
homeland come by granting dual citizenship and long-distance voting
rights. Eva Østergaard-Nielsen argues, for instance, that the Turkish government's decision to grant migrants dual citizenship rights and waive
their military obligations came about with the realization that, by the
1990s, most of Turkey's once-temporary labor emigrants were not plan-
ning to return home. Turkey, like many other migrant-origin countries,
also extends political rights to expatriates to stall the assimilation process somewhat and reinforce an origin identity, reminding migrants that
as members of the origin polity they also remain members of the origin
society—with all its economic needs.[51]

Another way governments can maintain ties with their diasporas is by creating migrant-oriented institutions. The Institute for Mexicans Abroad, for example, provides emigrants a formal channel for communicating with the Mexican government and runs immigrant integration programs in the United States.[52] Other migrant institutions seek to reinforce homeland identity through culture, language, and education. Morocco and Tunisia, for example, established the Hassan II Foundation and the Office for Tunisians Abroad, which send teachers to destination countries to offer Arabic-language classes, hold summer camps in Morocco and Tunisia for the children of emigrants, and publish newsletters on homeland culture and society. These institutions remind expatriates and their foreign-born children that they remain members of the homeland society and economy and encourage them to invest in their communities back home.[53]

REMITTANCES, DEVELOPMENT, AND THE FUTURE OF THE WELFARE STATE

The spread of neoliberal policies over the past three decades has caused a rethinking of the state's role in the economy. Austerity has replaced the ethos of the Keynesian welfare state that dominated during the postwar era. As globalization and austerity create economic losers, people must improvise solutions for coping with economic, environmental, and life course risks. Emigration has long performed an important safety-valve function in developing economies by relieving labor market pressures. But the effects of emigration do not end with the exit of people. Many millions of emigrants continue to send money home. In some areas, they have become the chief providers of social welfare, complementing the efforts of governments that are unable or unwilling to provide adequate social protections. The question is whether this outsourcing of social welfare is a long-term solution that governments will continue to count on as time goes on, or if governments will assume greater social welfare responsibilities as their economies develop and tax revenues increase.

While the political and economic implications of remittances will continue to be debated long after the publication of this book, what cannot be disputed is the fact that remittances are a critical source of relief to millions of poor families throughout the developing world. These flows of money are impressive as well—not only in terms of their volume but also because they tend to originate with humble people who make long, sometimes-dangerous journeys to new societies to work difficult jobs that few others want to do. They go years without seeing their loved ones, and many are marginalized and discriminated against in their new countries. While their wages may be low, they work long hours and manage to save enough from their paychecks to support friends and family members back home. It is an amazing thing that, in combination, these individual contributions have, in increments of one and two hundred dollars at a time, become a leading source of social welfare in the modern global economy and a significant force for economic, political, and social stability in developing countries.

Methodological Appendix

This appendix discusses the methodology behind the survey data I collected and in-depth interviews I conducted in Michoacán, Mexico. These data and interviews are referenced in chapters 2, 3, and 6. This appendix also discusses the rationale behind the index that I developed to measure remittances in chapters 3 and 6.

SURVEY METHODOLOGY

The goal of the survey was to collect individual-level data on remittance income, economic assessments, political attitudes, and political behavior from people living in high-emigration communities in Mexico. I decided to focus on a relatively small geographical area rather than conduct a national survey for a few reasons. First, I needed to conduct this survey face-to-face because many people in rural areas of Mexico do not have access to telephones or the internet. The cost of conducting a national face-to-face survey was prohibitive. Another reason I focused on a relatively narrow geographical area was that I wanted to make sure our sample had a large subsample of remittance recipients. In fact, very few existing public opinion surveys focus on remittance recipients and seek to measure variation in that population. To achieve these ends, I followed the Mexican Migration Project (MMP)—a long-running household survey project founded by Douglas Massey and Jorge Durand—by conducting the survey in an area known to have high rates of out-migration to the United States.

I chose the state of Michoacán, which is located at the center of what has historically been Mexico's most important migrant-sending region, as the site for this study. I then used the probability proportionate to size (PPS) method to randomly select three of the twenty-eight municipalities in Michoacán that the Mexican Population Council has found to have "very high" rates of out-migration. Mexican municipalities are similar to U.S. counties in that they are made up of smaller units: cities, towns, communities, and villages. The catch-all name for these smaller units is "localities." Within each of the three municipalities, I again used PPS to select three or four localities for a total of ten localities. I then traveled to each of the ten localities accompanied by an eight-person research team, where we went block-by-block drawing detailed maps of each community to obtain the most accurate count of household units. Based on these censuses, I used simple random selection to select 768 households from the total population of households. The survey was conducted from January 2 to January 30, 2008. The survey was applied face-to-face by an experienced team of Mexican interviewers (some former MMP interviewers), supervised in the field by the author and the former field coordinator of the MMP. The response rate was 79.44 percent.

The questionnaire used a two-part design that combines approaches used in sociodemographic studies of emigration like the MMP and political science studies of public opinion. Part I of the interview was conducted with the head of the household and all other household members who were available and willing to participate. The main purpose of this half of the interview was to construct an in-depth profile of all household members' emigration experiences and income sources, including remittances. Part II of the interview was conducted with one randomly selected adult member of the household. The aim of this half of the interview was to understand an individual's political behaviors, political attitudes, and perspectives on the economy.

IN-DEPTH INTERVIEWS

To complement my statistical work, I draw on in-depth interviews I conducted in the Mexican states of San Luis Potosí, Morelos, and Michoacán between 2005 and 2008. Living in these small communities for between one and four weeks, I conducted interviews with dozens of farmers and return migrants about the intersection of remittances, economics, and politics in their towns. Often, these interviews would last about two or three hours. In Michoacán, I conducted dozens of in-depth interviews with mayors and mayoral candidates, local party leaders, peasant farmers, and return migrants in the ten rural towns where we collected survey data in January 2008. I also returned to Michoacán in April 2008 to conduct in-depth interviews with regional and state-level officials in Morelia, the state capital, including the regional director of the Ministry for Agrarian Reform (SRA), the state coordinator for the Oportunidades Program, the state director of statistics at the Ministry of Agriculture, Livestock, Rural Development, Fishing, and Nutrition (SAGARPA), the state technical director of the Ministry of Rural Development, and the director of the Michoacán Ministry for Migrants Abroad. Edited versions of many of these interviews can be viewed in my 2010 documentary film *The Other Side of Immigration*.[1] The methodology I used to edit the interviews is discussed in my 2014 article, "Analytic Filmmaking: A New Approach to Research and Publication in the Social Sciences."[2]

MEASURING REMITTANCES: THE REMITTANCES INDEX

When designing the survey, I gave a lot of thought to the question of how to measure remittances. Researchers commonly measure remittances in terms of volume or frequency. But how should we measure the extent to which remittances are a stable and enduring form of social insurance to a family? The more stable and enduring, the more likely the poor will feel insulated from market vicissitudes, and thus the less economically aggrieved they will feel compared to those in similar economic situations who do not have access to a reliable safety net. To see why this is important, imagine two poor households each received $1,200 in remittance income last year. On the basis of their remittance income alone, these two households are statistically indistinguishable. By digging deeper, however, we observe important differences in the extent to which this money serves as a buffer against economic crisis. Imagine, for instance, that Household A has only received remittances for one year and transfers were somewhat unpredictable: $700 arrived in January, another $400 was sent in October, and finally $100 was sent in November. Household B, on the other hand, has consistently received $100 every month from a family member abroad for the past ten years. Add to this that the head of Household A earns $12,000 per year teaching at a public school. Not only is his income consistent from month-to-month, but he is also covered by a health insurance and pension plan. The head of Household B, on the other hand, earns roughly $2,400 per year from small-scale agriculture. His income is unpredictable, and he does not have access to any public or employment-based social insurance plans. We can now see that the $1,200 these households receive from family members abroad means something vastly different to each. Household A does not depend on remittances; the money is more like an occasional gift than a reliable source of income. For Household B, on the other hand, the $1,200 it receives each year in remittances is an important and reliable safety net that likely means the difference between survival and abject poverty. It seems that if remittances have any impact on economic grievances and political behavior, they would reveal themselves more in Household B than in Household A.

Three important characteristics of remittances are thus their significance relative to normal household income (significance), how reliably and consistently family members abroad send remittances to the household (reliability), and the amount of time the household has consistently received remittances (enduringness).[3] Conceptualizing remittances in terms of their significance, reliability, and enduringness provides insight into the social insurance function of remittances at the household level.

To capture these qualities, my survey asked three questions about respondents' remittance income, which I used to create an index that measures the social insurance function of remittances. The first component of the index is the significance of remittances relative to other domestically earned sources of household income. If respondents reported that remittance income is "small" compared to other income sources, the interviewers gave them a score of one. If respondents reported that remittances are an "intermediate" or "substantial" share of normal income, interviewers gave them a score of two or three.[4] The second component is the degree to which the respondent can count on family members abroad to send money home in times of need. We gave respondents a score of one if they reported that remittances are "only sometimes sent" in times of need, a score of two if remittances are "almost always sent when needed," and a score of three if remittances are "always sent when needed." The purpose of this question was to measure respondents' feelings about emigrants' attentiveness to the economic needs of the household and therefore obtain a measure of the reliability of remittances as a source of social insurance. The final component is the number of years respondents reported that their household had consistently received remittances. Interviewers recorded the number of years reported. This measures the degree to which remittances have been a temporary or an enduring source of social insurance to the household.

I created the index by first assigning a score of zero on each of the three component variables to the 505 respondents who did not receive remittances at the time of the survey. Then, for the 262 respondents who reported receiving remittances, I combined scores on questions about the degree to which remittances are a relatively substantial, reliable, and enduring source of income. I then divided the number of years by a constant so that all three variables carried equal weight. Finally, I summed the three scores and divided by a constant to create a continuous index that ranges from 0 to 1.[5] This variable provides a much richer and more nuanced measure of the social insurance effect of remittances than a simple dichotomous variable or continuous variable measuring total dollar amounts. Specifically, it provides us with a continuum for understanding how substantial, reliable, and enduring remittances are to the respondent.

Statistical Appendix

This appendix includes statistical tables related to the figures presented in chapters 3–6. At the top of each table, I have listed figures for corresponding models in the text. With the exception of the multinomial logistic regressions discussed in chapter 6, the predicted probabilities I discussed in the book were based on binomial logistic regressions. With this type of analysis, the dependent variable is binary, taking a value of either 1 or 0 (e.g., bad/very bad = 1; good/very good = 0). I coded the dependent variables as binary variables to keep the figures simple and easy for readers to interpret. Key findings held up when I coded the dependent variables as ordinal variables and estimated ordered logit and ordered probit models (e.g., very good = 1; good = 2; bad = 3; very bad = 4). Key findings were also robust to different model specifications, as many of the following tables demonstrate. Standard errors were clustered by appropriate geographic units, depending on data set.

TABLE A1   REMITTANCES AND INCOME STABILITY IN MICHOACÁN, MEXICO
(BINOMIAL LOGIT). CORRESPONDS TO FIGURE 3.2

	(1)	(2)	(3)	(4)	(5)
VARIABLES	Considers Income Stable	Considers Income Stable	Considers Income Stable	Considers Income Stable	Considers Income Stable
Remittances	1.058** (0.502)	1.082** (0.478)	1.044** (0.495)	1.181** (0.478)	1.228** (0.488)
Income (log)	0.0619** (0.0241)	0.0697*** (0.0230)	0.0677*** (0.0235)	0.0586** (0.0241)	0.0492** (0.0236)
Agriculture		−0.599*** (0.173)	−0.746*** (0.203)	−0.626*** (0.213)	−0.551*** (0.204)
Number of Cows			0.0586** (0.0280)	0.0529** (0.0228)	0.0484** (0.0217)
Hectares Owned			0.0578 (0.0375)	0.0306 (0.0362)	0.0246 (0.0319)
Health Insurance				1.123*** (0.187)	1.014*** (0.213)
Female					0.0303 (0.171)
Education					0.0493*** (0.0174)
Age					0.00175 (0.00473)
Constant	−1.726*** (0.168)	−1.532*** (0.203)	−1.515*** (0.203)	−1.693*** (0.225)	−2.028*** (0.367)
Observations	749	749	749	749	749

Robust standard errors (clustered by town or village) in parentheses.
*** $p < 0.01$, ** $p < 0.05$, * $p < 0.1$.

TABLE A2   REMITTANCES AND THE LIKELIHOOD OF NAMING AN ECONOMIC
PROBLEM AS THE "MOST IMPORTANT PROBLEM FACING
MEXICO" (BINOMIAL LOGIT). CORRESPONDS TO FIGURE 3.3

VARIABLES	(1) Economic Issue Is "Most Important Problem"	(2) Economic Issue Is "Most Important Problem"	(3) Economic Issue Is "Most Important Problem"	(4) Economic Issue Is "Most Important Problem"
Remittances	−1.306***	−1.220***	−1.192***	−1.194***
	(0.267)	(0.231)	(0.209)	(0.215)
Income (log)	0.0131	−0.00420	−0.0106	−0.0105
	(0.0108)	(0.0121)	(0.0166)	(0.0167)
Age		−0.00198	0.00130	0.00138
		(0.00292)	(0.00363)	(0.00322)
Female		−0.441***	−0.423***	−0.423**
		(0.163)	(0.164)	(0.164)
Education		0.0447**	0.0691***	0.0696***
		(0.0210)	(0.0224)	(0.0207)
Agriculture			0.672***	0.670***
			(0.162)	(0.163)
Number of Cows			−0.0789**	−0.0788**
			(0.0390)	(0.0390)
Hectares Owned			−0.0786*	−0.0782*
			(0.0436)	(0.0451)
Health Insurance				−0.0238
				(0.170)
Constant	0.633***	0.892***	0.429	0.426
	(0.132)	(0.257)	(0.284)	(0.269)
Observations	759	759	759	759

Robust standard errors (clustered by town or village) in parentheses.
*** $p < 0.01$, ** $p < 0.05$, * $p < 0.1$.

TABLE A3   REMITTANCES AND POCKETBOOK ASSESSMENTS IN MICHOACÁN, MEXICO (BINOMIAL LOGIT). CORRESPONDS TO FIGURE 3.4A

VARIABLES	(1) Negative Prospective Pocketbook Assessment	(2) Negative Prospective Pocketbook Assessment	(3) Negative Prospective Pocketbook Assessment	(4) Negative Prospective Pocketbook Assessment
Remittances	−1.419*** (0.440)	−1.455*** (0.441)	−1.441*** (0.445)	−1.353*** (0.430)
Income (log)	0.0193 (0.0273)	0.0157 (0.0279)	0.0149 (0.0277)	0.0193 (0.0300)
Age	0.0325*** (0.0108)	0.0327*** (0.0111)	0.0322*** (0.0109)	0.0329*** (0.0104)
Female	0.150 (0.240)	0.192 (0.231)	0.189 (0.228)	0.140 (0.223)
Education	0.0187 (0.0201)	0.0240 (0.0237)	0.0206 (0.0246)	0.0216 (0.0234)
Agriculture		0.241 (0.191)	0.250 (0.183)	0.247 (0.183)
Number of Cows		−0.0151 (0.0321)	−0.0151 (0.0321)	−0.0119 (0.0301)
Hectares Owned		0.0283 (0.0377)	0.0261 (0.0397)	0.0236 (0.0421)
Health Insurance			0.129 (0.181)	0.154 (0.167)
Panista (Party ID)				−1.153*** (0.345)
Priista (Party ID)				−0.584 (0.395)
Perredista (Party ID)				0.0996 (0.209)
Constant	−2.703*** (0.639)	−2.871*** (0.636)	−2.844*** (0.634)	−2.764*** (0.622)
Observations	681	681	681	681

Robust standard errors (clustered by town or village) in parentheses.
*** p<0.01, ** p<0.05, * p<0.1.

TABLE A4 REMITTANCES AND SOCIOTROPIC ASSESSMENTS IN MICHOACÁN, MEXICO (BINOMIAL LOGIT). CORRESPONDS TO FIGURE 3.4B

VARIABLES	(1) Negative Prospective Sociotropic Assessment	(2) Negative Prospective Sociotropic Assessment	(3) Negative Prospective Sociotropic Assessment	(4) Negative Prospective Sociotropic Assessment
Remittances	−1.025**	−1.040**	−1.046**	−1.004**
	(0.487)	(0.495)	(0.488)	(0.491)
Income (log)	0.00585	0.00336	0.00369	0.00730
	(0.0168)	(0.0162)	(0.0159)	(0.0172)
Age	0.0229***	0.0221***	0.0224***	0.0228***
	(0.00634)	(0.00738)	(0.00752)	(0.00676)
Female	0.0223	0.0260	0.0271	−0.0193
	(0.169)	(0.184)	(0.184)	(0.187)
Education	0.0404***	0.0385*	0.0399*	0.0413*
	(0.0146)	(0.0209)	(0.0212)	(0.0211)
Agriculture		0.0337	0.0305	0.0221
		(0.154)	(0.156)	(0.154)
Number of Cows		0.0438*	0.0440*	0.0499**
		(0.0258)	(0.0261)	(0.0239)
Hectares Owned		0.0129	0.0138	0.0120
		(0.0622)	(0.0628)	(0.0648)
Health Insurance			−0.0546	−0.0247
			(0.175)	(0.219)
Panista				−0.820**
				(0.359)
Priista				−0.906*
				(0.478)
Perredista				0.0880
				(0.236)
Constant	−1.746***	−1.729***	−1.740***	−1.641***
	(0.372)	(0.455)	(0.455)	(0.479)
Observations	668	668	668	668

Robust standard errors (clustered by town or village) in parentheses.
*** p < 0.01, ** p < 0.05, * p < 0.1.

TABLE A5   REMITTANCES AND DEMAND FOR GOVERNMENT-PROVIDED
WELFARE IN MICHOACÁN, MEXICO (BINOMIAL LOGIT).
CORRESPONDS TO FIGURE 3.5

VARIABLES	(1) Respondent Has Asked Government Officials for Economic Assistance	(2) Respondent Has Asked Government Officials for Economic Assistance	(3) Respondent Has Asked Government Officials for Economic Assistance	(4) Respondent Has Asked Government Officials for Economic Assistance
Remittances	−1.152*** (0.416)	−1.113*** (0.410)	−1.142*** (0.400)	−1.199*** (0.417)
Income (log)	−0.0317 (0.0199)	−0.0282 (0.0186)	−0.0271 (0.0190)	−0.0305 (0.0201)
Age	0.00434 (0.00746)	0.00653 (0.00725)	0.00767 (0.00695)	0.00767 (0.00613)
Female	0.377 (0.232)	0.338 (0.228)	0.345 (0.226)	0.455* (0.233)
Education	−0.100*** (0.0300)	−0.0944*** (0.0286)	−0.0875*** (0.0274)	−0.0816*** (0.0253)
Agriculture		0.0137 (0.262)	−0.00870 (0.259)	−0.0105 (0.274)
Number of Cows		−0.115** (0.0488)	−0.111** (0.0489)	−0.123*** (0.0459)
Hectares Owned		−0.108** (0.0550)	−0.106* (0.0546)	−0.0991 (0.0604)
Health Insurance			−0.381 (0.314)	−0.442 (0.297)
Panista				0.780** (0.306)
Priista				0.821** (0.349)
Perredista				0.794*** (0.210)
Constant	−1.048** (0.502)	−1.101** (0.451)	−1.144** (0.449)	−1.519*** (0.389)
Observations	757	757	757	757

Robust standard errors (clustered by town or village) in parentheses.
*** p < 0.01, ** p < 0.05, * p < 0.1.

TABLE A6   REMITTANCES AND POCKETBOOK ASSESSMENTS IN LATIN
AMERICA AND THE CARIBBEAN (BINOMIAL LOGIT).
CORRESPONDS TO FIGURES 4.4A AND 4.5A

VARIABLES	(1) Negative Pocketbook Assessment	(2) Negative Pocketbook Assessment	(3) Negative Prospective Pocketbook Assessment	(4) Negative Prospective Pocketbook Assessment
Remittances	−0.0718***	−0.0749***	−0.0707***	−0.0720***
	(0.0215)	(0.0211)	(0.0256)	(0.0255)
Age	0.0125***	0.0127***	0.0142***	0.0142***
	(0.000881)	(0.000900)	(0.00199)	(0.00200)
Education	−0.0391***	−0.0374***	−0.0431***	−0.0432***
	(0.00340)	(0.00335)	(0.00585)	(0.00588)
Income	−0.168***	−0.171***	−0.0933***	−0.0922***
	(0.00913)	(0.00869)	(0.0129)	(0.0128)
Female	−0.00626	−0.00653	0.0238	0.0244
	(0.0176)	(0.0177)	(0.0452)	(0.0451)
Rural	−0.0504	−0.0514*	0.0672	0.0632
	(0.0308)	(0.0280)	(0.0737)	(0.0663)
Constant	−0.379***	−0.368***	−1.121***	−0.794***
	(0.0759)	(0.0984)	(0.194)	(0.212)
Country Fixed Effects	Yes	Yes	Yes	Yes
Year Fixed Effects	No	Yes	No	Yes
Observations	83,692	83,692	25,406	25,406

Robust standard errors (clustered by strata, province, or region) in parentheses.
*** $p < 0.01$, ** $p < 0.05$, * $p < 0.1$.

174

Appendix II

TABLE A7   REMITTANCES AND POCKETBOOK ASSESSMENTS IN SUB-
SAHARAN AFRICA (BINOMIAL LOGIT). CORRESPONDS
TO FIGURES 4.4B AND 4.5B

VARIABLES	(1) Negative Pocketbook Assessment	(2) Negative Pocketbook Assessment	(3) Negative Prospective Pocketbook Assessment	(4) Negative Prospective Pocketbook Assessment
Remittances	−0.0835*** (0.0147)	−0.108*** (0.0329)	−0.113*** (0.0189)	−0.0936*** (0.0345)
Age	0.00650*** (0.00119)	0.00723** (0.00287)	0.0143*** (0.00158)	0.0201*** (0.00399)
Education	−0.136*** (0.0121)	−0.204*** (0.0285)	−0.0125 (0.0165)	−0.00377 (0.0368)
Female	−0.0320 (0.0340)	−0.0939 (0.0842)	0.0568 (0.0357)	−0.00841 (0.0881)
Rural	0.0316 (0.0528)	0.145 (0.133)	0.00766 (0.0554)	−0.0159 (0.159)
Employment Status	−0.134*** (0.0250)	0.0211 (0.0490)	−0.0630 (0.0385)	0.0688 (0.0653)
High SES	−0.482*** (0.0817)		−0.0457 (0.114)	
Constant	0.647*** (0.243)	0.570* (0.306)	−1.878*** (0.256)	−2.269*** (0.309)
Country Fixed Effects	Yes	Yes	Yes	Yes
Sample	Full Sample	High SES Subsample	Full Sample	High SES Subsample
Observations	26,833	4,474	23,152	4,104

NOTE: High SES is defined as having running water in one's home.
Robust standard errors (clustered by region or province) in parentheses.
*** p < 0.01, ** p < 0.05, * p < 0.1.

TABLE A8   REMITTANCES AND SOCIOTROPIC ASSESSMENTS IN THE
            MIDDLE EAST AND NORTH AFRICA (BINOMIAL LOGIT).
            CORRESPONDS TO FIGURES 4.6A AND 4.7A

VARIABLES	(1) Negative Sociotropic Assessment	(2) Negative Prospective Sociotropic Assessment
Remittances	−0.187***	−0.268***
	(0.0471)	(0.0523)
Age	0.00203	0.00574**
	(0.00244)	(0.00282)
Female	0.0476	−0.114
	(0.0640)	(0.0692)
Education	0.0596*	0.0307
	(0.0314)	(0.0283)
Income (log)	−0.0380***	−0.0286**
	(0.0145)	(0.0144)
Rural	0.255**	0.200
	(0.100)	(0.131)
Constant	0.587***	−1.289***
	(0.191)	(0.212)
Country Fixed Effects	Yes	Yes
Observations	8,591	8,303

Robust standard errors (clustered by province, governorate, or state) in parentheses.
*** $p < 0.01$, ** $p < 0.05$, * $p < 0.1$.

TABLE A9   REMITTANCES AND SOCIOTROPIC ASSESSMENTS IN
SUB-SAHARAN AFRICA (BINOMIAL LOGIT). CORRESPONDS
TO FIGURES 4.6B AND 4.7B

VARIABLES	(1) Negative Sociotropic Assessment	(2) Negative Sociotropic Assessment	(3) Negative Prospective Sociotropic Assessment	(4) Negative Prospective Sociotropic Assessment
Remittances	−0.0599***	−0.0570**	−0.0907***	−0.102***
	(0.0124)	(0.0260)	(0.0191)	(0.0381)
Age	0.00193	0.00475	0.00997***	0.0129***
	(0.00139)	(0.00300)	(0.00168)	(0.00413)
Education	−0.0811***	−0.121***	0.0422**	0.0598*
	(0.0150)	(0.0339)	(0.0167)	(0.0322)
Female	0.126***	0.208**	0.0671*	0.0422
	(0.0288)	(0.0840)	(0.0358)	(0.0953)
Rural	−0.0822	−0.0281	−0.104*	−0.0405
	(0.0560)	(0.120)	(0.0570)	(0.124)
Employment Status	−0.0738*** (0.0247)	0.0400 (0.0498)	−0.00676 (0.0324)	0.0315 (0.0530)
High SES	−0.119		0.169*	
	(0.0822)		(0.101)	
Constant	0.666***	0.657**	−1.730***	−1.900***
	(0.255)	(0.311)	(0.249)	(0.300)
Country Fixed Effects	Yes	Yes	Yes	Yes
Sample	Full Sample	High SES Subsample	Full Sample	High SES Subsample
Observations	26,453	4,441	23,047	4,120

NOTE: High SES is defined as having running water in one's home.
Robust standard errors (clustered by region or province) in parentheses.
*** p < 0.01, ** p < 0.05, * p < 0.1.

TABLE A10   REMITTANCES AND POCKETBOOK ASSESSMENTS IN GHANA,
            MALI, AND SENEGAL (BINOMIAL LOGIT). CORRESPONDS
            TO FIGURE 4.8

	(1)	(2)	(3)
VARIABLES	Negative Pocketbook Assessment (GHANA)	Negative Pocketbook Assessment (MALI)	Negative Pocketbook Assessment (SENEGAL)
Remittances	−0.176***	−0.230***	−0.172***
	(0.0662)	(0.0494)	(0.0408)
Age	0.00999**	−0.00309	0.00871
	(0.00426)	(0.00489)	(0.00594)
Education	−0.164***	−0.173***	−0.189***
	(0.0336)	(0.0369)	(0.0541)
Female	−0.155	0.0719	0.0751
	(0.129)	(0.111)	(0.101)
Employment Status	−0.125*	−0.196*	−0.0542
	(0.0754)	(0.118)	(0.144)
High SES	−0.497**	0.181	−1.030***
	(0.249)	(0.190)	(0.202)
Constant	0.355	0.774***	1.435***
	(0.240)	(0.254)	(0.306)
Observations	1,151	1,214	1,130

Robust standard errors (clustered by district) in parentheses.
*** $p < 0.01$, ** $p < 0.05$, * $p < 0.1$.

TABLE A11   REMITTANCES AND POCKETBOOK ASSESSMENTS IN HAITI
(BINOMIAL LOGIT). CORRESPONDS TO FIGURE 4.9

VARIABLES	(1) Negative Pocketbook Assessment (HAITI 2006)	(2) Negative Pocketbook Assessment (HAITI 2008)
Remittances	−0.412***	−0.501***
	(0.0900)	(0.0806)
Age	−0.00230	0.00300
	(0.00739)	(0.00724)
Education	−0.0421**	−0.0571**
	(0.0196)	(0.0279)
Female	0.208	−0.0506
	(0.149)	(0.126)
Income	−0.0416	−0.167***
	(0.0450)	(0.0413)
Constant	1.439***	2.302***
	(0.442)	(0.480)
Observations	932	1,151

Robust standard errors (clustered by municipality) in parentheses.
*** $p < 0.01$, ** $p < 0.05$, * $p < 0.1$.

TABLE A12   REMITTANCES AND SOCIOTROPIC ASSESSMENTS
IN ALGERIA AND ZAMBIA (BINOMIAL LOGIT). CORRESPONDS
TO FIGURE 4.10

VARIABLES	(1) Negative Sociotropic Assessment (ALGERIA)	(2) Negative Sociotropic Assessment (ZAMBIA)
Remittances	−0.313**	−0.188***
	(0.127)	(0.0548)
Age	−0.00611	0.00589
	(0.00526)	(0.00524)
Education	−0.0571	0.0362
	(0.0454)	(0.0457)
Female	−0.158	0.217
	(0.140)	(0.147)
Employment Status		−0.140*
		(0.0815)
High SES		0.130
		(0.368)
Income (log)	−0.0822***	
	(0.00997)	
Constant	1.710***	0.595**
	(0.364)	(0.304)
Observations	1,119	1,172

Robust standard errors (clustered by province or district) in parentheses.
*** p < 0.01, ** p < 0.05, * p < 0.1.

TABLE A13 REMITTANCES AND PROSPECTIVE POCKETBOOK
ASSESSMENTS IN UGANDA, JAMAICA, AND GUYANA
(BINOMIAL LOGIT). CORRESPONDS TO FIGURE 4.11

VARIABLES	(1) Negative Prospective Pocketbook Assessment (UGANDA)	(2) Negative Prospective Pocketbook Assessment (JAMAICA)	(3) Negative Prospective Pocketbook Assessment (GUYANA)
Remittances	−0.273*** (0.0937)	−0.239*** (0.0817)	−0.205** (0.0803)
Age	0.0138*** (0.00488)	0.00219 (0.00603)	0.0268*** (0.00647)
Education	0.0364 (0.0289)	−0.0509 (0.0335)	−0.0845*** (0.0301)
Female	−0.0179 (0.0765)	−0.0275 (0.142)	0.00168 (0.162)
Employment Status	−0.132 (0.114)		
High SES	−0.392* (0.206)		
Income		−0.104*** (0.0328)	−0.163** (0.0818)
Constant	−1.186*** (0.226)	0.209 (0.457)	−1.315*** (0.439)
Observations	2,092	968	951

Robust standard errors (clustered by district or municipality) in parentheses.
*** p < 0.01, ** p < 0.05, * p < 0.1.

TABLE A14   REMITTANCES AND PROSPECTIVE SOCIOTROPIC
ASSESSMENTS IN LEBANON AND YEMEN (BINOMIAL LOGIT).
CORRESPONDS TO FIGURE 4.12

VARIABLES	(1) Negative Prospective Sociotropic Assessment (LEBANON)	(2) Negative Prospective Sociotropic Assessment (YEMEN)
Remittances	−0.388***	−0.306***
	(0.141)	(0.0884)
Age	−0.000251	−0.00312
	(0.00737)	(0.00565)
Education	−0.122***	0.0574
	(0.0395)	(0.0447)
Female	0.0873	−0.602***
	(0.168)	(0.216)
Income (log)	−0.155***	0.00762
	(0.0308)	(0.0154)
Constant	2.189***	0.206
	(0.388)	(0.364)
Observations	1,337	1,044

Robust standard errors (clustered by governorate) in parentheses.
*** p < 0.01, ** p < 0.05, * p < 0.1.

TABLE A15   EXPERIENCING HUNGER AND ASSESSMENTS OF GOVERNMENT
PERFORMANCE IN SUB-SAHARAN AFRICA (BINOMIAL LOGIT).
CORRESPONDS TO FIGURES 5.1, 5.2, AND 5.3

	(1)	(2)	(3)	(4)	(5)
VARIABLES	Respondent Experienced Hunger	Gov't Doing Bad Job: PRICES	Gov't Doing Bad Job: HUNGER	Gov't Doing Bad Job: POVERTY	Gov't Doing Bad Job: EQUALITY
Remittances	−0.0799***	−0.0719***	−0.0488***	−0.0544***	−0.0691***
	(0.0171)	(0.0214)	(0.0151)	(0.0171)	(0.0189)
Age	0.00521***	0.00285*	0.00164	−6.33e-05	0.00290*
	(0.00136)	(0.00163)	(0.00124)	(0.00123)	(0.00151)
Education	−0.170***	0.0163	−0.000274	−0.0201	0.0252
	(0.0151)	(0.0164)	(0.0149)	(0.0135)	(0.0153)
Female	0.0128	0.0517	0.0386	0.0254	−0.0107
	(0.0283)	(0.0408)	(0.0330)	(0.0319)	(0.0372)
Employment Status	−0.142***	−0.0826***	−0.0648**	−0.0597**	−0.0456
	(0.0310)	(0.0306)	(0.0291)	(0.0256)	(0.0312)
High SES	−0.546***	−0.135*	−0.152**	−0.0738	−0.0151
	(0.0643)	(0.0718)	(0.0647)	(0.0721)	(0.0759)
Rural	0.225***	−0.0899	−0.0462	−0.0948*	−0.144**
	(0.0492)	(0.0576)	(0.0518)	(0.0555)	(0.0580)
Political Interest		−0.0829***	−0.0985***	−0.105***	−0.0750***
		(0.0217)	(0.0193)	(0.0188)	(0.0201)
Sent by Government		−0.00794	−0.0733	−0.109**	−0.143***
		(0.0542)	(0.0473)	(0.0435)	(0.0523)
Constant	0.201	1.536***	0.996***	0.798**	1.412***
	(0.216)	(0.289)	(0.261)	(0.314)	(0.258)
Observations	26,917	25,882	25,638	25,851	25,214

All models estimated with country fixed effects (not shown).
Robust standard errors (clustered by region) in parentheses.
*** p < 0.01, ** p < 0.05, * p < 0.1.

TABLE A16   REMITTANCES AND SUPPORT FOR INCUMBENTS IN SUB-SAHARAN AFRICA (BINOMIAL LOGIT). FULL SAMPLE AND DEMOCRATIC/NONDEMOCRATIC SUBSAMPLES. CORRESPONDS TO FIGURES 5.4 AND 5.5

VARIABLES	(1) Would Vote Incumbent Party	(2) Would Vote Incumbent Party	(3) Would Vote Incumbent Party	(4) Would Vote Incumbent Party	(5) Would Vote Incumbent Party	(6) Would Vote Incumbent Party
Remittances	0.0379**	0.0458***	0.0483***	0.0397**	0.0544***	-0.0187
	(0.0156)	(0.0155)	(0.0154)	(0.0158)	(0.0177)	(0.0312)
Age	0.00273*	0.00333**	0.00329**	0.00238	0.000841	0.00850***
	(0.00153)	(0.00148)	(0.00147)	(0.00151)	(0.00178)	(0.00275)
Education	-0.0557***	-0.0404**	-0.0269*	-0.0304**	-0.0202	-0.0539**
	(0.0171)	(0.0161)	(0.0157)	(0.0153)	(0.0178)	(0.0263)
Female	-0.0534	-0.0434	-0.0358	0.00526	-0.0178	0.0754
	(0.0368)	(0.0371)	(0.0376)	(0.0384)	(0.0433)	(0.0808)
Employment Status	0.0205	0.0270	0.0324	0.0325	0.0564*	-0.0358
	(0.0277)	(0.0271)	(0.0271)	(0.0271)	(0.0331)	(0.0431)
High SES	-0.362***	-0.362***	-0.279***	-0.280***	-0.278**	-0.336***
	(0.0949)	(0.0949)	(0.0937)	(0.0929)	(0.110)	(0.124)

(continued)

TABLE A16 CONTINUED

VARIABLES	(1) Would Vote Incumbent Party	(2) Would Vote Incumbent Party	(3) Would Vote Incumbent Party	(4) Would Vote Incumbent Party	(5) Would Vote Incumbent Party	(6) Would Vote Incumbent Party
Rural			0.230***	0.195***	0.164**	0.284***
			(0.0579)	(0.0582)	(0.0678)	(0.108)
Political Interest				0.156***	0.149***	0.177***
				(0.0195)	(0.0241)	(0.0319)
Sent By Gov't				0.345***	0.299***	0.463***
				(0.0388)	(0.0463)	(0.0646)
Constant	0.0170	0.00434	−0.178	−0.662***	−0.568**	−0.644***
	(0.252)	(0.250)	(0.250)	(0.247)	(0.253)	(0.216)
Sample	Full Sample	Full Sample	Full Sample	Full Sample	Democracies	Nondemocracies
Observations	23,088	23,043	23,043	22,800	14,455	8,345

All models estimated with country fixed effects (not shown).

Respondents from Mali were omitted because president was not a member of a political party.

Robust standard errors (clustered by region) in parentheses.

*** p < 0.01, ** p < 0.05, * p < 0.1.

TABLE A17   REMITTANCES AND POLITICAL ENGAGEMENT IN SUB-SAHARAN AFRICA (BINOMIAL LOGIT). CORRESPONDS TO FIGURE 5.6

VARIABLES	(1) Interested in Public Affairs	(2) Never Watches TV News	(3) Likely Could Make Representative Listen	(4) Would Not Vote in Hypothetical Election
Remittances	0.0464***	−0.120***	0.0586***	−0.0981***
	(0.0133)	(0.0174)	(0.0160)	(0.0238)
Age	0.0104***	0.0109***	0.00329***	−0.00117
	(0.00133)	(0.00161)	(0.00127)	(0.00228)
Education	0.116***	−0.366***	0.0280**	0.0946***
	(0.0130)	(0.0191)	(0.0120)	(0.0243)
Female	−0.472***	0.226***	−0.124***	0.100
	(0.0344)	(0.0375)	(0.0309)	(0.0655)
Employment Status	0.110***	−0.174***	0.0947***	−0.0124
	(0.0263)	(0.0331)	(0.0304)	(0.0385)
High SES	0.0195	−1.155***	−0.0940	0.368***
	(0.0727)	(0.103)	(0.0684)	(0.107)
Rural	0.125**	1.437***	0.0197	−0.271***
	(0.0492)	(0.0770)	(0.0411)	(0.0673)
Political Interest		−0.106***	0.179***	−0.325***
		(0.0205)	(0.0209)	(0.0344)
Sent by Government				−0.139**
				(0.0660)
Constant	0.312**	−0.413^	−0.803^^^	−2.674^^^
	(0.152)	(0.220)	(0.160)	(0.330)
Observations	26,728	26,728	24,839	24,008

All models estimated with country fixed effects (not shown).
Robust standard errors (clustered by region) in parentheses.
*** p < 0.01, ** p < 0.05, * p < 0.1.

TABLE A18   REMITTANCES AND VOTE CHOICE IN MEXICO'S 2006
             PRESIDENTIAL ELECTION, NATIONAL SAMPLE (MULTINOMIAL
             LOGIT). PRD IS BASE CATEGORY. CORRESPONDS
             TO FIGURE 6.1

VARIABLES	Voted for the PAN	Voted for the PRI	Voted for Minor Party
Remittances	0.200**	0.364***	−0.277
	(0.100)	(0.107)	(0.245)
Age	0.000162	−0.00348	0.00995
	(0.0108)	(0.0108)	(0.0134)
Male	−0.631**	0.0821	−0.772*
	(0.255)	(0.335)	(0.409)
Education	0.0357	−0.0277	0.0936
	(0.0629)	(0.0916)	(0.0912)
Income	−0.0202	−0.0280	−0.0550
	(0.0492)	(0.0855)	(0.0791)
Panista	1.984***	0.827	0.474
	(0.304)	(0.548)	(0.513)
Priista	0.796**	3.291***	0.436
	(0.390)	(0.358)	(0.535)
Perredista	−2.385***	−2.113***	−2.118***
	(0.376)	(0.545)	(0.524)
Pocketbook Assessment	0.448**	0.255	0.00217
	(0.183)	(0.225)	(0.284)
Sociotropic Assessment	0.208	−0.215	−0.0208
	(0.153)	(0.227)	(0.262)
Prospective Assessment	0.500**	0.580**	0.510
	(0.219)	(0.257)	(0.333)
Approval of Vicente Fox	0.488***	−0.177	−0.0373
	(0.123)	(0.121)	(0.121)
Welfare Recipient	−0.451*	−0.0894	−0.453
	(0.273)	(0.351)	(0.448)
Constant	−2.052***	−1.580*	−1.754*
	(0.795)	(0.928)	(1.036)
Observations	633	633	633

Robust standard errors (clustered by municipality) in parentheses.
*** $p < 0.01$, ** $p < 0.05$, * $p < 0.1$.

TABLE A19   REMITTANCES AND VOTE CHOICE IN MEXICO'S 2006
PRESIDENTIAL ELECTION, MICHOACÁN SAMPLE
(MULTINOMIAL LOGIT). PRD IS BASE CATEGORY.
CORRESPONDS TO FIGURE 6.2

VARIABLES	Voted for the PAN	Voted for the PRI
Remittances (in 2006)	1.533*** (0.547)	0.0600 (0.931)
Age	−0.00672 (0.0157)	−0.00523 (0.0120)
Female	0.502* (0.279)	0.196 (0.403)
Education	0.0520** (0.0254)	−0.0592 (0.0461)
Income (log)	0.0295 (0.0280)	0.0619 (0.0608)
Panista	2.077*** (0.400)	0.409 (0.371)
Priista	1.738* (1.048)	3.085*** (0.831)
Perredista	−2.701*** (0.492)	−2.453*** (0.462)
Pocketbook Assessment	−0.161 (0.131)	−0.0591 (0.170)
Sociotropic Assessment	0.407*** (0.109)	0.286 (0.210)
Approval of Vicente Fox	0.314*** (0.0992)	0.0160 (0.0968)
Constant	−1.373** (0.679)	−1.170 (0.977)
Observations	411	411

Robust standard errors (clustered by town or village) in parentheses.
*** p < 0.01, ** p < 0.05, * p < 0.1.

TABLE A20   REMITTANCES AND INCUMBENT SUPPORT IN MEXICO,
             NATIONAL SAMPLES (BINOMIAL LOGIT). CORRESPONDS
             TO FIGURE 6.3

VARIABLES	(1) Would Vote for Incumbent (2008)	(2) Would Vote for Incumbent (2008)	(1) Would Vote for Incumbent (2010)	(2) Would Vote for Incumbent (2010)
Remittances	0.327**	0.359**	0.301**	0.313**
	(0.150)	(0.155)	(0.143)	(0.152)
Income	0.0364	0.0146	0.0287	0.00196
	(0.0405)	(0.0503)	(0.0369)	(0.0408)
Age	−0.00555	−0.00786	0.00317	0.00218
	(0.00566)	(0.00632)	(0.00479)	(0.00534)
Education	−0.0181	−0.0431**	−0.0278	−0.0376*
	(0.0205)	(0.0219)	(0.0197)	(0.0223)
Female	−0.0260	0.0756	0.516***	0.514***
	(0.147)	(0.172)	(0.155)	(0.164)
Rural	0.00486	−0.0977	0.137	0.266
	(0.229)	(0.243)	(0.210)	(0.216)
Panista		3.162***		2.366***
		(0.361)		(0.337)
Priista		−1.795***		−0.730**
		(0.351)		(0.300)
Perredista		−1.757***		−1.226**
		(0.380)		(0.588)
Constant	−0.136	0.0998	−1.301***	−1.205***
	(0.369)	(0.385)	(0.363)	(0.410)
Observations	894	894	925	925

Robust standard errors (clustered by municipality) in parentheses.
*** $p < 0.01$, ** $p < 0.05$, * $p < 0.1$.

TABLE A21   TALKING POLITICS WITH FAMILY MEMBER IN THE UNITED
            STATES, MICHOACÁN SAMPLE (BINOMIAL LOGIT)

VARIABLES	(1) Respondent Talks about Politics with Someone in the United States	(2) Respondent Talks about Politics with Someone in the United States
Remittances (Binary Variable)	0.182 (0.282)	
Remittances Index		0.789 (0.530)
Number of Relatives Abroad	0.192** (0.0835)	0.195*** (0.0713)
Age	−0.0152* (0.00871)	−0.0174** (0.00762)
Female	−0.341 (0.323)	−0.412 (0.290)
Education	0.133*** (0.0352)	0.131*** (0.0354)
Income (log)	−0.0339 (0.0375)	−0.0353 (0.0320)
Political Interest	0.713*** (0.187)	0.765*** (0.187)
Constant	−3.423*** (0.514)	−3.436*** (0.365)
Observations	702	695

Robust standard errors (clustered by town or village) in parentheses.
*** $p < 0.01$, ** $p < 0.05$, * $p < 0.1$.

NOTES

CHAPTER 1

1. Harold Alderman and Christina H. Paxson, "Do the Poor Insure? A Synthesis of the Literature on Risk and Consumption in Developing Countries" (World Bank, Agriculture and Rural Development Department, October 1992), WPS 1008.
2. Stefan Dercon, "Income Risk, Coping Strategies, and Safety Nets," *World Bank Research Observer*17, no. 2 (2002): 141–166.
3. Oded Stark and David Levhari, "On Migration and Risk in LDCs," *Economic Development and Cultural Change* 31, no. 1 (1982): 191–196.
4. For more on the social insurance function of remittances, see Robert E. B. Lucas and Oded Stark, "Motivations to Remit: Evidence from Botswana," *Journal of Political Economy* 93, no. 5 (1985): 901–918; Douglas S. Massey, Joaquin Arango, Graeme Hugo, Ali Kouaouci, Adela Pellegrino, and J. Edward Taylor, *Worlds in Motion: Understanding International Migration at the End of the Millennium* (Oxford: Oxford University Press, 1998); Reena Agarwal and Andrew W. Horowitz, "Are International Remittances Altruism or Insurance? Evidence from Guyana Using Multiple-Migrant Households," *World Development* 30, no. 11 (2002): 2033–2044; Flore Gubert, "Do Migrants Insure Those Who Stay Behind? Evidence from the Kayes Area (Western Mali)," *Oxford Development Studies* 30 no. 3 (2002): 267–287; and Dean Yang and HwaJung Choi, "Are Remittances Insurance? Evidence from Rainfall Shocks in the Philippines," *World Bank Economic Review* 21, no. 2 (2007): 219–248.
5. Author interview, January 2008.
6. Michael P. Todaro, "A Model of Labor Migration and Urban Unemployment in Less Developed Countries," *American Economic Review* 59, no. 1 (1969): 138–148; Carola Suarez-Orozco, Marcelo Suarez-Orozco, and Irina Todorova, *Learning a New Land: Immigrant Students in American Society* (Cambridge, MA: Harvard University Press, 2008); Hirokazu Yoshikawa, *Immigrants Raising Citizens: Undocumented Parents and Their Young Children* (New York: Russell Sage Foundation, 2011).

7. J. Edward Taylor, "The New Economics of Labour Migration and the Role of Remittances in the Migration Process," *International Migration* 37, no. 1 (1999): 65–86.

8. Author interview, August 2016.

9. Author interview, March 2016.

10. Author interview, September 2015.

11. See United Nations, "Trends in International Migrant Stock: The 2017 Revision," data available for download at http://www.un.org/en/development/desa/population/migration/data/estimates2/estimates17.shtml.

12. World Bank, *World Development Indicators* (January 2018): http://data.worldbank.org/data-catalog/world-development-indicators.

13. World Bank, *Migration and Remittances: Recent Developments and Outlook,* Migration and Development Brief 28 (October 2017), http://www.knomad.org/publication/migration-and-development-brief-28.

14. See World Bank, *Migration and Remittances: Recent Developments and Outlook;* and OECD, "Development Aid Stable in 2014 but Flows to Poorest Countries Still Falling," August 4, 2015: http://www.oecd.org/dac/stats/development-aid-stable-in-2014-but-flows-to-poorest-countries-still-falling.htm.

15. Data come from World Bank estimates (April 2017 revision). Available for download at http://pubdocs.worldbank.org/en/818981492713050366/remittancedatainflowsapr2017.xls. For the most recent estimates, see http://www.worldbank.org/en/topic/migrationremittancesdiasporaissues/brief/migration-remittances-data.

16. Devesh Kapur, "Remittances: The New Development Mantra?," in S. M. Maimbo and D. Ratha, eds., *Remittances: Development Impact and Future Prospects* (Washington, DC: World Bank, 2005): 331–360.

17. G. E. Johnson and W. E. Whitelaw, "Urban-Rural Income Transfers in Kenya: An Estimated-Remittances Function," *Economic Development and Cultural Change* 22, no. 3 (1974): 473–479; Lucas and Stark, "Motivations to Remit: Evidence from Botswana"; Ralph Chami, Connel Fullenkamp, and Samir Jahjah, "Are Immigrant Remittance Flows a Source of Capital for Development?" *IMF Staff Papers* 52, no. 1 (2005); Kapur, "Remittances: The New Development Mantra?"

18. See Jeffrey A. Frankel, "Are Bilateral Remittances Countercyclical?" NBER Working Paper w15419, October 2009; David Andrew Singer, "Migrant Remittances and Exchange Rates Regimes in the Developing World," *American Political Science Review* 104, no. 2 (2010): 307–323; Dilip Ratha, "Workers' Remittances: An Important and Stable Source of External Development Finance," in *Global Development Finance: Striving for Stability in Development Finance* (Washington, DC: World Bank, 2003): 157–175; Kapur, "Remittances: The New Development Mantra?"; Lucas and Stark, "Motivations to Remit: Evidence from Botswana"; Gubert, "Do Migrants Insure Those Who Stay Behind? Evidence from the Kayes Area (Western Mali)"; Yang and Choi, "Are Remittances Insurance? Evidence from Rainfall Shocks in the Philippines."

19. Kirk Semple, "Nepalis in New York Region Improvise Quake Relief Effort," *New York Times*, May 5, 2015, p. A18.

20. Asmita Naik, Elca Stigter, and Frank Laczko, "Migration, Development and Natural Disasters: Insights from the Indian Ocean Tsunami," IOM Migration Research Series, no. 30 (2007), http://publications.iom.int/bookstore/free/MRS30.pdf; Jake Maxwell Watts and Chester Yung, "After Typhoon Haiyan, Overseas Filipinos Raise Their Remittances," *The Wall Street Journal*, November 18, 2013, https://www.wsj.com/articles/in-the-wake-of-typhoon-haiyan-overseas-filipinos-raise-their-remittances-1384783466.
21. World Bank estimates, October 2015 revision, http://pubdocs.worldbank.org/pubdocs/publicdoc/2015/10/255871445543163508/remittancedata-inflows-october2015-0.xls.
22. World Bank, *Global Economic Prospects: Having Fiscal Space and Using It* (Washington DC: World Bank, January 2015), available online https://www.worldbank.org/content/dam/Worldbank/GEP/GEP2015a/pdfs/GEP15a_web_full.pdf.
23. Dilip Ratha, "Leveraging Remittances for Development," *Policy Brief* (Washington, DC: Migration Policy Institute, 2007), http://www.migrationpolicy.org/research/leveraging-remittances-development.
24. Similarly, a national survey conducted by the Bank of Mexico around the same time reported that Mexican households spent 92 percent of remittances on food, clothing, shelter, health, and education. See Banco de México, "Las Remesas Familiares en México. Inversión de los recursos de migrantes: resultados de las alternativas vigentes" (2007), http://www.ime.gob.mx/investigaciones/2006/estudios/economia/remesas_familiares.pdf.
25. Eliud George Ramocan, "Remittances to Jamaica: Findings from a National Survey of Remittance Recipients," Remittance Survey 2010 (Kingston, Jamaica: Bank of Jamaica, 2011), http://boj.org.jm/uploads/pdf/papers_pamphlets/papers_pamphlets_Remittances_to_Jamaica_-_Findings_from_a_National_Survey_of_Remittance_Recipients.pdf.
26. Ereblina Elezaj, Faton Bislimi, and Iris Duri, "Kosovo Remittance Study 2012" (United Nations Development Programme, July 2012), http://www.ks.undp.org/content/dam/kosovo/docs/Remittances/KRS2012_English_858929.pdf.
27. Manuel Orozco, *Migrant Remittances and Development in the Global Economy* (Boulder, CO: Lynne Rienner, 2013).
28. Bangladesh Bureau of Statistics, "Report on Survey on the Use of Remittances (SUR) 2013" (June 2014), http://www.bbs.gov.bd/WebTestApplication/userfiles/Image/LatestReports/SUR_2013.pdf.
29. International Organization for Migration, "International Migration and Migrant Workers' Remittances in Indonesia: Findings of Baseline Surveys of Migrant Remitters and Remittance Beneficiary Households" (2010), http://publications.iom.int/bookstore/free/indonesia_remittances.pdf.
30. Bangko Sentral ng Pilipinas Department of Economic Statistics, "Consumer Expectations Survey: Third Quarter 2009" (September 10, 2009), http://www.bsp.gov.ph/downloads/Publications/2009/CES_3qtr2009.pdf.
31. Dilip Ratha, Sanket Mohapatra, Caglar Özden, Sonia Plaza, William Shaw, and Abebe Shimeles, *Leveraging Migration for Africa: Remittances, Skills, and Investments* (Washington, DC: World Bank, 2011): chap. 2, http://siteresources.

worldbank.org/EXTDECPROSPECTS/Resources/476882-1157133580628/
AfricaStudyEntireBook.pdf.

32. Dilip Ratha, "The Impact of Remittances on Economic Growth and Poverty Reduction," Migration Policy Institute (September 2013), http://www.migrationpolicy.org/research/impact-remittances-economic-growth-and-poverty-reduction; Richard H. Adams Jr. and John Page, "Do International Migration and Remittances Reduce Poverty in Developing Countries?," World Development 33, no. 10 (October 2005): 1645–1669.

33. Jorge Durand, Emilio A. Parrado, and Douglas S. Massey, "Migradollars and Development: A Reconsideration of the Mexican Case," International Migration Review 30, no. 2 (1996): 423–444.

34. Ratha, "Leveraging Remittances for Development."

35. Lucas and Stark, "Motivations to Remit: Evidence from Botswana."

36. Because they are countercyclical and generally used to purchase basic goods and services, a number of political scientists have drawn parallels between remittances and social welfare benefits. See, e.g., Layna Mosley and David A. Singer, "Migration, Labor, and the International Political Economy," Annual Review of Political Science (2015): 283–301; Abel Escriba-Folch, Covadonga Meseguer, and Joseph Wright, "Remittances and Democratization," International Studies Quarterly (2015): 1–16; David Doyle, "Remittances and Social Spending," American Political Science Review 109, no. 4 (November 2015): 785–802; Roy Germano, "Migrants' Remittances and Economic Voting in the Mexican Countryside," Electoral Studies 32, no. 4 (December 2013): 875–885; Patrick M. Regan and Richard W. Frank, "Migrant Remittances and the Onset of Civil War," Conflict Management and Peace Science 31, no. 5 (November 2014): 502–520; Faisal Z. Ahmed, "The Perils of Unearned Foreign Income: Aid, Remittances, and Government Survival," American Political Science Review 106, no. 1 (2012): 146–165; David Andrew Singer, "Migrant Remittances and Exchange Rate Regimes in the Developing World," American Political Science Review 104, no. 2 (2010): 307–323; Yasser Abdih, Ralph Chami, Jihad Dagher, and Peter Montiel, "Remittances and Institutions: Are Remittances a Curse?," World Development 40, no. 4 (April 2012): 657–666; Claire L. Adida and Desha M. Girod, "Do Migrants Improve Their Hometowns? The Effects of Remittances on Public Goods in Mexico, 1995–2000," Comparative Political Studies 44, no. 1 (January 2011): 1–25; see also Massey et al., Worlds in Motion: Understanding International Migration at the End of the Millennium.

37. Nita Rudra, "Globalization and the Decline of the Welfare State in Less-Developed Countries," International Organization 56, no. 2 (2002): 411–445; Robert R. Kaufman and Alex Segura-Ubiergo, "Globalization, Domestic Politics, and Social Spending in Latin America: A Time-Series Cross-Section Analysis, 1973–97," World Politics 53 (2001): 553–587; Miguel Glatzer and Dietrich Rueschemeyer, eds., Globalization and the Future of the Welfare State (Pittsburgh, PA: University of Pittsburgh Press, 2005). Irfan Nooruddin and Nita Rudra argue that some developing countries have made up for shortfalls in the provision of social insurance by growing public-sector employment. They point out, however, that this approach largely bypasses the poor. See Nooruddin and Rudra, "Are Developing

Countries Really Defying the Embedded Liberalism Compact?," *World Politics* 66, no. 4 (2014): 603–640. See also Marcus J. Kurtz and Sarah M. Brooks, "Embedding Neoliberal Reform in Latin America," *World Politics* 60, no. 2 (2008): 231–280.

38. Robert H. Bates, *Markets and States in Tropical Africa* (Berkeley: University of California Press, 1981).

39. John Walton and David Seddon, *Free Markets and Food Riots: The Politics of Global Adjustment* (Oxford: Blackwell Publishers, 1994).

40. John Walton and Charles Ragin, "Global and National Sources of Political Protest: Third World Responses to the Debt Crisis," *American Sociological Review* 55, no. 6 (1990): 876–890.

41. Stiglitz, *Globalization and Its Discontents*.

42. World Bank, "Global Food Crisis Response Program," April 11, 2013, http://www.worldbank.org/en/results/2013/04/11/global-food-crisis-response-program-results-profile.

43. International Monetary Fund, "Exiting from Crisis Intervention Policies," February 4, 2010, https://www.imf.org/external/np/pp/eng/2010/020410.pdf.

44. Isabel Ortiz and Matthew Cummins, "The Age of Austerity: A Review of Public Expenditures and Adjustment Measures in 181 Countries," Initiative for Policy Dialogue and the South Centre, Working Paper (March 2013), http://policydialogue.org/files/publications/Age_of_Austerity_Ortiz_and_Cummins.pdf.

45. Lauren Q. Sneyd, Alexander Legwegoh, Evan D. G. Fraser, "Food Riots: Media Perspectives on the Causes of Food Protest in Africa," *Food Security* 5, no. 4 (2013): 485–497.

46. The United Nations, *The Global Social Crisis: Report on the World Situation, 2011* (New York: United Nations, 2011), http://www.un.org/csa/socdev/rwss/docs/2011/rwss2011.pdf.

47. Melani Cammett and Lauren M. MacLean, *The Politics of Non-state Social Welfare* (Ithaca, NY: Cornell University Press, 2014); Gosta Esping-Andersen, *Social Foundations of Post-Industrial Economies* (New York: Oxford University Press, 1999); Dani Rodrik, *Has Globalization Gone Too Far?* (Washington, DC: Institute of International Economics, 1997); Joan M. Nelson, "Poverty, Equity, and the Politics of Adjustment," in Steven Haggard and Robert Kaufman, eds., *The Politics of Economic Adjustment* (Princeton, NJ: Princeton University Press, 1992): 221–268.

48. See Daniel R. Reichman, *The Broken Village: Coffee, Migration, and Globalization in Honduras* (Ithaca, NY: Cornell University Press, 2011); Robyn Magalit Rodriguez, *Migrants for Export* (Minneapolis: University of Minnesota Press, 2010); Katrina Burgess, "Neoliberal Reform and Migrant Remittances: Symptom or Solution?," in John Burdick, Philip Oxhorn, and Kenneth M. Roberts, eds., *Beyond Neoliberalism in Latin America? Societies and Politics at the Crossroads* (New York: Palgrave Macmillan, 2009): 177–195. See also Massey, "Economic Development and International Migration in Comparative Perspective"; and Cammett and MacLean, *The Politics of Non-state Social Welfare*. David Doyle argues that the line of causality goes in the opposite direction—that remittances cause less social spending. While remittances may reduce their recipients' propensity to vote for left-wing populists,

I will show in the next chapter an example of how families in rural Mexico used remittances to cope with austerity. See Doyle, "Remittances and Social Spending."

49. Marc F. Bellemare, "Rising Food Prices, Food Price Volatility, and Social Unrest," *American Journal of Agricultural Economics* 97, no. 1 (2015): 1–21; Ray Bush, "Food Riots: Poverty, Power, and Protest," *Journal of Agrarian Change* 10, no. 1 (2010): 119–129; Kurt Weyland, "The Threat from the Populist Left," *Journal of Democracy* 24, no. 3 (July 2013): 18–32.

50. Karl Polanyi, *The Great Transformation* (New York: Farrar & Rinehart, 2001 [1944]); Gosta Esping-Andersen, *The Three Worlds of Welfare Capitalism* (Cambridge, UK: Polity Press, 1990); Geoffrey Garrett, "Global Markets and National Politics: Collision Course or Virtuous Circle?" *International Organization* 52 (1998): 787–824; So Young Kim, "Openness, External Risk, and Volatility: Implications for the Compensation Hypothesis," *International Organization* 61, no. 1 (2007): 181–216; Peter J. Katzenstein, *Small States in World Markets: Industrial Policy in Europe* (Ithaca, NY: Cornell University Press, 1985); David Cameron, "The Expansion of the Public Economy: A Comparative Analysis," *American Political Science Review* 72, no. 4 (1978): 1243–1261; Rodrik, *Has Globalization Gone Too Far?*; Dani Rodrik, "Why Do More Open Economies Have Bigger Governments?," *Journal of Political Economy* 106, no. 5 (1998): 997–1032; Daron Acemoglu and James A. Robinson, "A Theory of Political Transitions," *American Economic Review* 91, no. 4 (2001): 938–963; John Gerard Ruggie, "International Regimes, Transactions, and Change: Embedded Liberalism in the Postwar Economic Order," *International Organization*, 36, no. 2 (1982): 379–415; Matthew M. Singer, "Economic Voting and Welfare Programmes: Evidence from the American States," *European Journal of Political Research* 50, no. 4 (June 2011): 479–503; Marco Manacorda, Edward Miguel, and Andrea Vigorito, "Government Transfers and Political Support," *American Economic Journal: Applied Economics* 3, no. 3 (2011): 1–28; Norbert R. Schady, "The Political Economy of Expenditures by the Peruvian Social Fund (FONCODES), 1991–95," *American Political Science Review* 94, no. 2 (2000): 289–304; Kenneth M. Roberts and Moises Arce, "Neoliberalism and Lower-class Voting Behavior in Peru," *Comparative Political Studies* 31, no. 2 (1998): 217–247; Benjamin Radcliff, "The Welfare State, Turnout, and the Economy: A Comparative Analysis." *American Political Science Review* 86, no. 2 (1992): 444–454; Alexander Pacek and Benjamin Radcliff, "Economic Voting and the Welfare State: A Cross-National Analysis," *Journal of Politics* 57, no. 1 (1995): 44–61; Jude C. Hays, Sean D. Ehrlich, and Clint Peinhardt, "Government Spending and Public Support for Trade in the OECD: An Empirical Test of the Embedded Liberalism Thesis," *International Organization* 59, no. 2 (2005): 473–494; Edwin Eloy Aguilar and Alexander Pacek, "Macroeconomic Conditions, Voter Turnout, and the Working-Class/Economically Disadvantaged Party Vote in Developing Countries," *Comparative Political Studies* 33, no. 8 (2000): 995–1017.

51. Germano, "Migrants' Remittances and Economic Voting in the Mexican Countryside"; Regan and Frank, "Migrant Remittances and the Onset of Civil War."

52. See also Roy Germano, "The Political Economy of Remittances: Emigration, Social Insurance Provision, and Political Behavior in Mexico," PhD diss., University of

Texas at Austin (2010); Jorge Bravo, "Credit Where Credit Is Due? Remittances, Economic Assessments, and Presidential Approval in Latin America," unpublished paper, Niehaus Center for Globalization and Governance, Princeton University (2011/2012); Germano, "Migrants' Remittances and Economic Voting in the Mexican Countryside"; Regan and Frank, "Migrant Remittances and the Onset of Civil War"; Faisal Z. Ahmed, "Remittances and Incumbency: Theory and Evidence," *Economics and Politics* 29, no. 1 (March 2017): 22–47.

53. Germano, "Migrants' Remittances and Economic Voting in the Mexican Countryside"; Regan and Frank, "Migrant Remittances and the Onset of Civil War."

54. This is not to say that people evaluate government performance solely on the basis of personal consumption. Other factors, such as partisan attachments, media coverage, and government communication strategies matter in shaping how people interpret their economic circumstances and evaluate government performance. But there is little doubt that personal consumption matters a great deal. See, e.g., Austin Hart, *Economic Voting: A Campaign-Centered Theory* (New York: Cambridge University Press, 2016); Lynn Vavreck, *The Message Matters: The Economy and Presidential Campaigns* (Princeton, NJ: Princeton University Press, 2009); Marc J. Hetherington, "The Media's Role in Forming Voters' National Economic Evaluations in 1992," *American Journal of Political Science* 40, no. 2 (May 1996): 372–395.

55. Christopher H. Achen and Larry M. Bartels, *Democracy for Realists: Why Elections Do Not Produce Responsive Government* (Princeton, NJ: Princeton University Press, 2016).

56. Daniela Campello and Cesar Zucco Jr., "Presidential Success and the World Economy," *Journal of Politics* 78, no. 2 (2016): 589–602.

57. Bravo, "Credit Where Credit Is Due? Remittances, Economic Assessments, and Presidential Approval in Latin America"; Germano, "Migrants' Remittances and Economic Voting in the Mexican Countryside."

The idea that remittances make citizens less aggrieved and more likely to approve of government performance is particularly important since the relatives of emigrants are—in the absence of remittances—people we might expect to be more aggrieved and more likely to oppose their governments. Many people emigrate, in fact, because they are dissatisfied with economic conditions and unhappy with government performance. See Albert O. Hirschman, "Exit, Voice, and the State," *World Politics* 31, no. 1 (October 1978): 90–107. Because remittance recipients are often from the same families as people who emigrate, it stands to reason that they too would be unhappy with economic conditions and government performance. We could even imagine that some remittance recipients feel particularly dissatisfied if they blame the government for creating the economic, political, or social conditions that caused their loved ones to move abroad.

While there are reasons to expect that members of emigrant households would be predisposed to having economic and political grievances, I show throughout this book that the economic benefits of remittances ultimately reduce economic grievances to the extent that they make people less likely to react to economic crises by disapproving of or punishing political leaders. I expect this to be the case particularly in democracies. The relatives of a person who flees a violent or repressive autocratic regime, such as the Assad regime in Syria or the Afwerki regime in Eritrea, on the other hand, may never soften their opposition to the government even though they benefit economically from remittances. Remittances may even reduce their dependence on the regime for patronage and free them to support opposition parties, resulting in a hardening of attitudes toward the party in power. (See, e.g., Abel Escribà-Folch, Covadonga Meseguer, and Joseph Wright, "Remittances and Democratization," *International Studies Quarterly* (2015): 1–16; and Tobias Pfutze, "Does Migration Promote Democratization? Evidence from the Mexican Transition," *Journal of Comparative Economics* 40, no. 2 (2012): 159–175.) Most people in democracies, however, do not emigrate because they are fleeing a violent or repressive state but because, in a more diffuse sense, they hope to make a better life for themselves and their families. In some communities, emigration even becomes a rite of passage—something people aspire to do, not avoid. Remittance recipients miss their relatives dearly, but they also feel fortunate that their relatives had the opportunity to travel abroad and they are grateful for the money they send home.

58. Gary L. Goodman and Jonathan T. Hiskey, "Exit without Leaving: Political Disengagement in High Migration Municipalities in Mexico," *Comparative Politics* 40, no. 2 (2008): 169–188.

59. The bulk of my fieldwork involved interviews and participant observation research in sixteen high-emigration communities in the Mexican states of Michoacán, Morelos, and San Luis Potosí and the collection of new survey data from 768 households in ten communities in Michoacán, Mexico. I furthermore conducted participant observation and interview research in high-emigration communities in Honduras and Guatemala and in a number of communities in the United States, including Marshalltown, Iowa, Chicago, New York City, and Western New York state. The publicly available data that I use in this book comes from nationally representative surveys such as Afrobarometer, the Latin American Public Opinion Project, Arab Barometer, and the Mexico Panel Studies. Although large sections of this book are based on statistical analyses, I have tried to make them accessible to all readers by keeping my models simple and by presenting key statistical findings in the form of simple line graphs that show the size and direction of relationships. Readers who are interested can find regression tables in the Statistical Appendix and a discussion of topics like survey design and measurement in the Methodological Appendix. Both appendices are located in the back of the book.

60. Natasha Iskander, *Creative State: Forty Years of Migration and Development Policy in Morocco and Mexico* (Ithaca, NY: Cornell University Press, 2010).

61. Sarah Lynn Lopez, *The Remittance Landscape: Spaces of Migration in Rural Mexico and Urban USA* (Chicago: University of Chicago Press, 2015); Alex Rivera (dir.), *The Sixth Section* (DVD) (New York: Subcine, 2003).

62. Orozco, *Migrant Remittances and Development in the Global Economy.*

63. Robert Courtney Smith, *Mexican New York: Transnational Lives of New Immigrants* (Berkeley: University of California Press, 2006); Iskander, *Creative State.*

64. See, e.g., Escribà-Folch et al., "Remittances and Democratization"; Doyle, "Remittances and Social Spending"; Michael D. Tyburski, "The Resource Curse

Reversed? Remittances and Corruption in Mexico," *International Studies Quarterly* 56, no. 2 (2012): 339–350; Goodman and Hiskey, "Exit without Leaving: Political Disengagement in High Migration Municipalities in Mexico"; Germano, "Migrants' Remittances and Economic Voting in the Mexican Countryside"; Regan and Frank, "Migrant Remittances and the Onset of Civil War"; Burgess, "Neoliberal Reform and Migrant Remittances: Symptom or Solution?"; Pfutze, "Does Migration Promote Democratization? Evidence from the Mexican Transition"; Pfutze, "Clientelism versus Social Learning: The Electoral Effects of International Migration"; Ahmed, "The Perils of Unearned Foreign Income: Aid, Remittances, and Government Survival"; Singer, "Migrant Remittances and Exchange Rate Regimes in the Developing World"; Perez-Armendariz and Crow, "Do Migrants Remit Democracy? International Migration, Political Beliefs, and Behavior in Mexico"; Adida and Girod, "Do Migrants Improve Their Hometowns? The Effects of Remittances on Public Goods in Mexico, 1995–2000"; Angela O'Mahony, "Political Investment: Remittances and Elections," *British Journal of Political Science* 43, no. 4 (2013): 799–820; Devesh Kapur, *Diaspora, Development, and Democracy: The Domestic Impact of International Migration from India* (Princeton: Princeton University Press, 2010); Mosley and Singer, "Migration, Labor, and the International Political Economy"; Devesh Kapur, "Political Effects of International Migration," *Annual Review of Political Science* (2014): 479–502; David Leblang, "Harnessing the Diaspora: Dual Citizenship, Migrant Return Remittances," *Comparative Political Studies* 50, no. 1 (2017): 75–101; Benjamin James Waddell and Matias Fontenla, "The Mexican Dream? The Effect of Return Migrants on Hometown Development," *Social Science Journal* 52, no. 3 (2015): 386–396; Michael D. Tyburski, "Curse or Cure? Migrant Remittances and Corruption," *Journal of Politics* 76, no. 3 (July 2014): 814–824; Covadonga Meseguer, Sebastián Lavezzolo, and Javier Aparicio, "Financial Remittances, Trans-border Conversations, and the State," *Comparative Migration Studies* 13, no. 4 (2016): 1–29; Ahmed, "Remittances and Incumbency: Theory and Evidence"; Francisco Javier Aparicio and Covadonga Meseguer, "Collective Remittances and the State: The 3x1 Program in Mexican Municipalities," *World Development* 40, no. 1 (2012): 206–222; Benjamin Nyblade and Angela O'Mahony, "Migrants' Remittances and Home Country Elections: Cross-National and Subnational Evidence," *Studies in Comparative International Development* 49, no. 1 (March 2014): 44–66.

65. Stephan Haggard and Robert R. Kaufman, *The Political Economy of Democratic Transitions* (Princeton, NJ: Princeton University Press, 1995); Stephan Haggard and Robert R. Kaufman, eds., *The Politics of Economic Adjustment: International Constraints, Distributive Conflicts and the State* (Princeton, NJ: Princeton University Press, 1992); Kurt Weyland, *The Politics of Market Reform in Fragile Democracies: Argentina, Brazil, Peru, and Venezuela* (Princeton, NJ: Princeton University Press, 2002); Adam Przeworski, *Democracy and the Market: Political and Economic Reforms in Eastern Europe and Latin America* (New York: Cambridge University Press, 1991); Nooruddin and Rudra, "Are Developing Countries Really Defying the Embedded Liberalism Compact?"

66. Noam Lupu, *Party Brands in Crisis: Partisanship, Brand Dilution, and the Breakdown of Political Parties in Latin America* (New York: Cambridge University Press, 2016); Campello and Zucco, "Presidential Success and the World Economy."

67. Jaimie Bleck and Nicolas Van de Walle, "Valence Issues in African Elections: Navigating Uncertainty and the Weight of the Past," *Comparative Political Studies* 46, no. 11 (November 2013): 1394–1421; Timothy Hellwig, "Constructing Accountability: Party Position Taking and Economic Voting," *Comparative Political Studies* 45, no. 1 (January 2012): 91–118; Matthew M. Singer, "Economic Voting in an Era of Non-Crisis: The Changing Electoral Agenda in Latin America, 1982–2010," *Comparative Politics* 45, no. 2 (January 2013): 169–185; Rachel Beatty Riedl, *Authoritarian Origins of Democratic Party Systems in Africa* (New York: Cambridge University Press, 2014).

68. Chami et al., "Are Immigrant Remittance Flows a Source of Capital for Development?"; Pablo A. Acosta, Emmanuel Lartey, and Federico S. Mandelman, "Remittances and the Dutch Disease," Federal Reserve Bank of Atlanta Working Paper, 2007–08 (April 2007).

69. Durand et al., "Migradollars and Development: A Reconsideration of the Mexican Case."

70. Ratha, "Leveraging Remittances for Development."

CHAPTER 2

1. Some of these interviews and observations were captured in my 2010 documentary film *The Other Side of Immigration*. See Roy Germano, *The Other Side of Immigration* (DVD), Roy Germano Films (2010), www.theothersideofimmigration.com.

2. Jonathan Fox, *The Politics of Food in Mexico: State Power and Social Mobilization* (Ithaca, NY: Cornell University Press, 1993); Antonio Yunez-Naude, "The Dismantling of CONASUPO, a Mexican State Trader in Agriculture," *World Economy* 26, no. 1 (2002): 97–122.

3. Fox, *The Politics of Food in Mexico: State Power and Social Mobilization*; Diego Abente Brun and Larry Diamond, eds., *Clientelism, Social Policy, and the Quality of Democracy* (Baltimore, MD: Johns Hopkins University Press, 2014).

4. Neil Harvey, "Rebellion in Chiapas: Rural Reforms and Popular Struggle," *Third World Quarterly* 16, no. 1 (1995): 39–72.

5. Yunez-Naude, "The Dismantling of CONASUPO, a Mexican State Trader in Agriculture"; Andrés Casco Flores, "CONASUPO: A Case Study on State-Trading Deregulation," *Canadian Journal of Agricultural Economics* 47, no. 4 (1999): 495–506.

6. Andres Espinosa-Carmona, "Evolución de la Industria Mexicana de Fertilizantes y su Impacto en la Agricultura," paper prepared by the Director of the Department of Fertilizers, Secretaría de Agricultura, Ganadería, Desarrollo Rural, Pesca y Alimentación (SAGARPA), June 2002.

7. *Mexican Agricultural Policies: An Immigration Generator?: Hearing before the Employment, Housing, and Aviation Subcommittee of the Committee on Government Operations, House of Representatives, One Hundred Third Congress, First Session, October 28, 1993* (Washington, DC: U.S. G.P.O, 1994).

8. *Mexican Agricultural Policies: An Immigration Generator?*, 60.
9. Timothy A. Wise, "The Impacts of U.S. Agricultural Policies on Mexican Producers," in Jonathan Fox and Libby Haight, eds., *Subsidizing Inequality: Mexican Corn Policy since NAFTA* (Woodrow Wilson International Center for Scholars; Centro de Investigación y Docencia Económicas; University of California, Santa Cruz, 2010), 163–171; Yunez-Naude, "The Dismantling of CONASUPO, a Mexican State Trader in Agriculture."
10. Wise, "The Impacts of U.S. Agricultural Policies on Mexican Producers."
11. Oxfam, "Dumping without Borders: How US Agricultural Policies Are Destroying the Livelihoods of Mexican Corn Farmers," Oxfam Briefing Paper 50, August 2003.
12. Author interview, February 2008.
13. Author interview, January 2008.
14. Wise, "The Impacts of U.S. Agricultural Policies on Mexican Producers."
15. Author interview, January 2008.
16. Author interview, January 2008.
17. Interviewees included Oswaldo Rodríguez Gutierrez at the Michoacán Ministry of Rural Development, David Niño Zavala at the Ministry of Social Development (SEDESOL), Jorge Porcayo Tirso at the Ministry of Agriculture (SAGARPA), Francisco Javier Cañada Melecio at the Ministry of Agricultural Reform (SRA), and Alma Griselda Valencia Medina at the Institute for Mexicans Abroad (IME). Interviews conducted April 2008.
18. Author interview with Porcayo Tirso at SAGARPA, the government ministry that administered PROCAMPO, April 2008.
19. Survey of 768 household conducted in rural communities of Michoacán, Mexico, January 2008. Methodology described in the Methodological Appendix.
20. Casco Flores, "CONASUPO: A Case Study on State-Trading Deregulation."
21. Manuel Pastor and Carol Wise, "State Policy, Distribution, and Neoliberal Reform in Mexico," *Journal of Latin American Studies* 29 (1997): 419–456.
22. Casco Flores, "CONASUPO: A Case Study on State-Trading Deregulation."
23. Author interview, January 2008.
24. Author interview with Cañada Melecio, director of the Michoacán office of the Secretaría de Reforma Agraria (Mexican government agency responsible for agricultural policy at the time), April 2008.
25. Author interview at SAGARPA, April 2008.
26. In 1990, a point in which the Mexican government had already begun to reduce its investment in the agricultural sector, producers bought urea directly from FERTIMEX for about 460 pesos per metric ton. Meanwhile, the market price of corn in Mexico was officially 707 pesos per metric ton. However, CONASUPO paid Mexican producers a guaranteed price for surplus corn that generally amounted to two to four times the market rate. Farmers who sold to CONASUPO therefore earned in the neighborhood of 2,000 pesos per metric ton. Between 1991 and 1992, FERTIMEX was privatized and by 1995 producers were paying 1,343 pesos per metric ton for urea. The market price for urea continued to rise over the following decade and hit a high of about 3,400 pesos per metric ton by 2008. Then CONASUPO phased out guaranteed prices for most crops in 1990 and for corn and beans by 1995.

According to official data, producer prices for corn reached 2,010 pesos per metric ton in 2006. Private buyers, however, usually pay below-market rates in the countryside. In communities where I conducted fieldwork in 2007–2008, the going rate for corn was 1,200 pesos per metric ton. See Andres Espinosa-Carmona, "Evolución de la Industria Mexicana de Fertilizantes y su Impacto en la Agricultura"; Food and Agriculture Organization data; Yunez-Naude, "The Dismantling of CONASUPO, a Mexican State Trader in Agriculture."

27. Author interviews with various community members, July 2005.
28. Jorge Hernández Díaz, "The New Top-Down Organizing: Campesino Coffee Growers in the Chatino Region of Oaxaca," in Richard Snyder, ed., *Institutional Adaptation and Innovation in Rural Mexico* (La Jolla: Center for U.S.-Mexican Studies, University of California, San Diego, 1999): 83–107.
29. Robert H. Bates, *Open-Economy Politics: The Political Economy of the World Coffee Trade* (Princeton, NJ: Princeton University Press, 1997).
30. Harvey, "Rebellion in Chiapas: Rural Reforms and Popular Struggle."
31. Author interviews, July 2005 and February 2008.
32. In some of Mexico's major coffee-producing states like Oaxaca and Guerrero, well-organized growers worked with state and local governments to provide production support and purchase crops in INMECAFÉ's absence. Coffee, however, is not a major crop in the area where La Victoria is located, and there was not the same impetus there to establish new state-level institutions to replace INMECAFÉ. Growers in La Victoria were thus left to compete in a declining market saturated with superior varieties without the cheap inputs or high guaranteed prices they had become so accustomed to receiving. See Richard Synder, "After Neoliberalism: The Politics of Reregulation in Mexico," *World Politics* 51, no. 2 (January 1999): 173–204.
33. This is not to argue that austerity and market reforms were the only cause of Mexican migration to the United States, but that these economic forces greatly exacerbated existing emigration pressures.
34. *Mexican Agricultural Policies: An Immigration Generator?*
35. Rodriguez, *Migrants for Export*; Reichman, *The Broken Village*.
36. Author interview, January 2008.
37. Author interview, January 2008.
38. Ginger Thompson, "Nafta to Open Floodgates, Engulfing Rural Mexico," *New York Times*, December 19, 2002.
39. Wise, "The Impacts of U.S. Agricultural Policies on Mexican Producers."
40. *Índice de Intensidad Migratoria: México-Estados Unidos, 2000* (Mexico, DF: Consejo Nacional de Población, 2002).
41. A total of 116 out of 353 households in the municipality of Huadacareo received remittances and 56 out of 175 households in the town of Huadacareo (the center of the municipality) received remittances.
42. Author interviews, January 2008.
43. Author interviews, January 2008.
44. Author interviews, January 2008.

45. Author interview, January 2008.
46. Author interview, January 2008.
47. *World Development Indicators,* February 2015.
48. Massey et al., *Worlds in Motion: Understanding International Migration at the End of the Millennium*; Douglas S. Massey and Kristin E. Espinosa, "What's Driving Mexico-U.S. Migration? A Theoretical, Empirical, and Policy Analysis," *American Journal of Sociology* 102, no. 4 (1997): 939–999; Douglas S. Massey, Rafael Alarcon, Jorge Durand, and Humberto González, *Return to Aztlan: The Social Process of International Migration from Western Mexico* (Berkeley: University of California Press, 1987).
49. Author interviews with Marshalltown residents from Villachuato, April 2012.
50. Pew Hispanic Center State and County Databases, Latinos as a Percent of the Population, http://www.pewhispanic.org/states/.
51. Douglas S. Massey, Jorge Durand, and Nolan J. Malone, *Beyond Smoke and Mirrors: Mexican Immigration in an Era of Economic Integration* (New York: Russell Sage Foundation, 2003).
52. Massey, Durand, and Malone, *Beyond Smoke and Mirrors.*
53. Data comes from Mexico Secretaría de Gobernación, Observatorio de Migración Internacional, http://www.omi.gob.mx/es/OMI/8_Remesas.
54. Data comes from Mexico's Consejo Nacional de Población (CONAPO), Cuadro VIII.2.2., www.conapo.gob.mx/work/.../remesas/08_02_02.xlsx.
55. CONAPO, *Índice de Intensidad Migratoria: México-Estados Unidos, 2000* (Mexico, DF: Consejo Nacional de Población, 2002).

CHAPTER 3

1. Paul Pierson, *Dismantling the Welfare State? Reagan, Thatcher, and the Politics of Retrenchment* (New York: Cambridge University Press, 1994).
2. Beatriz Magaloni and Vidal Romero, "Partisan Cleavages, State Retrenchment, and Free Trade: Latin America in the 1990s," *Latin American Research Review* 43, no. 2 (2008): 107–135; Pierson, *Dismantling the Welfare State?*
3. Ronald Rogowski, *Commerce and Coalitions* (Princeton, NJ: Princeton University Press, 1989); Michael J. Hiscox, *International Trade and Political Conflict: Commerce, Coalitions, and Mobility* (Princeton, NJ: Princeton University Press, 2001).
4. Polanyi, *The Great Transformation*; Esping-Andersen, *The Three Worlds of Welfare Capitalism*; Garrett, "Global Markets and National Politics: Collision Course or Virtuous Circle"; Kim, "Openness, External Risk, and Volatility: Implications for the Compensation Hypothesis"; Katzenstein, *Small States in World Markets*; Cameron, "The Expansion of the Public Economy: A Comparative Analysis"; Rodrik, *Has Globalization Gone Too Far?*
5. J. F. Hornbook, *Trade Adjustment Assistance (TAA) and Its Role in U.S. Trade Policy* (Washington, DC: Congressional Research Service, 2013), https://www.fas.org/sgp/crs/misc/R41922.pdf.
6. Ruggie, "International Regimes, Transactions, and Exchange: Embedded Liberalism in the Postwar Economic Order."

7. Katzenstein, *Small States in World Markets.*
8. Walton and Seddon, *Free Markets and Food Riots: The Politics of Global Adjustment.*
9. Tim Golden, "Rebel Attacks Hit 4 Towns in Mexico," *New York Times,* January 2, 1994, https://nyti.ms/2Fk0nyj.
10. Tim Golden, "Old Scores; Left Behind, Mexico's Indians Fight the Future," *New York Times,* January 9, 1994, https://nyti.ms/2FfNDsw.
11. Jonathan Fox and Xochitl Bada, "Migrant Organizations and Hometown Impacts in Rural Mexico," *Journal of Agrarian Change* 8, nos. 2/3 (2008): 435–461.
12. Jeffrey D. Sachs, "Social Conflict and Populist Policies in Latin America," NBER Working Paper, no. 2897, 1989; Susan Stokes, "Globalization and the Left in Latin America," Yale University, unpublished manuscript, http://www.yale.net/macmillanreport/resources/Stokes_GlobalizationLeft.pdf.
13. Author interview, April 2008.
14. Goodman and Hiskey, "Exit without Leaving: Political Disengagement in High Migration Municipalities in Mexico"; Abdih et al., "Remittances and Institutions."
15. Author interview, January 2008.
16. See the Methodological Appendix for more on survey methodology and study design.
17. See, e.g., Lopez, *The Remittance Landscape.*
18. Elisabeth Malkin, "Thousands in Mexico City Protest Rising Food Prices," *New York Times,* February 1, 2007.
19. *El Chamuco y los Hijos del Averno,* no. 140, January 14, 2008.
20. Susan Stokes, *Public Support for Market Reforms in New Democracies* (Cambridge, UK: Cambridge University Press, 2001).
21. It makes sense that remittances would have stronger effects on pocketbook assessments than sociotropic assessments. Remittance recipients feel more optimistic about their personal economic position because remittances offer their household a buffer against poverty and economic volatility. In the process, they may generalize their improved circumstances to the economy as a whole. Still, respondents know that remittances benefit certain households more than the economy as a whole.
22. Goodman and Hiskey, "Exit without Leaving: Political Disengagement in High Migration Municipalities in Mexico"; Ahmed, "The Perils of Unearned Foreign Income: Aid, Remittances, and Government Survival"; Abdih et al., "Remittances and Institutions."

CHAPTER 4

1. This dataset is publicly available at http://www.afrobarometer.org/data/merged-round-4-data-20-countries-2008 and http://doi.org/10.3886/ICPSR33701.v1. Afrobarometer Round 6 also collected data on remittances; however, at the time of writing, Round 6 data has not been released.
2. This question corresponds closely with the reliability dimension of the remittances index variable I developed in the last chapter. Unfortunately, Afrobarometer did not ask additional questions regarding the size of remittances relative to other income sources or how long respondents had received remittances. This precluded

the development of a full remittances variable like the one used in the last chapter. The reliability dimension of the index, however, is highly correlated with the full index. In the survey data I collected in Michoacán, Mexico, for instance, there is a very strong (r = .94) correlation between the full index and respondents' scores on the question about how frequently they receive remittances.

3. Arab Barometer Wave II data is available at http://www.arabbarometer.org/instruments-and-data-files. Saudi Arabia was a tenth country surveyed, but has been excluded from this analysis since very few respondents received remittances.

4. LAPOP datasets are available for download at http://vanderbilt.edu/lapop/rawdata.php.

5. This question is similar to a question I asked in Michoacán, Mexico. Recall that in Michoacán, we asked respondents to report whether remittance income was small, moderate, or large compared to domestic sources of income. In the Methodological Appendix, I explain that this kind of relative measure helps us understand the significance of remittances as a source of social insurance to the household. After controlling for overall income levels, this variable tells us something about a household's exposure to or insulation from local economic conditions. Take two very poor households, both with income levels near the line of subsistence. A household that depends on remittances "little" or "nothing" by default depends more heavily on a locally earned income. A household with an equivalent income overall that depends on remittances "a lot" derives much of its income from family members abroad. Therefore, in the event of some local economic crisis, the household that depends heavily on a locally earned income should in theory feel the pain of the crisis more than the household that depends more heavily on remittances. Unfortunately, the Latin American Public Opinion Project data did not measure how reliable or enduring a respondent's remittance income is, again preventing the development of a full remittances index variable like I used in chapter 3. In survey data I collected in Mexico, however, I found a very strong (r = 0.92) correlation between the remittances index and the component measuring remittances' relative significance as a source of income.

6. World Bank, *Migration and Remittances Factbook 2016* (Washington, DC: World Bank, 2016): http://siteresources.worldbank.org/INTPROSPECTS/Resources/334934-1199807908806/4549025-1450455807487/Factbookpart1.pdf.

7. Ana Gonzalez-Barrera and Mark Hugo Lopez, "A Demographic Portrait of Mexican-Origin Hispanics in the United States," Pew Research Center, 2013: http://www.pewhispanic.org/2013/05/01/a-demographic-portrait-of-mexican-origin-hispanics-in-the-united-states/.

8. This estimate is based on U.S. Border Patrol statistics on apprehensions of people from countries other than Mexico at the Southwest border. Apprehensions are not immigration figures, but they can provide us with a sense of immigration trends in the absence of reliable data. At the Southwest border, people from countries other than Mexico who are apprehended by the U.S. Border Patrol are overwhelmingly from Central America. The number of people in this category rose from 45,283 in 2009 to 252,600 in 2014. See U.S. Border Patrol Statistics: https://www.cbp.gov/

sites/default/files/assets/documents/2016-Oct/BP%20Total%20Apps%2C%20
Mexico%2C%20OTM%20FY2000-FY2016.pdf.

9. Migration Policy Institute Data Hub, Table: "United States, Immigrant Population by Country of Birth, 2000–Present," http://www.migrationpolicy.org/sites/default/files/datahub/MPI-Data-Hub-Region-birth_1960-2014.xlsx.

10. Orozco, *Migrant Remittances and Development in the Global Economy.*

11. Anna Brown and Renee Stepler, "Statistical Portrait of the Foreign-Born Population in the United States," Pew Research Center, April 19, 2016: http://www.pewhispanic.org/2016/04/19/statistical-portrait-of-the-foreign-born-population-in-the-united-states/ph_2016_stat-portrait-fb-current-05/.

12. Randall Hansen, *Citizenship and Immigration in Postwar Britain* (New York: Oxford University Press, 2000); Rita Chin, *The Crisis of Multiculturalism in Europe: A History* (Princeton, NJ: Princeton University Press, 2017).

13. United Nations, "Trends in International Migrant Stock: The 2017 Revision."

14. Orozco, *Migrant Remittances and Development in the Global Economy.*

15. World Bank, *Migration and Remittances Factbook 2016.*

16. Orozco, *Migrant Remittances and Development in the Global Economy.*

17. D'Vera Cohn, Ana Gonzalez-Barrera, and Danielle Cuddington, "Remittances to Latin America Recover—but Not to Mexico," Pew Research Center, November 15, 2013: http://www.pewhispanic.org/2013/11/15/remittances-to-latin-america-recover-but-not-to-mexico/.

18. Data come from World Bank estimates, April 2017 revision, http://pubdocs.worldbank.org/en/818981492713050366/remittancedatainflowsapr2017.xls.

19. World Bank, *Migration and Remittances Factbook 2016.*

20. UNHCR, "Regional Refugee, and Resilience Plan 2016–2017: 2016 Annual Report," http://data.unhcr.org/syrianrefugees/download.php?id=13223.

21. World Bank, *Migration and Remittances Factbook 2016.*

22. Ibid.

23. World Bank estimates, April 2017 revision.

24. World Bank, *Migration and Remittances Factbook 2016.*

25. See, e.g., David Ngaruri Kenney and Philip G. Schrag, *Asylum Denied* (Berkeley: University of California Press, 2008).

26. World Bank, *Migration and Remittances Factbook 2016.*

27. Sonia Plaza, Mario Navarrete, and Dilip Ratha, "Migration and Remittances Household Surveys in Sub-Saharan Africa: Methodological Aspects and Main Findings," background paper prepared as part of the Africa Migration Project, March 31, 2011. See Table 4.9 in particular.

28. Lucas and Stark, "Motivations to Remit: Evidence from Botswana."

29. Gubert, "Do Migrants Insure Those Who Stay Behind? Evidence from the Kayes Area (Western Mali)"; Sanjeev Gupta, Catherine A. Pattillo, and Smita Wagh, "Effect of Remittances on Poverty and Financial Development in Sub-Saharan Africa," *World Development* 37, no. 1 (January 2009): 104–115; Sanket Mohapatra, George Joseph, and Dilip Ratha, "Remittances and Natural Disasters: Ex-Post Response and Contribution to Ex-Ante Preparedness," *World Bank Policy Research Working Paper No. 4972* (2009); Peter Quartey, "The Impact of Migrant Remittances on

Household Welfare in Ghana," African Economic Research Consortium Research Paper 158 (2006), http://www.csae.ox.ac.uk/conferences/2006-eoi-rpi/papers/csae/quartey.pdf.

30. Peter Quartey and Theresa Blankson, "Do Migrant Remittances Minimize the Impact of Macro-Volatility on the Poor in Ghana?" Final Report Submitted to the Global Development Network (2004), https://www.imf.org/external/np/res/seminars/2005/macro/pdf/quarte.pdf.

31. Afrobarometer asked the same questions across the different country samples while LAPOP varied the questions it asked by survey year and country. The LAPOP survey asked pocketbook and sociotropic questions with reference to current economic conditions to all respondents. The prospective questions, however, were asked less frequently. Prospective pocketbook questions were included on the 2004 Mexico questionnaire and questionnaires for all countries in 2010. Prospective sociotropic questions were included on the 2004 Mexico and 2004 El Salvador questionnaires and on the questionnaires for all countries in 2010.

32. Afrobarometer surveys did not ask respondents to report their cash income, so I included two variables as proxies: (1) a variable for employment status (unemployed, part-time employed, full-time employed) and (2) a dummy variable to identify respondents whose living conditions signal relatively high socioeconomic status. Respondents fell into the high socioeconomic subsample if they had running water inside their homes. Only 16.6 percent of respondents fell into this category. To make sure that remittance recipients from high socioeconomic status households were not driving the results, I also reran all Afrobarometer analyses on a subsample of high-socioeconomic-status respondents.

33. The LAPOP data were also estimated with and without year fixed effects. The results were nearly identical whether or not year fixed effects were included in the model.

CHAPTER 5
1. Marc F. Bellemare, "Rising Food Prices, Food Price Volatility, and Social Unrest," *American Journal of Agricultural Economics* 97, no. 1 (2015): 1–21; Ray Bush, "Food Riots: Poverty, Power, and Protest," *Journal of Agrarian Change* 10, no. 1 (2010): 119–129.

2. Diadie Ba, "Senegal's Wade Threatens to Sue U.N.'s FAO over Costs," Reuters, May 9, 2008, http://www.reuters.com/article/us-food-africa-wade-idUSL0910986720080509.

3. Yawn Bar-Yam, Marco Lagi, and Yaneer Bar-Yam, "South African Riots: Repercussion of the Global Food Crisis and US Drought," in Philip Vos Fellman, Yaneer Bar-Yam, and Ali. A Minai, eds., *Conflict and Complexity* (New York: Springer, 2015): 261–267; Barry Bearak and Celia W. Dugger, "South Africans Take Out Rage on Immigrants," *New York Times*, May 20, 2008, http://www.nytimes.com/2008/05/20/world/africa/20safrica.html.

4. Julia Berazneva and David R. Lee, "Explaining the African Food Riots of 2007–2008: An Empirical Analysis," *Food Policy* 39 (April 2013): 28–39.

5. Emmanuel Gyimah-Boadi, "Another Step Forward for Ghana," *Journal of Democracy* 20, no. 2 (2009): 138–152.

6. As a possible alternative, Afrobarometer asked respondents if they have ever participated in a protest. There are two problems with this variable. One is that there is no way to know if those who say yes are referring to a recent protest related to the food crisis, or if they protested for some other reason. Another is that since there are no timelines associated with either the question about protesting or receiving remittances, there is no way to know if people who have a history of protest received remittances at the time that they protested. For example, a respondent who receives remittances now may have used protest in the past as a tool for trying to resolve economic problems. Finding protest ineffective, he began turning to a relative abroad for economic relief. This is different than a person who concurrently receives remittances and engages in protest.

7. Recall from chapter 4 (n. 32) that Afrobarometer did not ask a question about cash income. In an effort to control for income level, I included a variable for employment status (unemployed, employed part-time, employed full-time) and a dummy variable to identify the minority of survey respondents (16.6 percent) who reported having running water inside their homes. I consider having running water inside the home as a proxy for relatively high socioeconomic status.

8. Elizabeth Carlson, "Social Desireability Bias and Reported Vote Preferences in African Surveys," Afrobarometer Working Paper No. 144 (2014).

9. Food and Agriculture Organization, "Lesotho Faces Deep Food Crisis after One of Its Worst Droughts in 30 Years" (Rome: Food and Agriculture Organization of the United Nations, 2007): http://www.fao.org/Newsroom/en/news/2007/1000597/index.html.

10. Samuel Hauenstein Swan, Sierd Hadley, and Bernardette Cichon, "Crisis behind Closed Doors: Global Food Crisis and Local Hunger," *Journal of Agrarian Change* 10, no. 1 (2010): 107–118.

11. Channing Arndt, M. Azhar Hussain, Vincenzo Salvucci, and Lars Peter Østerdal, "Effects of Food Price Shocks on Child Malnutrition: The Mozambican Experience 2008/2009," *Economics & Human Biology* 22 (2016): 1–13.

12. Porter Anderson, "Selling Precious Assets for Food in Ghana," World Food Programme, January 26, 2009: https://www.wfp.org/stories/selling-precious-assets-food-ghana.

13. Doyle, "Remittances and Social Spending."

14. World Bank, "Global Food Crisis Response Program."

15. Variables on past political activity have been used in other papers that use Afrobarometer data to analyze the effects of remittances on political participation. I disagree with this approach, however, because it is impossible to know if respondents received remittances in the time periods these questions reference. See Kim Yi Dionne, Kris L. Inman, and Gabriella R. Montinola, "Another Resource Curse? The Impact of Remittances on Political Participation," Afrobarometer Working Paper No. 145.

16. Respondents from Mali were dropped from the analysis because the country's president at the time of the survey was an independent and it was unclear which party, if any, could be considered the incumbent.

17. I used 2008 data from the Polity IV Annual Time Series to split the Afrobarometer sample into democratic and nondemocratic subsamples. Polity scores range from -10 (strongly autocratic) to +10 (strongly democratic), with a democracy being a country with a score of +6 or higher. Sixty-five percent of respondents in the Afrobarometer sample were living in a country with a Polity score of +6 or greater at the time of the survey. See http://www.systemicpeace.org/polityproject.html.

18. Escribà-Folch et al., "Remittances and Democratization"; Pfutze, "Clientelism versus Social Learning: The Electoral Effects of International Migration"; Pfutze, "Does Migration Promote Democratization? Evidence from the Mexican Transition."

19. Pfutze, "Does Migration Promote Democratization? Evidence from the Mexican Transition"; Pfutze, "Clientelism versus Social Learning: The Electoral Effects of International Migration"; Escribà-Folch et al., "Remittances and Democratization."

20. Regan and Frank, "Migrant Remittances and the Onset of Civil War."

21. Abdih et al., "Remittances and Institutions: Are Remittances a Curse?"; Ahmed, "The Perils of Unearned Foreign Income: Aid, Remittances, and Government Survival."

22. Doyle, "Remittances and Social Spending."

23. Goodman and Hiskey, "Exit without Leaving: Political Disengagement in High Migration Municipalities in Mexico."

24. Ibid., 172.

25. Ibid., 183.

26. Jorge Bravo, "Emigración y Compromiso Político en México," *Política y Gobierno* 16, no. 1b (2009): 273–310; See also Germano, "Migrants' Remittances and Economic Voting in the Mexican Countryside."

27. Abdih et al., "Remittances and Institutions: Are Remittances a Curse?," 664.

28. Ibid.; Ahmed, "The Perils of Unearned Foreign Income: Aid, Remittances, and Government Survival"; Ahmed, "Remittances Deteriorate Governance."

29. Brady et al., "Beyond SES: A Resource Model of Political Participation."

30. Goodman and Hiskey, "Exit without Leaving: Political Disengagement in High Migration Municipalities in Mexico."

31. Tyburski, "The Resource Curse Reversed? Remittances and Corruption in Mexico"; Lopez, *The Remittance Landscape*; Iskander, *Creative State*; Lauren Duquette-Rury, "Migrant Transnational Participation: How Citizen Inclusion and Government Engagement Matter for Local Democratic Development in Mexico," *American Sociological Review* 81, no. 4 (2016): 771–799; Orozco, *Migrant Remittances and Development in the Global Economy*.

32. Henry E. Brady, Sidney Verba, and Kay Lehman Schlozman, "Beyond SES: A Resource Model of Political Participation," *American Political Science Review* 89, no. 2 (1995): 271–294.

33. Smith, *Mexican New York*; Pfutze, "Does Migration Promote Democratization? Evidence from the Mexican Transition"; Escribà-Folch et al., "Remittances and Democratization"; O'Mahony, "Political Investment: Remittances and Elections."

34. Iskander, *Creative State*; Lopez, *The Remittance Landscape*.

35. Abby Córdova and Jonathan Hiskey, "Shaping Politics at Home: Cross-Border Social Ties and Local-Level Political Engagement," *Comparative Political Studies* 48, no. 11 (2015): 1454–1487.

36. Ralph Chami, Connel Fullenkamp, and Samir Jahjah, "Are Immigrant Remittance Flows a Source of Capital for Development?" IMF Working Paper. Available at SSRN 880292 (September 2003).

37. Sanket Mohapatra and Dilip Ratha, "Migrant Remittances in Africa: An Overview," in Sanket Mohapatra and Dilip Ratha, eds., *Remittance Markets in Africa* (Washington, DC: World Bank Publications, 2011), 3–70.

38. Adida and Girod, "Do Migrants Improve their Hometowns? Remittances and Access to Public Services in Mexico, 1995–2000."

CHAPTER 6

1. Although ultimately not a very competitive election, survey data on remittances and vote choice was also collected by the Latin American Public Opinion Project three weeks after El Salvador's 2004 election. In a published article, I show that remittance recipients were more likely to vote for the incumbent party in that election and more likely to make positive pocketbook assessments. The context of this election, however—and therefore, the mechanisms by which remittances may have influenced vote choice—was complicated by the fact that some members of the U.S. House of Representatives made a widely publicized threat to restrict the flow of remittances to El Salvador if voters elected the opposition party. These House GOP members made the threat less than a week before the election, and some observers believed it influenced the outcome, although I find no evidence to support that belief. See Roy Germano, "Remittances as Diplomatic Leverage? The Precedent for Trump's Threat to Restrict Remittances to Mexico," *Research & Politics* 4, no. 2 (May 2017).

2. See Chappell Lawson et. al., The Mexico 2006 Panel Study (2007), available for download at http://mexicopanelstudy.mit.edu.

3. Kathleen Bruhn and Kenneth F. Greene, "Elite Polarization Meets Mass Moderation in Mexico's 2006 Elections," *PS: Political Science & Politics* 40, no. 1 (2007): 33–38.

4. Andy Baker, "Public Mood and Presidential Election Outcomes in Mexico," in Jorge I. Domínguez, Kenneth F. Greene, Chappell Lawson, and Alejandro Moreno, eds., *Mexico's Evolving Democracy: A Comparative Study of the 2012 Elections* (Baltimore: Johns Hopkins University Press, 2015).

5. Baker, "Public Mood and Presidential Election Outcomes in Mexico."

6. Steven Levitsky and Kenneth M. Roberts, "Latin America's 'Left Turn': A Framework for Analysis," in Steven Levitsky and Kenneth M. Roberts, eds., *The Resurgence of the Latin American Left* (Baltimore, MD: Johns Hopkins University Press, 2011).

7. See Consejo Nacional de Población, México, International Migration Series, Table 8.2.2. Data available at http://www.conapo.gob.mx/en/OMI/Series_de_Migracion_Internacional.

8. Results were similar when I included controls for voters' positions on issues like trade, social spending, and privatization.

9. I used CLARIFY software to create these simulations in Stata. See Michael Tomz, Jason Wittenberg, and Gary King, "CLARIFY: Software for Interpreting

and Presenting Statistical Results," *Journal of Statistical Software* 8 (2003), Copy at http://j.mp/2oSx5Pc; and King, Tomz, and Wittenberg, "Making the Most of Statistical Analyses: Improving Interpretation and Presentation," *American Journal of Political Science* 44, no. 2 (April 2000): 341–355.

10. Jorge I. Domínguez and Chappell Lawson, eds., *Mexico's Pivotal Democratic Election: Candidates, Voters, and the Presidential Campaign of 2000* (Stanford, CA: Stanford University Press, 2004); Chappell Lawson and James McCann, "Television News, Mexico's 2000 Elections and Media Effects in Emerging Democracies," *British Journal of Political Science* 35, no. 1 (2005):1–30; Kenneth Greene, "Images and Issues in Mexico's 2006 Presidential Election," in Jorge I. Dominguez, Chappell Lawson, and Alejandro Moreno, eds., *Consolidating Mexico's Democracy: The 2006 Presidential Campaign in Comparative Perspective* (Baltimore, MD: Johns Hopkins University Press, 2009).

11. Jorge Buendía, "Economic Reform, Public Opinion, and Presidential Approval in Mexico, 1988–1993," *Comparative Political Studies* 29, no. 5 (1996): 566–591; Jorge Buendía Laredo, "Economic Reforms and Political Support in Mexico, 1988–1997," in Susan C. Stokes, ed., *Public Support for Market Reforms in New Democracies* (New York: Cambridge University Press, 2001): 131–159; Greene, "Images and Issues in Mexico's 2006 Presidential Election"; Matthew M. Singer, "'Defendamos lo que hemos logrado': Economic Voting in the 2006 Mexican Presidential Election," *Política y Gobierno* 15 (2009): 199–236; Beatriz Magaloni and Alejandro Poiré, "The Issues, the Vote, and the Mandate for Change," in Jorge I. Domínguez and Chappell Lawson, eds., *Mexico's Pivotal Democratic Election: Candidates, Voters, and the Presidential Campaign of 2000* (Stanford, CA: Stanford University Press, 2004); Alejandro Poiré, "Retrospective Voting, Partisanship, and Loyalty in Presidential Elections: 1994," in Jorge I. Domínguez and Alejandro Poiré, eds., *Toward Mexico's Democratization: Parties, Campaigns, Elections, and Public Opinion* (New York: Routledge, 1999): 24–56.

12. Lau, "Two Explanations for Negativity Effects in Political Behavior"; Weyland, "Swallowing the Bitter Pill: Sources of Popular Support for Neoliberal Reform in Latin America."

13. Doyle, "Remittances and Social Spending."

14. Lopez, *The Remittance Landscape*.

15. Douglas S. Massey, Rafael Alarcon, Jorge Durand, and Humberto Gonzalez, *Return To Aztlan* (Berkeley: University of California Press, 1990).

16. Pérez-Armendáriz and Crow, "Do Migrants Remit Democracy? International Migration, Political Beliefs, and Behavior in Mexico."

17. Roberto Suro and Gabriel Escobar, "Survey of Mexicans Living in the U.S. on Absentee Voting in Mexican Elections" (Washington, DC: Pew Hispanic Center, 2006).

18. The survey found that the average remittance recipient was 44 years old and that the average nonrecipient was 41.5 years old. In terms of income and education, the survey used categories. For education, respondents received a score of 3 if they had completed elementary school and a score of 4 if they had completed some middle school/technical school requirements. Remittance recipients had an average

score of 3.17 on this variable and nonrecipients had an average score of 3.9. For the income variable, respondents received a score of 4 if their income was 2,600–3,999 pesos per month and a score of 5 if their income was 4,000–5,199 pesos per month. Remittance recipients had an average score of 4.1 on the income variable compared to 4.56 for nonrecipients.

19. Joseph L. Klesner, "A Sociological Analysis of the 2006 Election," in Jorge I. Domínguez, Chappell Lawson, and Alejandro Moreno, eds., *Consolidating Mexico's Democracy: The 2006 Presidential Campaign in Comparative Perspective* (Baltimore, MD: Johns Hopkins University Press, 2009).

20. However, other important remittance-receiving states in these regions such as Michoacán, Zacatecas, and Guerrero have leaned PRD and PRI.

21. Jorge G. Castaneda, *Ex Mex: From Migrants to Immigrants* (New York: New Press, 2008).

CHAPTER 7

1. Author interview, July 2014. For more on Olga's story, see a documentary I wrote and directed called "Immigrant America: Murder and Migration in Honduras" (2014), available at https://video.vice.com/en_us/show/immigrant-america.

2. Author interview, November 2013. The Jesus family's story is part of another documentary I wrote and directed called "Immigrant America: The High Cost of Deporting Parents" (2014). This piece is available online at https://video.vice.com/en_us/show/immigrant-america.

3. OECD, "Social Expenditure Update," Insights from the OECD Social Expenditure Database (SOCX), November 2014, https://www.oecd.org/els/soc/OECD2014-Social-Expenditure-Update-Nov2014-8pages.pdf.

4. Ahmed, "The Perils of Unearned Foreign Income: Aid, Remittances, and Government Survival"; Doyle, "Remittances and Social Spending"; Germano, "Migrants' Remittances and Economic Voting in the Mexican Countryside."

5. Regan and Frank, "Migrant Remittances and the Onset of Civil War."

6. Rodrik, *Has Globalization Gone Too Far?*; Stiglitz, *Globalization and Its Discontents*; United Nations Development Programme, *Fighting Climate Change: Human Solidarity in a Divided World* (New York: Palgrave Macmillan, 2007).

7. George Avelino, David S. Brown, and Wendy Hunter, "The Effects of Capital Mobility, Trade Openness, and Democracy on Social Spending in Latin America, 1980-1999," *American Journal of Political Science* 49, no. 3 (2005): 625–641; Alìcia Adserà and Carles Boix, "Trade, Democracy, and the Size of the Public Sector: The Political Underpinnings of Openness," *International Organization* 56, no. 2 (2002): 229–262; David S. Brown and Wendy Hunter "Democracy and Social Spending in Latin America, 1980–92," *American Political Science Review* 93, no. 4 (1999): 779–790; Rudra, "Globalization and the Decline of the Welfare State in Less-Developed Countries"; Barbara Stallings, "International Influence on Economic Policy: Debt, Stabilization, and Structural Reform," in Stephan Haggard and Robert R. Kaufman, eds., *The Politics of Economic Adjustment* (Princeton, NJ: Princeton University Press, 1992): 41–88; Erik Wibbels, "Dependency

Revisited: International Markets, Business Cycles, and Social Spending in the Developing World," *International Organization* 60, no. 2 (2006): 433–468.

8. Lupu, *Party Brands in Crisis*; Kenneth Roberts, *Changing Course in Latin America: Party Systems in the Neoliberal Era* (New York: Cambridge University Press, 2014).

9. Campello and Zucco, "Presidential Success and the World Economy"; Noam Lupu and Susan Stokes, "Democracy, Interrupted: Regime Change and Partisanship in Twentieth-Century Argentina," *Electoral Studies* 29, no. 1 (2010): 91–104.

10. Roberts, *Changing Course in Latin America*; Weyland, "The Threat from the Populist Left."

11. Doyle, "Remittances and Social Spending."

12. Weyland, "The Threat from the Populist Left."

13. Katrina Burgess, "Migrants, Remittances, and Politics: Loyalty and Voice after Exit," *Fletcher Forum of World Affairs* 36, no. 1 (2012): 43–55.

14. Abdih et al., "Remittances and Institutions: Are Remittances a Curse?"

15. Albert O. Hirschman, *Exit, Voice, and Loyalty: Responses to Decline in Firms, Organizations, and States* (Cambridge, MA: Harvard University Press, 1970).

16. Goodman and Hiskey, "Exit without Leaving: Political Disengagement in High Migration Municipalities in Mexico."

17. Melani Cammett and Lauren M. MacLean, "The Political Consequences of Non-State Social Welfare: An Analytical Framework," in Cammett and MacLean, eds., *The Politics of Non-State Social Welfare* (Ithaca, NY: Cornell University Press, 2014), 31–53.

18. Abdih et al., "Remittances and Institutions: Are Remittances a Curse?"; Ahmed, "The Perils of Unearned Foreign Income: Aid, Remittances, and Government Survival."

19. Brady et al., "Beyond SES: A Resource Model of Political Participation"; Tyburski, "The Resource Curse Reversed? Remittances and Corruption in Mexico."

20. Smith, *Mexican New York*; O'Mahony, "Political Investment: Remittances and Elections"; Escribà-Folch et al., "Remittances and Democratization"; Tobias Pfutze, "Clientelism versus Social Learning: the Electoral Effects of International Migration," *International Studies Quarterly* 58, no. 2 (2014): 295–307.

21. Iskander, *Creative State*; Duquette-Rury, "Migrant Transnational Participation: How Citizen Inclusion and Government Engagement Matter for Local Democratic Development in Mexico."

22. Melani Cammett and Lauren M. MacLean, "The Political Consequences of Non-State Social Welfare: An Analytical Framework."

23. Robert Kaestner and Ofer Malamud, "Self-Selection and International Migration: New Evidence from Mexico," *Review of Economics and Statistics* 96, no. 1 (2014): 78–91; George Borjas, "Self-Selection and the Earnings of Immigrants," *The American Economic Review* 77, no. 4 (1987): 531–553; see also statistical tests in chapter 6.

24. Kapur, "Remittances: The New Development Mantra?"

25. Michael Birnbaum, "Smuggling Refugees into Europe is a New Growth Industry," *Washington Post*, September 3, 2015.

26. Author interview, July 2014.

27. See the World Bank's Migration and Development Brief, no. 21 (October 2, 2013): http://siteresources.worldbank.org/INTPROSPECTS/Resources/3349341288 990760745/MigrationandDevelopmentBrief21.pdf.

28. Author interview, July 2014.

29. Graeme Hugo, "Information, Exploitation, and Empowerment: The Case of Indonesian Overseas Workers," *Asian and Pacific Migration Journal* 12, no. 4 (2003): 439–466.

30. Jacqueline Bhabha, *Child Migration and Human Rights in a Global Age* (Princeton, NJ: Princeton University Press, 2014); Louise Shelley, *Human Trafficking: A Global Perspective* (New York: Cambridge University Press, 2010).

31. Hugo, "Information, Exploitation, and Empowerment: The Case of Indonesian Overseas Workers."

32. Bhabha, *Child Migration and Human Rights*.

33. An copy of the Guide is available at: https://www.cfif.org/htdocs/legislative_issues/ federal_issues/hot_issues_in_congress/immigration/mexican-booklet.pdf.

34. Amy Waldman, "Sri Lankan Maids' High Price for Foreign Jobs," *New York Times*, May 8, 2005.

35. Manuel Orozco and Rachel Fedewa, "Regional Integration: Trends and Patterns of Remittance Flows within South East Asia," Southeast Asia Workers Remittance Study, TA 6212-REG (Manila, Philippines: Asian Development Bank, 2005).

36. Nadine Sika, "Egypt: Socio-Political Dimensions of Migration," Consortium for Applied Research on International Migration, 2011, http://www.ilo.org/dyn/ migpractice/docs/146/EUI.pdf.

37. Riccardo Faini, "Remittances and the Brain Drain: Do More Skilled Migrants Remit More?" *World Bank Economic Review* 21, no. 2 (2007): 177–191; see also Massey et al., *Worlds in Motion*.

38. Stephen Castles, Hein de Hass, and Mark J. Miller, *The Age of Migration: International Population Movements in the Modern World* (New York: Guilford Press, 2013); Saskia Sassen, *Guests and Aliens* (New York: New Press, 1999).

39. Graziano Battistella and Maruja M. B. Asis, *Country Migration Report: The Philippines 2013* (Makati City, Philippines: International Organization for Migration, 2013), https://www.iom.int/files/live/sites/iom/files/Country/docs/ CMReport-Philipines-2013.pdf.

40. World Bank, *Global Economic Prospects: Having Fiscal Space and Using It*.

41. Author's calculations based on historical remittance data published by The Central Bank of the Philippines. Raw data available at http://www.bsp.gov.ph/statistics/efs_ ext3.asp.

42. Cohn, Gonzalez-Barrera, and Cuddington, "Remittances to Latin America Recover—but Not to Mexico."

43. Manolo Abella, "The Role of Recruiters in Labor Migration," in Douglas S. Massey and J. Edward Taylor, eds., *International Migration: Prospects and Policies in a Global Market* (New York: Oxford University Press, 2004).

44. Philip Martin, Manolo Abella, and Elizabeth Midgley, "Best Practices to Manage Migration: The Philippines," *International Migration Review* 38, no. 4 (2004): 1544–1559.

45. Data comes from the World Bank's Remittance Prices Worldwide database: http://remittanceprices.worldbank.org.

46. Orozco, *Migrant Remittances and Development in the Global Economy.*

47. Miriam Jordan, "U.S. Banks Woo Migrants, Legal or Otherwise," *Wall Street Journal,* October 11, 2006, B5.

48. Comisión Nacional de Vivienda, "Gobierno Federal Presenta Esquema de Vivienda Para Apoyar a Migrantes y Sus Familias," Press Release, June 24, 2016. See https://www.gob.mx/conavi/prensa/gobierno-federal-presenta-esquema-de-vivienda-para-apoyar-a-migrantes-y-sus-familias.

49. Barbara Schmitter Heisler, "Sending Countries and the Politics of Emigration and Destination," *International Migration Review* 19, no. 3 (1985): 469–484.

50. Jesús Martínez-Saldaña, "Los Olvidados become Heroes: The Evolution of Mexico's Policies toward Citizens Abroad," in Eva Østergaard-Nielsen, ed., *International Migration and Sending Countries: Perceptions, Policies, and Transnational Relations* (New York: Palgrave Macmillan, 2003), 35.

51. Eva Østergaard-Nielsen, "Turkey and the 'Euro Turks': Overseas Nationals as an Ambiguous Asset," in Eva Østergaard-Nielsen, ed., *International Migration and Sending Countries: Perceptions, Policies, and Transnational Relations* (New York: Palgrave Macmillan, 2003); see also Leblang, "Harnessing Diaspora: Dual Citizenship, Migrant Return Remittances."

52. Alexandra Délano, "Immigrant Integration vs. Transnational Ties? The Role of the Sending State," *Social Research* 77, no. 1 (Spring 2010): 237–268.

53. Laurie A. Brand, *Citizens Abroad: Emigration and the State in the Middle East and North Africa* (New York: Cambridge University Press, 2006); Jonathan Laurence, *The Emancipation of Europe's Muslims: The State's Role in Minority Integration* (Princeton: Princeton University Press, 2012).

APPENDIX I

1. Roy Germano, *The Other Side of Immigration* (DVD), Roy Germano Films (2010). See also www.theothersideofimmigration.com.

2. Roy Germano, "Analytic Filmmaking: A New Approach to Research and Publication in the Social Sciences," *Perspectives on Politics* 12, no. 3 (September 2014): 663–676.

3. Germano, "Migrants' Remittances and Economic Voting in the Mexican Countryside."

4. I believe asking respondents to make a quick assessment of remittances' relative significance as a source of income is an improvement over self-reports of remittance income for the following reasons: (1) incomes in communities like those where the survey was applied are highly unstable, changing month-to-month, and often coming from a variety of formal and informal sources. As a result, many respondents are not able to quickly or accurately recall what their domestically

earned income is; (2) There is a high level of distrust of outsiders in rural communities like these, and respondents often feel uncomfortable reporting their
incomes; (3) Respondents are known to mistakenly include a count of remittances
in responses about their domestically earned income in surveys about remittances
(see, e.g., Lucas and Stark 1985). Asking respondents to think about remittances as
a small, medium, or substantial share of their total income (1) saves respondents
from having to try to recall specific financial information that they likely do not
know off the top of their head; (2) is much less invasive; and (3) makes it clear to
the respondent that their income from remittances should be distinguished from
their other income sources.

5. To test the validity of the index, I compared it and its component parts to similar constructs. I find strong correlations, which suggest that the index is indeed
measuring the constructs that we are interested in. First, I find that the correlation between the index and a continuous variable measuring households' annual
income from remittances is .6452 (statistically significant at $p < 0.01$). Respondents'
answers about whether remittance income was small, medium, or substantial when
compared to domestically-earned income was strongly and positively correlated
with a variable that divided annual income from remittances by total household
income ($r = 0.72$, statistically significant at $p < 0.01$). Reports about the reliability
of remittances as a source of social insurance are strongly and positively correlated
with data collected on a question about whether migrants remit once a week, once
a month, once every two months, etc. ($r = 0.66$, statistically significant at $p < 0.01$).
Data on this question, on the other hand, is not correlated with self-reported levels
of income stability ($r = 0.08$, not statistically significant). The implication, then, is
that this variable is more effectively measuring the degree to which migrants are
attentive to the household's needs, not how needy the household is in general.

World Bank, 4, 18, 77, 79, 80, 156
WorldRemit, 4

xenophobia, 100, 154

Yemen
  economic grievances, 97, 99, 181
  migration from, 76, 77
  remittances, 6, 7–8, 78, 97, 99, 181
  social unrest, 8–9, 99

Zambia
  economic grievances, 94–95, 179
  migration from, 79
  political preferences, 111
  remittances, 12, 81, 94–95, 179
  social unrest, 12
Zapatista uprising, 13, 50–51, 52,
    55, 56, 70
Zedillo, Ernesto, 28, 32
Zimbabwe, 7–8, 79, 80, 81